COOK WITH JOAN ROCA

COOK WITH JOAN ROCA

Step-by-Step Preparation and Cooking Techniques

GRUB STREET • LONDON

This English language edition published in 2022 by
Grub Street
4 Rainham Close
London
SW11 6SS

Email: food@grubstreet.co.uk
Web: www.grubstreet.co.uk
Twitter: @grub_street
Facebook: Grub Street Publishing

First published in Spanish as *Cocina con Joan Roca , Técnicas Básicas Para Cocinar en Casa*

Interior photographs © Joan Pujol-Creus, except pp. 41 (Thinkstock), 46-47 (Shutterstock) and 49, photo no. 2 (Shutterstock)
Interior design and composition: Sàpiens Publicacions (Cuina)

A CIP catalogue record for this book is available from the British Library.

ISBN 978-1-911667-41-4

Printed and bound in Czech Republic by Finidr

INTRODUCTION

WHEN WE COOK WE COMBINE A MULTITUDE OF INGREDIENTS: EXPERIENCE, TECHNIQUE, TRADITION, EXPRESSION, VALUES, INNOVATION, EXPERIMENTATION AND MORE. EACH CHEF BASES HIS OR HER CUISINE ON DIFFERENT FACTORS, WHICH ARE OFTEN DIFFICULT TO EXPLAIN BUT THAT UNDOUBTEDLY MAKE THEIR DISHES AND MENUS STAND OUT. THESE ARE JUST SOME OF THE GREAT VALUES THAT BRING DIVERSITY AND UNIQUENESS TO QUALITY CUISINE.

The goal of this book is to bring techniques and processes to domestic kitchens to enable home cooks to acquire knowledge, improve their skills and ensure that their dishes are prepared with the greatest efficiency. It is not a recipe book, even if it contains a selection of preparations, but a book that tries – from my professional and teaching experience, and with the support of my team – to explain in a didactic way the techniques and principles that allow every cook to have an optimal base. To this end, we list the essential kitchen equipment, offer an informed knowledge on products, and finally – from a technical, qualitative, gustatory and healthy point of view – explain how these products can be treated and cooked to get the most out of them.

We are convinced that the correct application of culinary techniques is essential to evolve in any type of cuisine, along with being able to understand the characteristics and peculiarities of each of the ingredients that contribute to and are part of our dishes. Mastering these techniques and knowing how to treat the products will give any cook a solid base to reproduce, adapt or create recipes with greater success, which along with their own vision for cooking, can lead to exceptional results.

The experience acquired at the School of Hospitality and Tourism of Girona allows us to contribute to and share our technical knowledge. However, we do not wish to turn this book into an encyclopedic cooking school, but rather want it to be a useful tool to help all those who wish to advance in their understanding and knowledge because they feel that cooking is a fundamental part of their daily lives, a universe of creative possibilities or, simply, an activity that they are passionate about.

For us, cooking is what ultimately invites us to share, to prepare a small act of conviviality around the table, where food gives us a means for spending time with loved ones, an opportunity to express our feelings and passions, and an excuse to talk, reflect, look at each other and feel.

Cooking is an emotional experience and we, therefore, consider it very important to cook with a sense of purpose and values. On the one hand, we want to maintain the gastronomic culture of our region, its uses, customs and traditions. We cook with local products because by using them we value and help to maintain our environment. We also cook with seasonal products because in this way we respect the cycles of nature and can enjoy the products at the optimum point of maturity and fullness of flavour. On the other hand, we like to enjoy the culinary experience and its ability to nourish us in a healthy way.

We offer you a book that will allow you to incorporate new habits and processes and reassess your own routines and practices. This is a guide to being organised in the kitchen and other related activities such as making shopping lists. We give an overview of the products we use in our cuisine (and those of other cultures) and of the essential tools and most suitable appliances for each technique. There is also advice – a key pillar of the book – on getting to know and putting into practice the main techniques of food preparation, cooking and storage. In addition, we offer a review of the essential bases for a multitude of preparations as well as a selection of dishes for you to experiment with and obtain different results depending on the techniques used. Above all, we invite you to cook with generosity and love, to provide that finishing touch, that pinch of salt, that turns any dish, whether simple or grand, into a source of happiness.

Joan Roca

HEALTHY COOKING

EVERY DAY WE ARE MORE AND MORE AWARE OF THE NEED TO FOLLOW A BALANCED DIET TO PROMOTE BOTH OUR PHYSICAL AND MENTAL WELL-BEING. HERE ARE THE KEYS TO A HEALTHY DIET.

Eating a healthy and balanced diet is a very common preoccupation in today's society. Catering professionals also have this same concern and, increasingly, we are trying to offer our customers dishes that promote a sense of well-being and healthy eating, without renouncing tasty cuisine.

Indeed, long gone are the days when people went to restaurants to enjoy heavy, hearty dishes. The world of professional catering has been working for years on an evolving cuisine in which healthy ingredients, harmonious combinations, light cooking and limited portions are triumphant. For this reason, this cookery book, while describing all kinds of products and cooking procedures, is also full of delicious but healthy ideas.

It is always well worth to start by seeking expert advice. Mireia Anglada, cook, consultant and nutrition specialist, as well as good friend and collaborator of El Celler de Can Roca, shares with us her tips and suggestions for healthy cooking and eating. In the following pages we set out her recommendations.

RESPONSIBLE EATING

ACHIEVING A HEALTHY AND BALANCED DIET IS MUCH EASIER THAN IT SOUNDS: SIMPLY GET INTO THE HABIT OF EATING A VARIETY OF FOODS, AND IN THE RIGHT PROPORTIONS OF EACH ESSENTIAL FOOD GROUP.

According to the World Health Organization, 80 per cent of today's diseases are related to poor nutrition. This is why we need to realise, once and for all, that our diet is a key determining factor in our health.

The nutrients that our body needs for its proper development are not found in just any type of food, and that is why nutritionists say that eating is not the same as nourishment. For this reason, it is worthwhile to occasionally take a moment to think about what we eat and how we eat. This will allow us to become aware of the habits that are leading us to making small errors or big mistakes in our daily diet that are likely already affecting our health in one way or another.

Eating consciously, with natural, local, fresh and additive-free products, cooking ingredients using the right methods for preserving their nutritional properties, and, finally, eating calmly and enjoying the experience are the keys that help us to improve our health – and they are the starting point for responsible eating.

THE IMPORTANCE OF NUTRIENTS

Nutrients are necessary elements for our body to be able to function in a balanced way. Some of these substances, particularly carbohydrates and fats, have an energetic value that enables us to carry out our daily activities. Other nutrients, especially proteins, are structural – that is, they build the structure of our body and its different tissues. Finally, there are the regulating components: vitamins and minerals, which enable our body to use the aforementioned functions correctly.

Since no single food can provide all of these nutrients, the key to proper nutrition is having variety in the diet.

MAIN NUTRIENTS

- **Carbohydrates.** They are the main source of the energy that our body needs, and should represent between 50 and 60 per cent of the calories we ingest daily (between 4 and 6 servings). They are found in cereals, fruits, pulses (also called legumes) and vegetables. However, although they are essential for exercise or physical exertion, excessive consumption can lead to unnecessary fat storage. It is advisable to prioritise wholegrain cereals over refined products (white pasta, white bread, etc.) as they have a higher nutritional and fibre content.

■ **Proteins.** They are found mainly in meat, eggs and fish. Although we are accustomed to a high consumption of animal protein, it should not exceed 15 per cent of the total calories we eat per day. They can be substituted by foods rich in vegetable protein, such as pulses and certain cereals, such as quinoa.

■ **Fats.** Although our body needs a daily intake of fats — they should represent approximately 30 per cent of the calories consumed per day — an excessive intake of animal fats is detrimental to our cardiovascular system. For this reason, it is preferable to prioritise fats from a vegetable origin, such as those provided by olive oil and seeds (sunflower, pumpkin, sesame, etc.).

■ **Vitamins.** Essential for multiple vital functions, they are present in any balanced diet. Each vitamin has a role: vitamin A, abundant in peppers and carrots, keeps the skin healthy; the B vitamins, found in nuts and dairy products, protect the immune, digestive and nervous systems; vitamin C, found in citrus fruit, is an antioxidant. To preserve the vitamins in food, it is important to use appropriate cooking methods.

■ **Minerals.** Very important for the formation of bones and other tissues, some of the main minerals are calcium, abundant in dairy products, nuts and seeds; phosphorus, found in eggs and wholegrain bread; sodium, found in salt; iron in meat and green leafy vegetables, and many other sources. They are present in any varied diet, although excessive consumption of refined sugars or fats hinders their absorption.

■ **Water.** With 60 per cent of our body being water, let's remember to drink regularly. The recommendation is to drink about 2 litres per day, although it should be taken into account that when we eat foods such as fruit, vegetables and stocks, we are also consuming it.

WEEKLY DIET PLANNING

Our diet should not lack the basic foods that guarantee energy and essential nutrients for our body. To ensure we get them, there are certain rules that should not be ignored.

We should include all kinds of fruit, vegetables, pulses and cereals. It is also important to eat fish and consume a moderate amount of meats, as well as restrict the consumption of sugars as much as possible. It is not advisable to have either excesses or deficiencies in any food group.

It is recommended to eat 4–5 times a day and not skip meals to avoid snacking between meals and having too abundant intakes.

The first meal of the day, breakfast, is one of the most important. We should start the day with a complete breakfast based on cereals – which are much better if they are wholegrains without added sugars – fruit and some product containing calcium such as nuts, dairy products or seeds like sesame. These are the ingredients that will nourish our body and provide it with the energy it needs to start the day.

SERVINGS FOR THE WEEK

- **Fruit and vegetables.** The recommendation is to consume a minimum of 5 servings a day (3 pieces of fruit and 2 servings of vegetables) to obtain the necessary vitamins, minerals, water and fibre.
- **Fish and meat.** To ensure an adequate amount of protein, it is recommended we eat oily fish (tuna, salmon, bonito, sardines, mackerel) 2-3 times a week. This type of fish is very rich in omega-3 fatty acids and essential nutrients. We should round off the week with good-quality animal protein: opt for red meat (lamb, beef, veal, pork) once a week and white meat (chicken, turkey) 2 days a week.
- **Eggs.** Preferably organic, they can be consumed regularly (3-4 per week).
- **Pulses.** They are a great source of protein and essential amino acids. They should be consumed a minimum of 2 times per week.
- **Rice, pasta and bread.** Carbohydrates are the basis of our energy intake and, therefore, 5-6 servings per day are necessary. Wholegrain flours and rice are preferable.
- **Dairy products, seeds and nuts.** A daily intake of calcium is necessary and can be obtained by consuming 2-4 daily servings of dairy products, if not lactose intolerant, or through nuts, seeds and green leafy foods.

TOMATO, ONION, AND OLIVE SALAD

Time: 1 hr | Level: easy

INGREDIENTS FOR 4 PEOPLE

Tomatoes of different varieties (beefsteak, plum, heirloom, cherry tomatoes)
Assorted onions (red, yellow and spring onions)
Young garlic
Assorted black and green olives
Olive oil
Sherry vinegar
Thyme
Rosemary
Zest 1 lemon
Salt and pepper
Sugar

METHOD

1 To marinade the olives, soak them in olive oil for a few hours and add the thyme and lemon zest.

2 To prepare the vinaigrette, mix 3 parts oil with 1 part sherry vinegar and add salt and pepper. The oil-vinegar mixture can then be adjusted to the taste of each diner.

3 We will treat the tomatoes in different ways: peel those that are especially tasty, smooth and have a tomato aroma. You can blanch them to peel them more easily, but if they are for salads, even if it is more difficult, it is preferable to peel them with a knife. You can use the core and seeds from the juiciest tomatoes for tomato 'caviar'.

4 Cut the outer part of the juiciest tomatoes into wedges and cook them in a gentle oven for 30 minutes with olive oil, salt, pepper, thyme, rosemary and a little sugar.

5 Halve the cherry tomatoes and sauté them quickly in a frying pan.

6 Allow the sautéed tomatoes to marinate by soaking them in oil and vinegar for a few minutes. Afterwards, add the remaining liquid from the marinade to the vinaigrette prepared previously.

7 Cut the onions and young garlic into julienne strips and immerse them in water and ice to reduce their excessive potency.

8 Carefully arrange the different salad ingredients in a bowl or on plates, and dress generously with the vinaigrette.

This recipe is simple, fresh and nutritious. However, you can use it as a guide: walk around the market and choose the best seasonal products picked at their peak ripeness. Allow yourself to be inspired by their colours and aromas.

RESPECTING THE PRODUCTS

IN COOKING, INGREDIENTS OFTEN UNDERGO GREAT TRANSFORMATIONS, WHICH IS WHY IT'S NOT ENOUGH TO CHOOSE THE BEST PRODUCTS — WE MUST ALSO USE THE RIGHT TECHNIQUES TO COOK THEM.

If you have purchased the freshest produce, it makes sense to ensure that they are cooked in a way that allows you to get the most benefit from the properties they offer. For this reason, they must be preserved in the best conditions, as we will discuss in the next chapter. But this is not enough: we must also cook them with respect.

By cooking food we modify its biochemical components, so that, although we make it more digestible and safer for our consumption, it also loses part of its nutrients. The more a product is cooked, and the higher the cooking temperature, the more nutrients it loses. Food must, therefore, be cooked to just the right doneness. Each product has its own optimum cooking time, although the type of cut and the size of the piece also influence this factor.

Of course, some products – basically fruit, vegetables and salad leaves – can be eaten raw, so they can provide us with all their nutritional richness. Wash them beforehand but never soak them, as some of the vitamins and minerals would be lost in the water.

If the product isn't eaten fresh, sometimes preparation processes are used that do not require the application of heat – such as cured, marinated or pickled products – which preserve their nutrients.

When boiling vegetables, you should not put too much water in the pot. Add the vegetables to the boiling water and cover them, to take advantage of the steam. It is estimated that at 100°C, after 20 minutes of cooking, 50 per cent of the vitamin C will be destroyed, so it is important to avoid boiling vegetables more than necessary, both to preserve their nutrients and to achieve a pleasant texture. Once cooking is finished, in order to preserve the vitamins and minerals, do not allow the vegetables to cool in the water; drain them as soon as possible, even if they are not going to be consumed immediately.

CULINARY SOLUTIONS

The cooking of dried pulses, in contrast, must be long and progressive. For many people, their skins are difficult to digest. So these people do not have to give up pulses, an alternative is to eat them in the form of purées or creams. Meanwhile, gastronomic globalisation has provided us with other interesting solutions: today we can more easily find kombu seaweed (on sale in health-food shops and shops specialising in Asian and gourmet products), which is common in oriental cooking. This seaweed softens the pulses' fibre, making them more digestive, and also provides valuable minerals. Simply introduce a portion to the cooking water to enjoy the pulses without problems.

For eggs, try to cook the white part of the eggs well, to make it more digestible but keep the yolk runny, to retain its nutrients. Don't boil for more than 10 minutes and eat immediately.

As for the preparation of meats, you should avoid overcooking them over direct heat (grilling or smoking), which can produce toxins that are harmful to health. Nor should you overcook oily fish, since high temperatures destroy its omega-3 content. For both poultry and fish, it can be useful to cook them with their skin on, as this protects them, seals the meat with its juices and prevents them from drying out. Once the cooking is finished, remove the skin to avoid the fat.

GENTLE COOKING

The use of low-temperature cooking introduces a culinary culture based on respect for the product's nature and its nutritional properties.

- **Cooking in a salt crust.** The food is covered with coarse salt, which allows it to cook evenly and also protects it from high temperatures.
- **Steaming.** This cooking method preserves all of the food's natural flavour and it can be easily flavoured by adding seasonings to the water (*see p. 216*).
- **Cooking en papillote.** This cooking occurs when heat is applied to the product while wrapped in a vegetable or in a sheet of greaseproof paper or baking parchment. The result is similar to that of steaming.
- **Grilling.** Although it can reach very high temperatures, the grill provides interesting results for cooking fish: it consists of placing the fish on grill skin-side down, so that the skin protects the meat from direct heat and prevents it sticking to the grill. Turn the piece only when the flesh changes colour so that the back of the fish finishes cooking slightly (*see p. 274*).
- **Sous vide.** The product remains vacuum-packed in a bag during the cooking process, which is carried out at controlled, usually low, temperatures and thus retains most of its nutritional and organoleptic properties. It is a procedure used in professional kitchens, but specialist suppliers have sous vide equipment for domestic use available to the home cook (*see p. 298*).

NUTRITIOUS FOOD

CERTAIN INGREDIENTS ARE RECOGNISED FOR THEIR HIGH CONTENT OF SPECIFIC NUTRIENTS — SUCH AS ESSENTIAL FATTY ACIDS, ANTIOXIDANTS AND FIBRE — AND THEIR REGULAR CONSUMPTION BRINGS EXTRAORDINARY HEALTH BENEFITS.

Some ingredients stand out for their exceptional properties, especially since some strengthen our immune system. Garlic and onion are part of our gastronomic heritage, for example, whereas newer, imported ingredients, such as miso or seaweed, are an opportunity to discover new flavours and approaches to cooking that at the same time provide us with a high nutritional quality. Try being adventurous and incorporate them into your diet. They will surprise you with their culinary possibilities.

SOME SUPERFOODS

- **Olive oil.** If it is first cold pressed, it is rich in monounsaturated fatty acids (omega-9) and antioxidants, which provide a cleansing and protective action upon the circulatory system.
- **Garlic.** Contains a potent natural antibiotic, but to take advantage of it, garlic must be consumed raw. The protective substance is destroyed when a cooking temperature of 60°C is exceeded.
- **Nuts and seeds.** These products are rich in fat, but they do not contribute towards cholesterol; rather, they are a good cardiovascular protector.

- **Seaweeds.** In oriental cuisine they are as common as vegetables are for Europeans and, in spite of the fact that there is no gastronomic custom in the West, they are a very interesting food due to their high nutritional qualities. Just one tablespoon of seaweed per day supplies the body with all the essential minerals and trace elements that are essential for proper cellular metabolism. Because of their culinary possibilities, seaweeds are capable of causing a revolution in our cuisine. Herbalists and specialist shops can guide us on incorporating them into our regular diet.
- **Onion.** When raw, it helps to eliminate mucus from the respiratory system and is useful for colds, coughs and flu. It also prevents the formation of blood clots. However, like garlic, once cooked it loses its antibiotic properties.
- **Endive, escarole and artichoke.** They keep the liver healthy and are ideal for diabetics.
- **Ginger.** This root is a great natural anti-inflammatory, ideal for circulation and for the respiratory systems. To take full advantage of its properties, add it to preparations at the end of cooking.
- **Miso.** An oriental condiment made from fermented soybeans and other cereals, use it as a flavour enhancer. It is endowed with multiple properties: it favours the balance among the intestinal flora, the hormonal balance in women and the cardiovascular system, and it is a powerful antioxidant. Add it at the end of cooking to avoid boiling.
- **Radish.** It is a natural depurative. It helps us to reduce fat and to eliminate fluid retention.
- **Watermelon.** A great cleanser, it is refreshing, cleanses the blood and helps eliminate liquids.

PULSE SALAD WITH ITS OWN COOKING EMULSION

Time: 4 hrs | Level: easy

INGREDIENTS FOR 4 PEOPLE

600 g various dried pulses (chickpeas, lentils, beans, soya beans), if possible of different varieties
100 g spring onions
100 g green and red peppers
6 baby radishes
Assorted black and green olives
Cherry tomatoes (yellow and red)
Olive oil
Cooking water from the pulses
For the vinaigrette
Oil
Vinegar
Parsley
Chives
Chervil
Fresh coriander leaves
Salt and pepper

METHOD

1 Cook the pulses the day before, remembering that they must be cooled in their own broth. Reserve some of the cooking liquid to prepare an emulsion with water and oil, which will provide flavour and nutrients (and to make it bind well and add a little thickness).

2 To make the vinaigrette, chop all the herbs, mix them with oil and vinegar, and season with salt and pepper.

3 Cut the vegetables into julienne strips. Cut the tomatoes in halves or quarters and stone a few olives. If you wish, also halve some olives and allow them to marinate in oil.

4 Set some vegetables aside to garnish the dish at the end, then mix the remaining vegetables with the pulses in a bowl. Add olive oil and allow to marinate for 1 hour. At this point, add a few drops of the cooking water emulsion.

5 Place a generous spoonful of the emulsion at the base of a slightly deep dish to give the salad some smoothness and flavour. Place the pulse and vegetable mixture on top, and finish by garnishing with the reserved vegetables and dressing with the vinaigrette.

This recipe allows us to enjoy the energy from the pulses, combined with the freshness of seasonal vegetables. It is a dish cooked with hardly any fat, making it a healthy, nutritious and tasty dish.

SALMON CONFIT WITH CITRUS MARINADE AND QUINOA

Time: 1 hr | Level: moderate

INGREDIENTS FOR 4 PEOPLE

100 g white quinoa
100 g black quinoa
100 g carrots
100 g courgette
4 spring onions
1 baby onion
15 ml vinegar
5 g pink peppercorn
5 g cardamom
Salt and pepper
Flower petals

For the citrus marinade

125 ml sunflower oil
25 g sugar
1 lemon
1 lime
1 grapefruit

To confit the salmon

4 x 125 g salmon supremes
100 ml sunflower oil

METHOD

1 Wash the quinoa or leave it in water for a few minutes to remove any bitterness it may have, then boil it in double its volume of water for about 15 minutes. Strain and transfer it to a bowl. Stir to cool quickly and set aside.

2 To prepare the citrus marinade, peel a couple of strips of peel from each citrus fruit, remove all the white pith and blanch the strips 3 times — that is, submerge them in cold water and, as soon as it starts to boil, remove and cool them. Cut them into very fine julienne or brunoise.

3 Squeeze the citrus fruit, set aside some of it, and prepare a reduction with 100 ml of juice and the sugar over a low heat until a concentrated juice is obtained. Allow it to cool.

4 Sear a whole spring onion in the frying pan and set it aside for finishing. Cut the other spring onions with the remaining vegetables into brunoise.

5 Cook the vegetables in a frying pan with a tablespoon of sunflower oil. Start with the onion, followed by the carrots and, finally, the courgette, which has been previously sweated with a pinch of salt to eliminate its bitterness.

6 When the vegetables begin to colour, add about 100 ml of sunflower oil, the vinegar, the reserved citrus juice, the blanched zest, the pink peppercorns and cardamom, and cook for 5 minutes over a very low heat and allow to cool. The citrus-marinated vegetables are ready.

7 Season the quinoa with part of the marinade and add salt and pepper.

8 To confit the salmon, put it into a saucepan with sunflower oil and some citrus peel, then cook at 50°C for 15 minutes. Drain the salmon from the oil and serve it with the seasoned quinoa and the seared onion.

9 To finish the dish, dress the salmon with the marinade and garnish with a few dots of citrus juice concentrate and flower petals.

Joan Roca
LO QUE HEMOS COMIDO
MARC VEYRAT

KITCHEN ORGANISATION

THE ACT OF COOKING DOES NOT BEGIN AT THE HOB, BUT LONG BEFOREHAND. HAVING A WELL-ORGANISED KITCHEN, PLANNING, BUYING, ORDERING AND PRESERVING ARE ALL ESSENTIAL PARTS OF COOKING.

Good organisation is the first step to success in the kitchen. Before putting on an apron and embarking on the instructions for a recipe, it is important to ensure you have all the essential equipment and necessary ingredients, as well as understanding the instructions. What preparations are necessary, what needs to be purchased and where? Check for even the most basic ingredients: don't take for granted that salt will always be at your disposal in its salt shaker, nor that the bag of flour previously used has remained in perfect condition at the back of a cupboard.

First analyse what type of cooking you like and what type of food suits you, the time you have available for cooking, and the utensils and ingredients available to you. You should also think about for whom and why you are going to cook: cooking for an everyday meal is not the same as cooking for a festive occasion, nor is it the same to cook for oneself as it is for a whole family.

Plan your shopping in advance, and once it is at home, think about how to store the products to have them at hand and to make sure they will be perfectly preserved.

PLANNING

WE OFTEN IMPROVISE IN THE KITCHEN, BUT IF WE WANT TO PREPARE BALANCED MENUS COOKED IN A THOUGHTFUL WAY AND ENJOY SEASONAL PRODUCTS, IT IS WELL WORTH DEVISING A WEEKLY MENU.

By adopting a few simple planning habits, you will always have a stock of essential foods for preparing an appetising dish; having plans and knowing what to expect are essential for making a meal with the least fuss. Although fewer people these days decide to plan a weekly menu, it is a very useful way to get organised, whether you are cooking for yourself or want to feed a whole family. Based on this menu, you can plan your shopping and prepare tasty meals that contribute to a consistent, varied and balanced diet.

If a change of circumstances or your appetite leads to a change of menu, then go for it, because, of course, you should occasionally allow yourself the luxury of forgetting the plans and improvising, both in shopping and in the kitchen. The important thing is that you will already be organised in a way that can be adapted to your convenience.

IDEAS FOR YOUR MENUS

- **Appealing menus.** Get used to thinking about menus that are as attractive as they are healthy.
- **Seasonal and local products.** Give priority on your menus to seasonal and local products that ensure freshness, taste, nutritional quality and the opportunity to vary your diet.
- **Balanced combinations.** Don't just plan the main dish, but the whole evening dinner, depending on what you have eaten at lunch. Think about your nutritional balance.
- **New recipes.** If you aren't sure which dishes to choose for a weekly menu, take inspiration from recipe books. Escape boredom and try cooking new dishes from time to time. Friends, family, books, the internet, retailers, etc. all can help you bring new ideas to the kitchen.
- **Necessary ingredients.** Review the ingredients needed for each dish, checking what you have available at home and what you need to buy. Remember to check the store cupboard periodically: it should be up to date with the basic products. When planning the menu, and before going out to buy new fresh produce, also check the stock in the fridge; you may have forgotten a product in the fridge that you need to consume immediately.

- **Preparations.** Pay attention to foods that need prior preparation, so that they are ready when you are ready to cook. If you have to defrost any food, think about it the day before, as well as if you have to soak it, marinate it, etc.
- **Condiments and garnishes.** Remember that the complements — such as spices, vinaigrettes or some special garnishes — can liven up the most common menus. A small touch of a condiment or a sauce can create a new and amazing dish.
- **Your personal recipe book.** It never hurts to get into the habit of saving your recipes, even for the most basic weekly menus. This way, when you don't know what to cook, you will have an easy and quick resource to consult.

SHOPPING

ALL GOOD COOKS KNOW HOW TO SHOP WISELY AND KNOW THE PRODUCT THEY WILL BE COOKING WELL. GOING TO THE SHOPS IS PART OF THE CULINARY PROCESS AND OFFERS THE OPPORTUNITY TO CHOOSE THE BEST PRODUCTS.

For many cooks, gastronomic pleasure begins at the time of purchase. Indeed, being surrounded by the colour and aromas of fresh produce and the liveliness of a market can be an intoxicating experience. It is not only the time to choose the ingredients, but also the opportunity to deal with the traders, to exchange ideas and to be advised by those who know the products best – especially if you find small producers who sell their own products. It is an ideal occasion to meet, learn, exchange and be inspired, and is an indispensable part of good cuisine.

Buying in a planned way, taking advantage of the time and looking for the best shops, and taking an interest in the product, its quality and origin, will help you to make a responsible purchase. In this way, through the act of shopping, you can not only improve the way you understand your kitchen and your food, but you can also contribute to improving your environment.

BUYING THOUGHTFULLY

- **Make a shopping list.** It is indispensable. Not only so that you don't forget anything, but also so that you don't let yourself get carried away with impulse purchases.
- **Ask.** It is wise to ask. Most retailers will be happy to explain the features of a product or how you can get the most out of it. Curiosity is fundamental to enjoying cooking.
- **Read the labels.** They will inform you about the nutritional composition of the products, the use-by date, their origin, their price per kilogram, etc. By reading the labels, you will learn to buy better and more consciously.
- **Go to the best shops.** Through experience, you'll learn where to find the most interesting products, the freshest and the best value for money.
- **Try new products.** As a result of the cultural mix of our society and globalisation, there are more and more exotic products available at the markets. Take an interest in these ingredients, as they can provide you with ideas for the next menu or to try new experiences.
- **Pack the purchases well.** Leave the heavier items — such as fruit — and, especially, the freshest and most delicate ones — fish — for the end of the shopping process. Bring your own shopping trolleys, baskets, insulated bags and shopping bags to contribute to the conservation of the environment.

FRUIT AND VEGETABLES

Prioritise fresh and seasonal fruit and vegetables, and go for local. Traders are obliged to indicate the origin of their products, so you will have the opportunity to choose according to their origin. Purchase the necessary quantities to be able to consume them at their best state of ripeness.

FISH

When it comes to fish, it is also better to opt for local and seasonal species. It is important to buy it from a reliable fishmonger. Knowing how to buy it is an art: it is often worthwhile to choose a fresh fish, just arrived at the fishmonger's, even if it forces you to change your menu plans.

Fresh fish should be purchased the same day it will be cooked. Ask the fishmonger for help in cleaning, gutting or cutting the fish: no one will do it better than him. And don't forget to use insulated bags to transport it.

MEATS

For each type of dish or recipe there is usually a type of meat, including the most suitable cut. If you are not sure, ask the sellers which option is the best. They can also prepare it for you (tenderising, cutting, chopping, stuffing, etc.).

Minced meat is not preserved in the same way as a whole piece of meat. If the meat will not be consumed on the same day it is purchased, and if it is not packaged and does not have a use-by date, it is important to ask about when it should be consumed.

ALL IN ORDER

AFTER SHOPPING, EACH PRODUCT MUST BE STORED IN THE PROPER LOCATION TO ENSURE ITS BEST PRESERVATION. A WELL-ORGANISED REFRIGERATOR, FREEZER AND STORE CUPBOARD WILL HELP YOU TO BE A BETTER COOK.

Once you have finished shopping, the journey home should be as quick as possible. A wide range of fresh produce needs to be kept within an optimal and safe temperature range for preservation. If measures are already taken to preserve products before they reach the consumer (during transport, storage and also in the shop), you should also take care to respect the cold chain as much as possible. This means transporting fresh groceries in insulated bags, not delaying on the way home and putting each product away properly as soon as possible.

IN THE REFRIGERATOR

It is important to organise any purchases that need to be refrigerated well. Newly purchased products should be placed in the refrigerator behind those that are already in it to prevent older products being hidden and forgotten at the back. Remember this rule: the first thing that goes into the refrigerator is the first thing that should come out.

Overfilling the refrigerator is not recommended, because if you do so the air does not circulate properly and this affects refrigeration. In this sense, you should not refrigerate foods that, in reality, do not need refrigeration and that even, in most cases, lose quality if you do so. This is the case of tomatoes, green beans, cucumbers, avocados and, in general, all exotic fruit. Fruit and vegetables that still need to ripen should be left at room temperature.

You should wrap or cover food in the refrigerator well to preserve its flavour and freshness and to prevent odours being transmitted from one food to another. As for leftovers, it is convenient to store them in shallow containers with airtight lids.

The temperature inside the refrigerator is not the same in all zones: as a general rule, it is cooler at the back and bottom than at the top and front. Based on this principle, you should find an appropriate place for each type of product.

1 The upper shelf

It is usually about 8°C, and it is here that dairy products — milk, cream, cheeses and yogurts — are usually stored.

2 Middle shelf

It is the most versatile, and its temperature should be between 4 and 5°C. Sausages, cakes, leftovers and all foods on which it is specified 'Once opened, keep refrigerated' can be stored here.

3 The lower shelf

Located just above the vegetable bin, it is the coldest point, where the temperature reaches about 2°C. It is here that you should store fresh meat and fish.

4 The lower bins

The temperature is usually 10°C; they are designed to preserve fruit and vegetables but to avoid excessive cold.

5 The compartments and door shelves

These are the least cold area of the refrigerator (between 10 and 15°C) and are intended for storing products that need little refrigeration, such as mustards, eggs, butters, beverages, etc.

1

2

IN THE FREEZER

In the freezer, where the temperature is -18°C, deterioration of food stuffs is halted. This will allow you to preserve them for a long time – up to 4 months in a domestic freezer – and in a safe way. This is a preservation measure that involves little loss of nutrients and moderate alteration of the food, although not all foods tolerate the freezing process well. For example, rice, potatoes and pasta lose their texture and their flavour deteriorates; sauces such as mayonnaise, béchamel sauce, Marie Rose sauces and all those containing cream will split when frozen; the cream itself can be frozen, but cannot be used for whipping. And while most vegetables will accept freezing, many of them must be blanched before freezing.

Taking all this into account, as a general rule, if you foresee that you will keep a preparation in the refrigerator for a number of days, it is better to freeze it.

- **Keep in portions.** Before freezing, it is worth thinking about how the product will be used and in what quantities it will be consumed. This will allow you to organise the freezing process according to your needs. It is easy to find resources for freezing precise portions: freeze liquids in plastic cups or bottles, in individual portions in freezer bags, in vacuum-seal bags or in ice cube trays (*photo 1*).
- **Maintenance standards.** To make sure it works properly, you must keep the freezer clean: check the door seals, prevent ice forming, do not overload it and do not introduce hot food.
- **Fast process.** Freezing should be rapid, to avoid the formation of large ice crystals that affect the texture of the product. To do this, place the fresh product in the freezer as soon as possible.

- **Suitable containers.** Products should be protected in freezer bags or suitable containers to avoid freezer burn and losing moisture (*photo 2*). Polyethylene trays are not recommended because they are porous containers that leach moisture. Rigid containers are suitable for freezing foods with liquids; remember to leave a few centimetres free at the top of the container to allow for expansion.
- **Labelling the products.** Providing the best-before date is a useful and necessary requirement to control the use-by date (*photo 2*).
- **Freeze in order.** Placing products as flat and spread out as possible promotes faster freezing and efficient storage. Rectangular containers and freezer bags make better use of space. Remember to extract the air from inside.

SAFE DEFROSTING

- **In the refrigerator.** The most appropriate defrosting method consists of placing the product in the refrigerator the day before use, in a container that separates it from the water that will be expelled (*photo 3*). However, if the product has been frozen in freezer bags, you can thaw the food without removing it from the bags.
- **In the microwave.** This oven has a defrosting programme that can be useful, but you must be very attentive to the timer, since it is easy for the product to overheat or even cook incorrectly.
- **In water.** Do not immerse food in water to thaw; only fish can eventually be thawed in water with ice and salt, but never in warm or hot water.
- **Products that don't require thawing.** Some foods, such as vegetables and some preparations (croquettes, chips, pizzas), can be cooked directly without defrosting (*photo 4*).

THE STORE CUPBOARD

A good store cupboard is always a useful source of ingredients and we should learn to make the most of it. In general, products in sealed containers and certain common produce that do not need refrigeration can be kept here, although they do need to be properly stored. It is advisable to check the cupboard periodically so that nothing indispensable is missing.

- **Rice, pasta, flours, dried beans and nuts.** In general, all dried or dehydrated foods should be stored at room temperature in a cool, dark and completely dry place. Once opened, they are best stored in airtight containers.
- **Tinned food.** As long as they are sealed, tinned food will keep for a long time in the store cupboard. However, once opened, tinned foods should be treated as perishable foods and stored in the refrigerator in a sealed plastic container.
- **Bread.** It is best kept in a cloth bag or in a bread basket covered with a cloth.
- **Potatoes and other tubers.** They should be stored in a well-ventilated and dark place.
- **Oil.** Store it in a dark place, either in its own bottle or in any other container that seals well, to prevent oxidation and rancidity.
- **Other foods.** You can also store pickles (spring onions, gherkins, etc.), commercial sauces, jars of jam, etc. in the store cupboard

FOOD SAFETY

PROPER FOOD PRESERVATION, BEFORE AND AFTER HANDLING IT, BY APPLYING BASIC HYGIENE RULES IS ESSENTIAL TO KEEP MICROORGANISMS AWAY FROM PRODUCTS AND PREPARATIONS.

Normally, after buying food items they are stored in the correct places, whether in the store cupboard, refrigerator or freezer. However, cooking and the activities associated with it can lead to a thousand circumstances and unforeseen events.

For example, when at the market, you might be attracted by the quality and good price of a product and decide to buy more than usual, with the plan to freeze it. Or you might prepare a product ahead of time and keep it in the refrigerator for a few hours, or days, before cooking.

Circumstances such as these are frequent in the kitchen, and we are not always aware that they involve some health risks. Depending on how we solve them, this will affect the final quality of the food – and also our safety. It is, therefore, important to apply food handling and other hygienic measures.

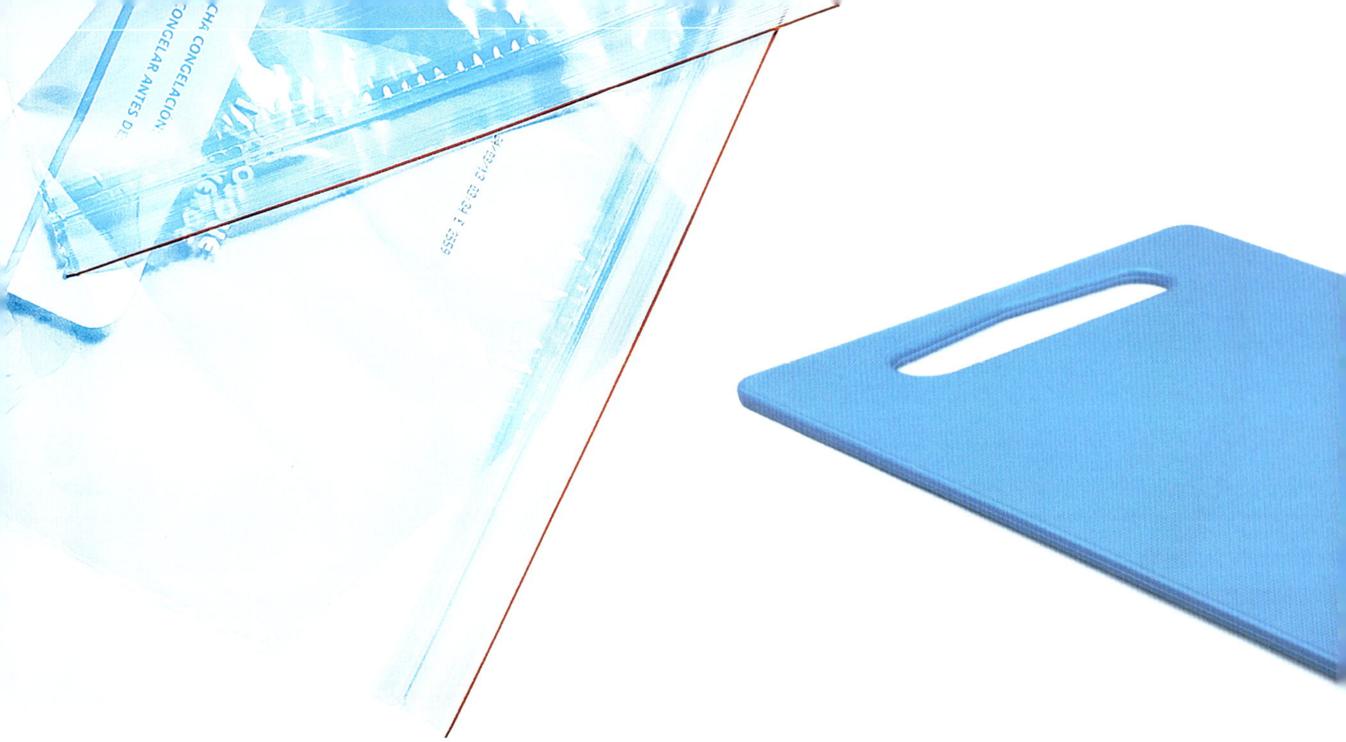

PRESERVATION MEASURES

Among the various factors that can alter and deteriorate food, the action of microorganisms is one of the main ones. Unfortunately, the food preferences of these tiny living creatures are similar to those of people, so they turn first to the richest and most digestible products. That is why a piece of hake spoils before a piece of garlic, or an egg yolk before a potato, as well as a stew before dried lentils.

We also know that there are certain foods in which it is easier for pathogens to lodge, which is sometimes very dangerous for people. This is the case of egg products, in which the toxic bacteria that causes salmonellosis can proliferate if they are not properly preserved.

Of course, the issue is more complex than it seems. The factors that can influence the microorganisms' food preferences are diverse, such as the pH (acidity or alkalinity) or absence of inhibitory substances in the product. So you cannot always determine at a glance whether a food is in good condition or not, nor can you know for sure how long its shelf life lasts.

For the purposes of food safety, it will suffice to bear in mind that all food is a rich source of nutrients for microbes and that you must always preserve them properly. Being meticulous in food handling, procedures and hygiene will ensure good preservation of food products.

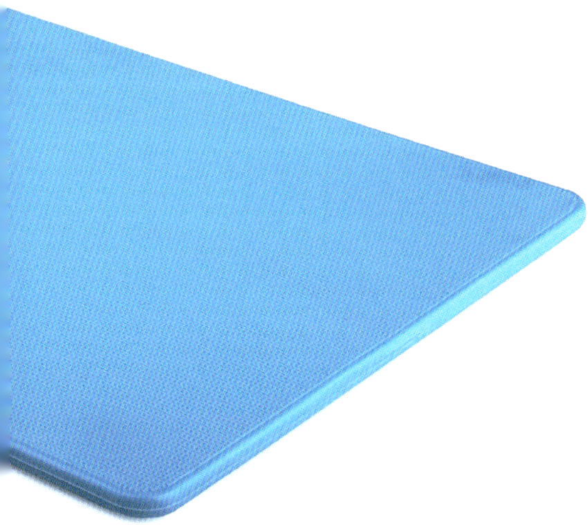

▪ **Keep the refrigerator and freezer up to date.** Periodically check their temperature, keep them clean, do not overfill them and open the doors only as long as necessary. In the event that ice accumulates in the freezer, you will need to defrost and clean it thoroughly.

▪ **Maintain scrupulous hygiene.** It is important to wash your hands and wrists thoroughly before starting to handle any items in the kitchen, as well as to remove rings, tie back hair, don't smoke and dress in appropriate clothing for cooking.

▪ **Use fresh products.** Buying products of the highest quality and freshness will help guarantee the effectiveness of the conservation measures that you carry out later.

▪ **Clean the equipment.** Cooking utensils and cloths should always be perfectly clean and dry. Plastic and especially wooden elements are difficult to clean and dry and can harbour microorganisms. Make sure that wooden utensils, such as spoons, are not soaked so that they do not retain moisture.

▪ **Observe the food's use-by date.** It indicates the cut-off day for optimal consumption from a health safety point of view.

▪ **Choose the chopping boards.** To avoid cross-contamination of food, it is preferable to use one board for raw products and another for cooked products. Avoid using wooden ones, which are not very hygienic; that is why they are forbidden in professional kitchens.

▪ **Control the storage temperature.** Most microorganisms are happy in mild temperatures, where they find a favourable climate to multiply. For this reason, the refrigerator is essential in the kitchen: perishable foods — especially meat, dairy products and fish — must be kept at a temperature of no more than 5°C.

■ **Rapid freezing and thawing.** By freezing food we can kill some microorganisms, such as the dreaded anisakis, which can live in the guts of fish. But there are many other harmful microbes that are not killed by freezing: they simply go into dormancy and stop multiplying. This is why it is essential to defrost and cook products without delay, because this will deny these microorganisms enough time to reactivate and multiply more vigorously, taking advantage of the aqueous medium. It is also important not to refreeze a previously frozen product, since there is nothing more stimulating for microbes than temperature fluctuations.

■ **Heat to the required temperature.** Another way to keep microorganisms at bay is the opposite of freezing them: it is by subjecting them to high temperatures of above 65°C. You must ensure, however, that this temperature is exceeded not only in the periphery of the product but also in the centre. To know for certain, use a kitchen thermometer, a very useful, inexpensive and easy-to-use utensil. With practice, you will learn to detect whether a food has reached the desired temperature with the naked eye.

■ **Reheat safely.** There is a certain risk involved in reheating a previously cooked dish. It is important to heat it to a safe temperature, since microorganisms may have grown in the food during the time it has been cooling, perhaps outside the refrigerator.

■ **Cool adequately.** If you need to cool a preparation quickly, you can immerse it in a container in a water bath of cold water, or place it in a cool place. It is not advisable to cool hot products in the refrigerator, not so much because of how this may damage the product, but because this will cause a sudden rise in temperature and an increase in humidity inside the refrigerator that may affect its contents.

■ **Wash fresh produce.** It is essential. In the chapter 'Preparation Methods' you will learn about food cleaning procedures. Vegetables in particular should be washed thoroughly, whether eaten raw or cooked.

■ **Labelling of products and processes.** If you mark the products with their name and the date of purchase, opening of the package, preparation or freezing, it will help you to remember the consumption priorities and use-by dates (*photo 1*).

2

1

- **Use suitable containers.** It should be noted that dehydrated products keep for a long time, while fresh products deteriorate easily. This is due to humidity. Since water is a vital element for microorganisms, you should avoid humid containers and spaces, where microbes proliferate with joy. Using plastic bags specified for food preservation, storing food in clean, dry and airtight containers, or packing them in vacuum-seal bags are some possibilities (*photo 2*).
- **Avoid exposure to air.** Not all microorganisms need oxygen to live, but a large part of them do, so eliminating oxygen will prevent them surviving. This is achieved with the vacuum-packing technique, which removes oxygen from the containers to slow the multiplication of microbes. However, the process involves certain specifics; for example, it makes no sense to vacuum-pack products that are not really fresh. In addition, it is not risk-free, since certain microorganisms — anaerobes — can develop in oxygen-deficient conditions. For these and other considerations, if you decide to buy a sous vide cooker to vacuum pack, it is best to have training beforehand.

MISE EN PLACE

BEFORE YOU BEGIN TO COOK, YOU MUST GATHER ALL THE INGREDIENTS, MEASURE THEIR PRECISE QUANTITY AND HAVE THE NECESSARY UTENSILS WITHIN YOUR REACH. YOU SHOULD MAKE SURE YOU LACK NOTHING TO COOK WITH PLEASURE.

There is a French expression used in all professional kitchens, 'mise en place', and it defines the preparation process prior to cooking a recipe. In other words, prepare all the ingredients in the correct quantities and prepare the work surfaces, all the equipment and the necessary accessories before getting into action in the kitchen.

Everything must be well organised and calculated so that nothing is missing at the last minute, and so that you do not waste time, which is usually an essential factor in the kitchen. Being meticulous always helps the preparation of any dish, no matter how simple, to be a success. The order will also be of vital importance for following the step-by-step instructions of a recipe.

FOLLOWING A RECIPE

It is not always easy to understand a recipe the first time; in fact, it almost never is. So before you start, you should read it carefully and make sure that you understand it perfectly, that you have mastered the proposed preparation and cooking techniques, and that you have the necessary time. It is important to work systematically to avoid making mistakes, especially when you have to combine different processes at the same time, such as boiling some vegetables while you start frying or cutting the garnishes.

However, following a recipe does not have to be a rigid process. Once the information is well assimilated, you can always play around with it, introducing modifications and adapting it to your ideas. If you wish to, try experimenting. Cooking, in short, is a creative process and the great chefs have been formed in large part thanks to curiosity and trial and error. In addition, if you note down your variations or observations, you will be able to improve the recipes and adapt them to your way of cooking.

CLASSIC ASSEMBLY OF A PLATE

1 Spread the sauce on the base of the dish.

2 Arrange the ingredients in a balanced way, with a variety of shapes, textures and colours.

3 Apply the complements, condiments and seasonings right before serving.

2

3

WEIGHTS AND MEASURES

In recipes, most ingredients are linked to numbers and measurements. Weights and volumes are combined and often lead to doubts. In addition, not all cultures use the same system of units, so sometimes interpreting the quantities to be used to prepare a dish is a challenge.

If you have suitable kitchen equipment for measuring and weighing (scales and measuring spoons and jug), it will be easier to apply the exact quantities proposed in the recipe, but you can also achieve their equivalence with common kitchen utensils (spoons, glasses, cups, etc.).

MOST COMMON MEASUREMENTS

Liquids

1 glass of water = 250 ml

1 cup of coffee with milk = 250 ml

1 cup of espresso = 100 ml

1 glass of wine = 150 ml

1 cup of tea = 150 ml

1 glass of yogurt = 150 ml

1 glass of cognac = 40-50 ml

1 tablespoon = 15 ml

1 teaspoon = 5 ml

1 serving ladle = 250 ml

Solids

Due to the texture and density of the food, although at equal volume, the weight may vary. Some indicative equivalences are as follows:

	1 GLASS (250 ml)	1 TBSP (15 ml)
RICE	190-200 g	10-12 g
SUGAR	200-220 g	12-15 g
BUTTER	225 g	8-10 g
WHEAT FLOUR	120-140 g	18-25 g
SALT	200-220 g	15-25 g

1

SERVICE

OF COURSE, PREPARING A FAMILY MEAL IS NOT THE SAME AS PREPARING AN INTIMATE DINNER FOR TWO. FOR EACH TYPE OF MEAL THERE IS AN APPROPRIATE WAY TO SERVE IT, WHICH WILL GREATLY INFLUENCE THE WAY IN WHICH YOU COOK IT.

Anticipating what you will need at the end of the process is as important as getting off to a good start. You should be prepared to finish the dish properly: if you are going to remove food from the oven, think about the necessary safety measures. Next, prepare the utensils with which you will serve your dishes (plates, cups or trays), and decide whether to use ladles, palatte knives or tongs to do so.

Don't forget the dining space: there should be clean surfaces ready to receive the dishes. You should also have the complements and decorative elements ready that you will incorporate to the final dish: herbs, spices, flowers, crunchy toppings, etc. And, finally, go over the dish or plate with a damp cloth or kitchen paper to present it clean of splashes. Your dish, the result of your effort, deserves a good presentation.

2

MENUS AND SERVICE

Depending on the type of food you are planning to cook, the prepared dishes can vary greatly in terms of shape, the necessary tableware, quantities and presentation. In professional kitchens we talk about types of services.

If you wish to organise a meal with a number of dishes for a full service, the recommendation is to offer the dishes that you are most comfortable and confident in preparing. It is not worthwhile getting involved in complicated recipes that prevent you from enjoying cooking. Fresh, healthy and simple cooking is always welcome.

- **Traditional service.** This is the most common type of service, based on first and second courses, or salad and main course.
- **Aperitif.** It consists of an arrangement of different dishes for sharing and nibbling on, offered to a group of diners before the main course.
- **Buffet.** It is a common choice for informal parties where food is generously laid out on tables for diners to serve themselves at their leisure. Monographic areas of prepared dishes can be organised: a salad buffet, an area with the most hearty dishes, a dessert buffet, etc. (*photo 1*).
- **Tasting menu.** It consists of a series of small-sized dishes that allow the diner to taste a considerable variety of options. It usually ranges from 4 to 10 plates. To prepare a tasting menu at home, 6 courses is a good option. Of course, this has its complexity: you will need to master their execution and be able to prepare and serve them in an appropriate time interval (*photo 2*).
- **Barbecue.** It is a casual occasion that allows you to savour a wide variety of products cooked on the spot. A few finger foods can be prepared to accompany the main course, cooked on the barbecue, with side dishes and sauces to share.

KITCHEN SAFETY

THE KITCHEN IS A PLACE WHERE ACCIDENTS CAN HAPPEN. HOWEVER, IF YOU FOLLOW A FEW SIMPLE SAFETY RULES, YOU CAN AVOID RISKS AND COOK MORE SAFELY WITH GREATER PEACE OF MIND.

Safety in the kitchen is part of the order required for proper cooking. This workspace entails risks that is often underestimated due to the daily routines in the kitchen. It is important to follow certain rules, especially regarding the use of sharp utensils, heat sources and electrical appliances. You can take advantage of the resources that the kitchenware industry has placed at our disposal to contribute to kitchen safety.

- **Avoid burns.** Keep kitchen oven gloves handy at all times. Do not use kitchen paper or wet cloths to pick up a hot pan. To avoid dangerous splashing, gently incorporate the food into the very hot oil or water. Protect yourself with long sleeves and an apron. If a frying pan catches fire, cover it immediately with a cloth or a lid and never pour water into it.

1

2

- **Ladles and wooden spoons.** Avoid leaving ladles and wooden spoons inside pots on the hob, and lift the lids carefully so as not to be burned by the steam.
- **Safe knives.** Keep knives sharp and dry, avoid allowing them to protrude from the work space and carry them carefully, never in a horizontal position.
- **Pot and pan handles.** Make sure that they never protrude from the hob (*photo 1*).
- **Chopping boards.** Get used to cutting and handling food on boards that fit the work surface well (*photo 2*).
- **Electrical appliances.** Check that you have turned off all controls when you finish cooking, and remember to unplug electrical appliances before cleaning them.
- **Smoke extraction.** The kitchen must have a good extraction system for the absorption of fumes, grease and moisture. Make sure that the hood and its ducts are clean of grease and are working properly.

Joan Roca

THE PRODUCE

THE VARIETY, RICHNESS AND QUALITY OF THE PRODUCE DETERMINE TO A LARGE EXTENT THE PERSONALITY OF EACH CUISINE. THEY ARE THE BASIS OF ANY PREPARED DISH, ALTHOUGH THEY DEPEND ON OUR KNOWLEDGE TO OFFER THEIR FULL POTENTIAL.

Today, it is easy to source a wide variety of products from around the world throughout the year. This allows us to expand our range of possibilities when it comes to cooking or tasting new dishes. However, without falling into dogmatism or rejecting the opportunities offered by market globalisation, we are in favour of starting by becoming aware of local products, of being sensitive and attentive to those that belong to our geographical and climatological region, and that are part of our memory and tradition.

Cooking with local products – that is, with food produced within a radius of around 100 kilometres around us – often provides us with unbeatable tastes, and it links us territorially with our culture, therefore allowing us to recall our gastronomic past. Food, like music, often has that great evocative power that serves to awaken sensations and memories hidden within us. Let's enjoy this pleasure.

In addition to the organoleptic quality of seasonal and local produce that allow them to be consumed at their optimum ripeness, we contribute, through our choice, to a sustainable consumption by avoiding the energy cost of long transports. At the same time, we promote agriculture in accordance with the rhythms of the seasons and support farmers, fishermen and livestock breeders.

However, we don't overlook certain very interesting products more typical of neighbouring cultures and gastronomies. Because, in spite of what has been said so far, knowing other ways of understanding cuisine and of treating products will also enrich our own gastronomic universe.

In the following pages, we will review the specifics of the main produce groups, the seasonal calendars that will help us to determine the best time of year for each of them (which means more flavour and, almost always, better price) and we will also point out some suggestions for processing or cooking them. However, we reiterate that curiosity and the desire to know exactly what we have in our hands are essential to expand our knowledge in the gastronomic universe, in which every small detail or variation can bring innovation to our dishes.

VEGETABLES

THE WORLD OF VEGETABLES OFFERS US A WIDE VARIETY OF PRODUCE WITH MULTIPLE AND SURPRISING FLAVOURS THAT ARE VERSATILE IN THE KITCHEN AND HAVE A GREAT RICHNESS OF NUTRIENTS.

This food group is very complex and lends itself to numerous classifications. The food items are referred to generically as vegetables because, although most of those presented are vegetables, also included are other plants that, without belonging to the gardener's world, also have an interesting use in the kitchen. From here on, their selection and description will be based on strictly culinary criteria.

There are many vegetables that are already incorporated regularly in most menus and daily diets. However, it is worth rediscovering some varieties that are used less frequently, despite their high gastronomic value. In general, they are all versatile in terms of their preparation: many vegetables can be used raw as a first course or as a salad; they can also be boiled, sautéed or grilled, or presented in the form of soups and creams. They can either be part of a second course as a garnish or complement, or be the essential element of a dish.

They are classified here according to the part of each vegetable that is consumed: leaves, roots, bulbs and underground tubers, stalks, fruit, and pods and seeds.

SALAD LEAVES

Rich in vitamins A and C, calcium, fibre and chlorophyll, leafy vegetables have great antioxidant power. Most of them are green, and their high water content provides hydration to our body. This group includes the entire lettuce family, which offers a wide range of textures – from fleshy to light – and very different flavours – from sweet to bitter. By simply combining them together, it is possible to create a delicious salad.

Vegetables that lend themselves to being cooked must be cooked in a way that enhances their flavour and at the same time respects their nutritional properties to the maximum. However, the leaves can also be used to prepare risky preparations, as a complement or garnish. Despite their apparent simplicity, they can add complexity and flavour to main dishes.

It is worth mentioning some somewhat forgotten plants, such as red chard and chicory, as they are as tasty and rich in minerals as the more familiar and nutritious spinach.

- Butterhead Lettuce
- Chard
- Chicory
- Cos lettuce
- Endive
- Escarole
- Iceberg Lettuce
- Lettuce
- Lollo green
- Lollo rosso
- Red chard
- Ruby gem lettuce
- Spinach
- Watercress

CABBAGES

There are different types of cabbages with different shades and tastes. Some varieties have a strong flavour, while others are mild, so when combined they offer interesting contrasts. If you wanted to, you could have one type of cabbage for each day of the week, and you can cook them in many different ways. Although you can boil and use them in broths and soups, a little creativity is enough to get more out of them. Their leaves, for example, can be used as a wrapper for preparations, and they can also be preserved as pickles.

- Broccoli
- Brussels sprouts
- Cabbage
- Cauliflower
- Chinese cabbage
- Red cabbage
- Romanesco cabbage
- Swede

ROOTS, BULBS & TUBERS

Roots, bulbs and underground tubers are often relegated as a side, but if you learn to take advantage of their intense earthy flavour, your preparations can acquire new nuances.

Roots and tubers are a great reservoir of nutrients and delicate, fleshy textures. Boiled, they are always delicious, and are essential in stews, broths and soups. If you fry them, you'll discover tasty appetisers and original garnishes. Thanks to their striking range of colours, you can create attractive creams or purées that combine well with herbs and spices. In contrast, bulbs such as garlic or onion are the basis for all kinds of sautéed foods and are ideal in salads for their refreshing qualities.

- Beetroot
- Carrot
- Celeriac
- Garlic
- Leek
- Onion
- Parsnip
- Potato
- Radish
- Shallot
- Salsify
- Spring onion
- Sweet potato
- Turnip

STALKS

To ensure freshness and fullness, the stalks should be firm and crisp, with leaves that are bright and vivid in colour and, especially in the case of celery, aromatic. The latter is very useful in all kinds of hot preparations, such as soups, braised dishes and stews, while raw it brings all its freshness to salads and even cocktails, such as Bloody Mary.

Another vegetable with a strong personality is asparagus, both white and green. It usually gains prominence when served either as a side dish or in a main course.

- Asparagus
- Cardoon
- Celery

FRUITING VEGETABLES

This group includes a good part of the most known and used vegetables in our cuisine. For each one you can find an infinity of varieties that will provide more and new flavours and textures. Many of them have an intense colour and taste, and their raw consumption provides a great amount of vitamins and minerals.

Many fruiting vegetables can be found practically all year round, but the recommendation is to consume them at their peak of ripeness, which is mostly in the warm months. This is when they will offer the most flavour, and also when you can find them at a good price. It is also when it will be time to take them into account in your recipes and menus, and even to preserve them so they are available when not in season or you cannot find them at the market.

They are the protagonists in a multitude of preparations: in stir-fries, as a base for all kinds of dishes, as garnishes or as a main dish.

- Avocado
- Aubergine
- Cayenne pepper
- Chilli pepper
- Courgette
- Cucumber
- Green pepper
- Red pepper
- Squash
- Tomato

PODS & SEEDS

The seeds and casings (pods) of some vegetables are edible. They belong to the legume family, and can be consumed as a vegetable (fresh) or also as a bean when they have undergone a drying process for later preservation.

They are very rich in nutrients and can be prepared in many ways. If the vegetable is fresh and tender, as in the case of mangetouts or peas, they should be boiled in water, or cooked in a stir-fry, very quickly.

- Fava bean
- Green bean
- Mangetout
- Pea

	JAN.	FEB.	MAR.	APR.	MAY	JUNE	JULY	AUG.	SEPT.	OCT.	NOV.	DEC.
Artichoke	■	■	■	■	■					■	■	■
Asparagus				■	■	■						
Aubergine	■	■	■	■	■	■	■	■	■	■	■	■
Borage	■	■	■							■		
Broccoli	■	■	■	■	■					■		■
Brussels sprouts	■	■	■								■	■
Cabbage	■											
Cabbage, red	■	■	■							■	■	■
Cardoon	■	■									■	■
Carrots	■	■		■	■	■	■	■	■	■	■	■
Cauliflower	■	■	■							■	■	■
Celery	■	■	■	■	■					■	■	■
Celeriac												■
Chard	■	■	■	■	■	■	■		■	■	■	
Courgette	■	■	■	■	■	■	■	■	■	■	■	■
Cucumber					■	■	■	■	■			
Endive	■	■	■								■	■
Escarole	■	■									■	■
Fava bean		■	■	■	■							
Fennel (bulb)								■	■	■	■	■
Garlic				■								
Garlic, young	■		■	■	■	■	■					
Green bean				■	■				■		■	■
Leek	■	■	■	■	■	■	■	■	■	■		
Lettuce	■	■	■	■	■	■	■	■	■	■		
Lettuce, cos						■	■	■				
Lettuce, oak leaf							■					
Lollo rosso							■					
Onion	■	■	■	■		■		■	■	■	■	■
Calçot	■	■	■	■	■							■
Pea		■	■	■	■							
Pepper, padron							■	■	■	■		
Pepper, red	■	■	■	■	■	■	■	■	■	■	■	■
Potato					■	■	■	■	■	■		
Radish	■	■	■	■	■	■	■					■
Rocket				■	■	■						
Spinach	■	■		■	■		■			■		
Spring onion		■	■	■	■							
Squash	■	■	■							■	■	■
Sweet potato	■	■	■	■								■
Tomato				■	■	■	■	■	■		■	■
Turnip	■	■	■	■	■						■	■

A vegetable's season is subject to variations depending on the climatic zones of cultivation.

MUSHROOMS

Being part of the amazing universe of fungi, mushrooms are not really plants. Regardless, they are highly regarded in the kitchen, as they offer intense and unique flavours. We even detect in them **umami**, a term that comes from the Japanese, meaning 'tasty' or 'savoury', and that designates one of the five basic tastes, along with sweet, sour, bitter and salty. The best way to savour them is lightly cooked. Because they release a large volume of water and lose a lot of weight, it is best to cook them quickly to enhance their fleshiness and their earthy, damp and fragrant undergrowth aromas.

The mushroom season is short and, although you can enjoy dried and cultivated varieties throughout the year, they don't compare to the aromatic strength and texture of the wild and seasonal varieties.

As for truffles, choose firm and aromatic ones to take advantage of their full potential. Use truffles that are in season rather than tinned products, which lose their aroma. Truffles should be kept in the refrigerator, but only for a short time. Truffles are rarely cooked. Normally, they are added grated or sliced to the dish or warmed, so that excessive heat doesn't destroy their aroma.

HOW TO STORE MUSHROOMS

Mushrooms and truffles are delicate. The refrigerator is a good refuge for their preservation and you should prepare them only just before cooking. Some varieties can be washed with water, but for others it is better to clean them by removing the remaining soil with a cloth or a soft brush. If you won't be using them immediately, some varieties withstand freezing well, although many others keep better if dried; they can also be preserved in salt, oil or vinegar, or sautéed and frozen.

WILD MUSHROOMS

- Morel (*Morchella esculenta*)
- Cep, porcini, or penny bun (*Boletus edulis*)
- Saffron milk cap (*Lactarius deliciosus*)
- Caesar's mushroom (*Amanita caesarea*)
- St George's mushroom (*Calocybe gambosa*)
- Chanterelle (*Cantharellus cibarius*)
- Horn of plenty (*Craterellus cornucopioides*)

CULTIVATED MUSHROOMS

- White button mushroom (*Agaricus bisporus*)
- King oyster mushroom (*Pleurotus eryngii*)
- Shiitake (*Lentinula edodes*)

FRUIT

RICH IN NUTRIENTS, THIS FOOD GROUP OFFERS A REPERTOIRE OF FLAVOURS THAT ARE AS EXTENSIVE AS THEY ARE VARIED IN TASTES, COLOURS, TEXTURES AND SHAPES.

Fruit do not need preparation or other ingredients to express their identity and virtues. However, they can also be a surprising yet harmonious, intense or mellow complement, providing contrast or perfectly accompanying an infinite number of preparations.

To select the best fruit, ideally you should choose them piece by piece. In this way you can appreciate its aroma, consider its degree of ripeness for when you will be consuming it and reject the specimens with bruises and other marks. Remember the criteria for seasonality and proximity to ensure a tastier fruit and that respecting them is important for the environment.

Fruit contains a wide variety of vitamins and minerals, as well as high amounts of fructose, a natural sugar. To take advantage of its nutrients, and also for better taste, take into account some storage tips.

STORAGE TIPS

- **Store fruit in a cool, ventilated place.** Ventilation prevents the accumulation of ethylene, the gas that the fruit produces to trigger its ripening, which also leads to spoilage. A cool environment slows down the ripening process.
- **Keep fruit in suitable containers.** Keep fruit in a container that permits transpiration. Remove fruit from plastic containers or plastic shopping bags as soon as possible.
- **To favour the optimum ripening point.** To delay the ripening of the fruit and preserve it for a longer period of time, store it in the refrigerator, in the bin at the bottom. If, however, you wish to accelerate the ripening process, mix immature fruit with ripe pieces. These, by generating ethylene, will accelerate the ripening process of nearby fruit.

- **Apples.** Fiji, Golden, Granny Smith, Gala.
- **Berries.** Raspberry, strawberry, currant.
- **Citrus.** Kuzu, lemon, lime, clementine, tangerine, blood orange, grapefruit, kumquat.
- **Melons.** Honeydew melon, cantaloupe melon, galia melon, watermelon.
- **Pears.** Conference, Williams, comice.
- **Stone fruits.** Apricot, plum, date, mango, peach, nectarine.
- **Others.** Pomegranate, kiwi, quince, persimmon, passion fruit.

	JAN.	FEB.	MAR.	APR.	MAY	JUNE	JULY	AUG.	SEPT.	OCT.	NOV.	DEC.
Apple	■	■	■	■	■				■	■		
Apple, Granny Smith												■
Apple, Reineta											■	■
Apricot					■	■						
Avocado									■	■	■	■
Banana	■	■	■	■	■	■			■	■	■	■
Blackberry						■	■					
Blueberry						■	■					
Chestnut											■	■
Cherry						■	■					
Currant						■	■					
Custard apple	■	■			■					■	■	■
Date											■	■
Fig								■	■			
Grape, white							■	■	■	■	■	■
Grape, red								■	■	■	■	■
Grapefruit	■	■	■	■	■					■	■	■
Lemon	■	■	■	■	■					■	■	■
Mandarin	■	■	■							■	■	■
Mango									■	■	■	■
Medlar					■	■						
Melon						■	■	■	■			
Melon, galia							■	■				
Nectarine						■						
Orange	■	■	■	■	■					■	■	■
Orange, blood	■	■										
Peach						■	■	■	■			
Peach, flat						■	■					
Pear, comice	■	■	■							■	■	■
Pear, conference	■	■	■	■					■	■	■	■
Pear, Williams							■	■	■			
Persimmon	■											
Plum, green								■	■			
Plum, red						■	■	■	■			
Plum, yellow						■	■	■				
Pomegranate									■	■	■	■
Quince										■	■	
Raspberry						■	■					
Strawberry			■	■	■							
Watermelon						■	■	■	■			

A fruit's season is subject to variations depending on the climatic zones of cultivation.

HERBS, SPICES, FLOWERS, SPROUTS

THE VEGETABLE WORLD OFFERS US AN ENDLESS NUMBER OF AROMAS AND FLAVOURS, THANKS TO THE PLANTS WE USE AS CONDIMENTS. AS WELL AS ENHANCING THE FLAVOUR OF THE FOOD, THEY ADD UNIQUENESS TO EACH DISH WITH A TOUCH OF DISTINCTION.

Aromatic herbs, flowers, sprouts and spices add personality to our recipes. Sometimes they take centre stage and add character to the dish; other times they only offer a small nuance. Moreover, the ability to grow many of these herbs, flowers and sprouts ourselves adds a very rewarding element to the act of cooking. Let's take a look at the uses of the main groups.

HERBS

It is easy to grow aromatic herbs in gardens or in flowerpots on balconies and windows. In this way, you will have them available when you need them, and they will bring fresh aromas to your home. You can also purchase them in bunches from greengrocers and supermarkets, and keep them already prepared in trays in the fridge. When refrigerated, it is best to store them in half-open bags or wrapped in kitchen paper or cloth that absorbs moisture well and prevents the proliferation of microorganisms.

You can also use dried herbs and, like spices, they can help you to season all kinds of preparations. Their fresh version is clearly superior, but having them always available in your kitchen is an advantage.

Herbs can also be freeze-dried, and in many cases these are of a higher quality than the dried ones, since they maintain their properties better. This is the case for dill and rosemary.

- Basil
- Bay
- Chervil
- Chives
- Coriander
- Dill
- Fennel
- Lemon verbena
- Marjoram
- Melissa
- Mint
- Oregano
- Parsley
- Rosemary
- Sage
- Tarragon
- Thyme

FLOWERS

Because of their delicacy, beauty and flavour, flowers are used in many professional kitchens and, despite their widespread use, they never cease to amaze. A wide variety and quality of edible flowers are available. Their use, however, should give meaning to the dish beyond mere decoration, so their presence should be well measured and contribute aroma and nuances that round off the dish.

Edible flowers are sold in specialist shops, but you can also use the flowers of many aromatic herbs, such as rosemary, thyme, basil and fennel.

- Almond blossom
- Carnation
- Borage
- Courgette
- Elder
- Geranium
- Marigold
- Nasturtium
- Pansy
- Pea
- Rose
- Salsify
- Squash
- Violet

SPROUTS AND MICROGREENS

Representatives of the world of micro vegetables, sprouts and microgreens bring gustatory, aesthetic and nutritional qualities to our dishes. They come from naturally occurring plants, and yet they contain more nutrients than their adult version, since it is in the seeds where all their nutritional properties are concentrated, which are diluted as the plant grows.

There are more than 40 varieties of sprouts. You can grow your seeds according to hydroponics procedures – that is, the cultivation of plants by means of a nutrient solution dissolved in water. When the sprouts begin to grow and acquire the ideal size, flavour and texture, you can use them.

- Alfalfa
- Basil
- Borage
- Cabbage, red
- Lentils
- Mooli
- Mustard
- Mustard, red
- Radish
- Rocket
- Samphire
- Sesame
- Shiso
- Soya bean, green
- Turnip
- Wheat

SPICES AND OTHER CONDIMENTS

You could travel around the world through its aromas. Spices are evocative of landscapes and customs, and if you wish to discover their infinite possibilities, you could give your dishes all sorts of sensations: spark, freshness, warmth, vigour, etc. A slight increase in temperature is necessary to activate a spice's properties. In this way, its aromatic substances, which are volatile, act with greater intensity. However, you should use spices in small quantities, since their aromatic strength can be potent.

It is best to grind spices just before using them. You can make your own mixes. Salts, for example, can be characterised with different spices and herbs: with dill and lemon, or cumin and paprika.

- Cardamom
- Cayenne
- Cinnamon
- Cloves
- Coriander
- Cumin
- Curry powder
- Green anise
- Ground ginger
- Juniper berries
- Liquorice
- Nutmeg
- Paprika
- Pepper
- Saffron
- Star anise
- Vanilla
- Wasabi

THE STORE CUPBOARD

A GOOD STORE CUPBOARD WILL HAVE AN INEXHAUSTIBLE SUPPLY OF INGREDIENTS. IT IS WHERE ESSENTIAL INGREDIENTS ARE STORED, AS WELL AS THE OCCASIONAL TREAT. IT IS IMPORTANT TO CHECK IT FROM TIME TO TIME TO KEEP IT IN ORDER.

There are some basic products that should not be missing in any store cupboard but, of course, you can include treats. The important thing is to occasionally review the cupboard and replace items that are out of stock and check the use-by date of those that are in stock. The store cupboard is the place for foods that should be kept in a dry, dark place; it is well worth taking the precaution of putting the items that need to be consumed first in front, and it is a good idea to arrange the cupboard by food groups, which will help you in making a shopping list. In any case, the space allotted for each should be clean and well ventilated, and remember that tinned foods, once opened, should be transferred to a sealed plastic container and stored in the refrigerator.

Here are the main food groups and some suggestions for stocking the cupboard.

OILS AND SAUCES

- **Oils.** Almond, avocado, coconut, extra virgin olive, groundnut, hazelnut, sesame, soya, sunflower, truffle, vegetable.
- **Sauces and pastes.** Anchovy paste, mayonnaise, mustard, mint sauce, pesto, soy sauce, teriyaki, tahini, tapenade, tomato purée tomato sauce.
- **Vinagers.** Balsamic, cider, herbal, raspberry, sherry, wine.

GENERAL FOODS

- Coffee, tea and infusions
- Dried beans (pulses)
- Fermented cabbage
- Flours
- Gelatine
- Honey
- Jams
- Milk (UHT, instant)
- Olives
- Pasta
- Pickles
- Plant-based drinks
- Rice
- Stock cubes
- Sugar
- Table salt
- Tinned products

FISH

AS FAR AS ITS PRESERVATION IS CONCERNED, FISH IS A DELICATE AND FRAGILE PRODUCT, BUT IT IS ALSO VERY HEALTHY AND VARIED FOR ALL OCCASIONS AND MENUS. WHITE AND OILY FISH ARE ALSO ESSENTIAL IN A HEALTHY DIET.

Today, supermarkets can receive fish from anywhere in the world in less than 24 hours by means of fast transport methods that ensure its preservation. That's why we have an extraordinary variety at our disposal. The two large families of fish, white fish (containing about 2% fat) and oily fish (containing more than 5% fat), include many species. All have sensational nutritional properties.

However, if you are lucky enough to live near the coast, you can enjoy local and seasonal fish in all its freshness and splendour.

Like fruit and vegetables, fish also have a time of the year when they are tastiest, which usually coincides with their breeding season. Seek advice from your fishmonger to learn about the seasonality of each species and to help you clean and cut it, as advised in this book or as they recommend.

As fish is a perishable product, freshness is a decisive factor in its purchase. It is best to cook it on the same day you buy it or not to leave it in the refrigerator for more than one day. If it will not be consumed within a short period of time, it is better to buy frozen fish.

HOW TO RECOGNISE FRESH FISH

- **Bright eyes.** A fish fresh from the sea has bulging, crystalline eyes. If they are covered by a thin whitish layer and sunken, the fish has lost its freshness.
- **Red-hot gills.** This is another reflection of its freshness. When the gills lose colour or turn black, it is an unmistakable sign that the fish is no longer fresh.
- **Smell of the sea.** This is the normal smell of the fish when buying it. Avoid fish that smell too strong or even give off a bad odour.
- **Firmness.** The skin of the fish should be firm and the scales should be well adhered. Its flesh should be well attached to the spines, and the skin should show a more or less accentuated shine, depending on the species.

	JAN.	FEB.	MAR.	APR.	MAY	JUNE	JULY	AUG.	SEPT.	OCT.	NOV.	DEC.
Anchovy					■	■	■			■		
Bonito						■	■	■		■		
Cod	■	■	■	■	■							■
Conger eel					■				■		■	
Elver (glass eel)	■	■	■	■							■	■
Gilthead sea bream			■	■	■	■	■		■	■		
Hake					■	■	■					
Horse mackerel								■	■	■		
John Dory					■	■	■	■	■			
Lamprey		■	■	■								
Mackerel			■	■	■	■						
Monkfish	■	■	■	■	■	■						
Red mullet	■										■	■
River eel								■	■			
Salmon								■	■			
Sardine					■	■	■	■	■	■		
Scorpionfish					■	■	■	■				
Sea bass	■	■	■	■	■	■	■			■	■	
Sea bream	■	■	■	■							■	■
Shark							■	■	■			
Stingray					■	■	■					
Swordfish		■			■	■	■	■	■	■	■	■
Tuna					■	■						
Turbot			■			■	■					

A fish's season is subject to variations depending on the fishing areas.

SHELLFISH AND CEPHALOPODS

THESE ARE SOME OF THE MOST APPRECIATED AND DELICATE PRODUCTS THAT THE SEA HAS TO OFFER. AT THE TIME OF PURCHASE, IT IS ESSENTIAL TO RECOGNISE THE SIGNS OF FRESHNESS, AND SOMETIMES IT MAY BE BETTER TO PURCHASE THEM FROZEN.

Seafood is an exquisite and highly appreciated food. For this reason, and because of the difficulty involved in catching them and keeping them in good condition, their price tends to be high. You can also find good frozen seafood, often at more affordable prices, but it probably loses a little of the organoleptic qualities of the fresh product.

Today, it is easy to find seafood from different seas or oceans in the supermarket, and often at a better price than seafood from our local waters. It can sometimes be an interesting resource. But it is important to be well informed: although a Mediterranean lobster and a Canadian lobster provide the same nutritional qualities, they do not taste the same as they are not really the same species.

From a gastronomic point of view, the more interesting seafood groups are crustaceans and molluscs. The latter include three large groups of culinary interest: cephalopods (octopus, squid, cuttlefish), gastropods (snails, sea snails) and bivalves (mussels, clams, razor clams).

As in the case of fish, the group of shellfish, molluscs and cephalopods also requires some knowledge to make the right choice, both for their freshness and taste. In the fish market observe if the specimens that you are interested in show the unmistakable signs of freshness, although the ideal is to buy them alive.

CEPHALOPODS

- Cuttlefish
- Octopus
- Squid

CRUSTACEANS

- Brown crab
- Crab
- Crayfish
- Langoustine
- Lobster
- Prawn
- Rock lobster
- Shrimp
- Spider crab

MOLLUSCS

- Clam
- Cockle
- Mussel
- Oyster
- Razor clam
- Scallop

OTHERS

- Goose barnacle
- Sea snail
- Sea urchin

HOW TO RECOGNISE FRESH CEPHALOPODS

- **Firm flesh.** The flesh should be firm to the touch, moist, shiny and slippery.
- **Pearly colour.** Flesh colour should be white to pearly pink.
- **Strong tentacles.** They should be neither soft nor sticky.
- **Fresh smell.** Its odour should be clean and not too strong or offensive.

HOW TO RECOGNISE FRESH MOLLUSCS

- **Closed valves.** Reject specimens with valves that are open, but if they are ajar, you can check that they close on contact (indicating that the animal is alive).
- **Fresh smell.** The smell must be unmistakably of the sea of more or less intensity.

HOW TO RECOGNISE FRESH CRUSTACEANS

- **Firm joints.** Legs should not droop or have darkened joints.
- **Attentive antennas.** A fresh crustacean keeps its antennae very stiff.
- **Bright eyes.** The eyes, almost like little pins, should sparkle.
- **United body.** Head, abdomen and tail should not be dismembered.

	JAN.	FEB.	MAR.	APR.	MAY	JUNE	JULY	AUG.	SEPT.	OCT.	NOV.	DEC.
Brown crab	■	■	■	■	■	■	■	■	■	■	■	■
Clam	■	■	■				■	■	■			■
Cockle	■		■	■	■					■		■
Crab					■	■	■	■	■	■	■	
Cuttlefish				■	■	■	■					
Goose barnacle			■						■			■
Lobster					■	■	■	■				
Langoustine	■	■	■	■	■	■	■	■	■			
Mussel	■	■	■	■				■		■	■	■
Octopus									■	■		
Oyster	■	■	■					■	■	■	■	■
Prawn					■	■	■	■				
Razor clam	■	■	■								■	■
Rock lobster					■	■	■	■	■			
Scallop	■	■	■	■							■	■
Spider crab				■	■	■	■	■	■			
Squid							■	■	■			

A shellfish's or cephalopod's season is subject to variations depending on the fishing areas.

MEATS

WITH A STRONG PRESENCE IN OUR DIET AND OUR CULINARY TRADITION, THERE ARE A GREAT VARIETY OF MEATS AND MULTIPLE WAYS OF PREPARING AND COOKING THEM.

The main meats consumed in our culture are beef, pork and lamb, which are considered red meat, along with game; as well as poultry (and rabbit), called white meat. The classification in these two groups does not respond to a scientific criterion but specifically to a culinary criterion based on the colour of the raw meat. However, from a nutritional point of view, mammalian meat is considered red meat and poultry meat is considered white meat.

Whenever possible, it is better to purchase meat on the same day that you are planning to cook it, or at least make sure that it will be consumed in a short period of time. However, there are currently good storage systems, such as protective atmosphere packaging, which, when properly applied, will allow you to extend the meat storage period, as long as you are scrupulous and do not break the cold chain.

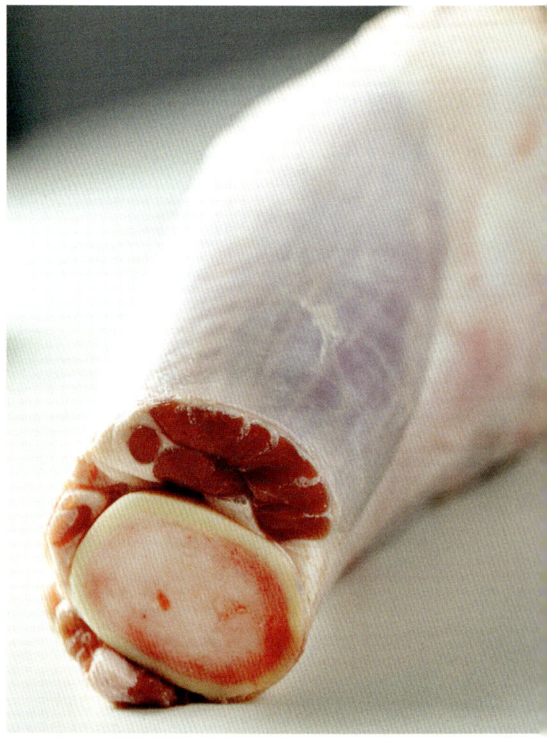

MEAT FROM CATTLE

There is an infinite number of veal and beef products available. It is a succulent meat suitable for all types of cooking, depending on the maturity of the meat and the part of the animal the cut is from. It can be prepared in different types of stews, casseroles, sautéed, grilled and even served prepared raw.

When you purchase red meat, opt for those with a bright colour, which is an unmistakable sign of freshness. The presence of streaks of fat infiltrated inside the meat, far from being a defect, is often a symptom of quality, and the meat should be flavoursome and creamy on the palate, as in the case of T-bone steaks.

MEAT FROM PORK

Pork is one of the most consumed meats in the world, despite the fact that some religions prohibit it. It is an extremely versatile meat, as almost all parts of the pig can be used in one way or another: in sausages, smoked and cured meats and countless other preparation methods.

There are parts of the pig, such as the loin or fillet, which offer tender meat for short cooking times, and others, such as trotters and bacon, very rich in gelatin, which require long cooking times.

Some pieces are perfect for grilling, such as chops and escalopes, and others make up a legion of deli meat products that can be used to complement and prepare a large number of dishes.

There are different breeds of pork, which provide different qualities and flavours. Iberian pork, for example, is one of the most appreciated.

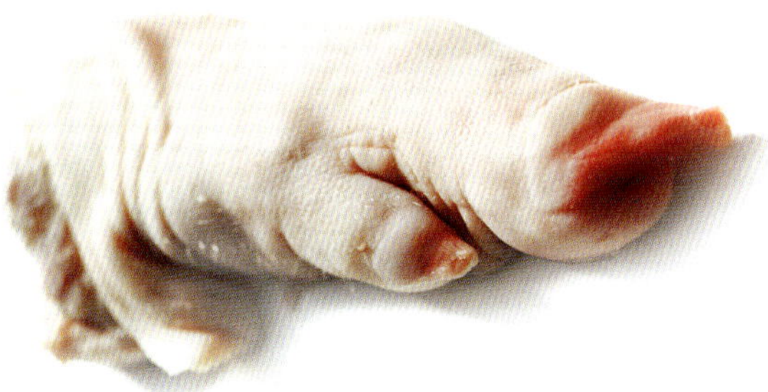

SHEEP AND GOAT

Lamb meat is rich in fat and has a marked personality. Tender in texture, it generally accepts short cooking times better; except for some cuts, such as the neck, skirt and leg, which require longer cooking times. Grilling and baking, and high-temperature cooking in general, enhance their flavour. Goat meat is very aromatic.

POULTRY

Whole, in supremes, diced, skewered, quartered, jointed, etc., there are many ways of preparing and cooking chicken: sautéed, roasted, marinated, stewed, etc. For the two main parts of the chicken, breasts and thighs, cooking often needs to be adjusted as they have different textures.

Game birds, which tend to have a more intense flavour, require some rest before cooking to tenderise their more fibrous and tougher meat.

OFFAL

Although offal, the parts of meat that are not considered noble, has fallen into disuse in domestic kitchens, it still has interesting uses. With a long culinary tradition, it often has powerful tastes and, in many cases, great nutritional value. Rediscovering offal in cooking can produce some very pleasant surprises.

Some very palatable pieces require long cooking to become tender, as is the case of pork rind or tripe, oxtail and veal tongue. In contrast, other offal meat, such as livers, brains and sweetbreads, require quick cooking processes.

KITCHEN EQUIPMENT

NOWADAYS, THERE ARE MANY UTENSILS AND OTHER EQUIPMENT AVAILABLE THAT MAKE IT MUCH EASIER TO COOK. UNDERSTANDING HOW TO TAKE ADVANTAGE OF THEM WILL HELP YOU TO FINE TUNE YOUR SKILLS AND EXPAND THE RANGE OF POSSIBILITIES IN THE KITCHEN.

Having a variety of kitchenware will make most kitchen tasks easier. It is not a matter of gathering the huge number of tools available in the shops today, nor of having the latest model of each machine, nor of owning the most sophisticated gadgets used in professional kitchens. The important thing is to have the appropriate tools for each type of preparation and cooking that you decide to undertake.

Sometimes, incorporating a new utensil, such as a simple thermometer, can open up the world of culinary possibilities, while returning to traditional hand utensils – such as a pestle and mortar, potato masher or coffee grinder – will allow you to obtain textures with greater control than those made with modern electrical appliances. You can experiment with new procedures and allow your imagination to run free, since kitchen utensils can give you the freedom to do so. They will also help you to improve your technique, to be more refined and precise in your preparations, which will contribute to achieving better dishes, more attractive presentations, improved results and, therefore, more delicious dishes.

1

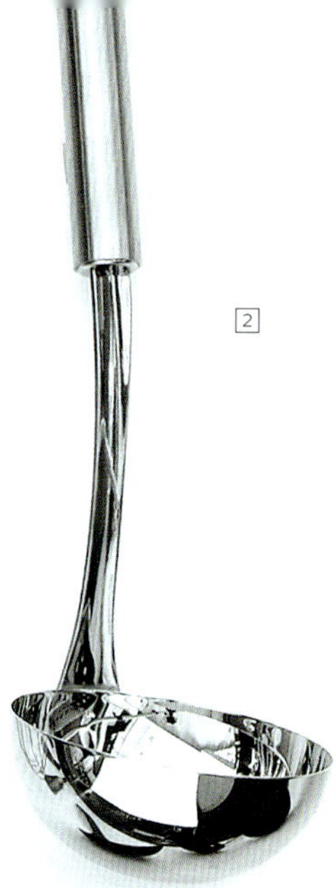
2

3

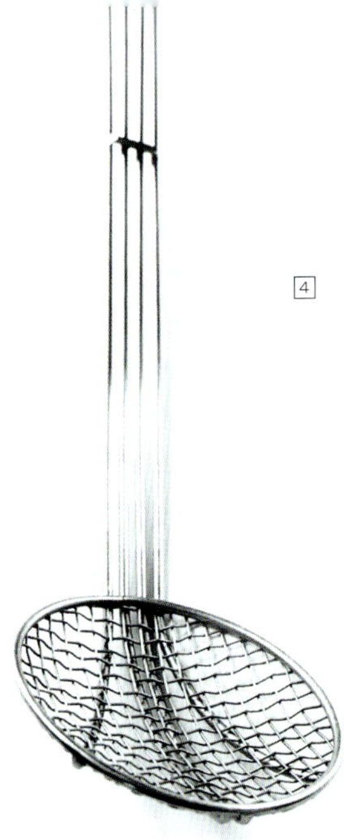
4

UTENSILS

FROM A RING TO GIVE AN ATTRACTIVE SHAPE TO A PREPARATION TO THE SERVING LADLE, FROM THE POTS AND PANS THAT GO ON THE HOB TO THE DEVICES THAT ALLOW BETTER CONTROL OF COOKING, EVERYTHING IS USEFUL IN THE KITCHEN.

There are different utensils for cooking and for different types of cuisine; each culture has a great variety. However, here is a review of some of the most common and necessary for the kind of preparations and products that are common in our gastronomic environment.

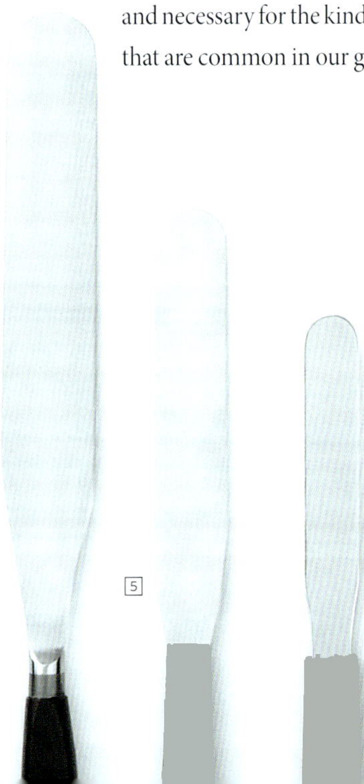
5

6

STIRRING, SCOOPING, SERVING

- **Whisk.** The curved wires, usually made of metal and linked to a handle, are used to mix or whisk foods (*photo 1*).
- **Ladle.** A spoon with elongated handle and deep bowl, used to serve soups (*photo 2*).
- **Skimmer.** A wide spoon used to skim stocks or broths, or for stirring and handling thick preparations (*photo 3*).
- **Spider.** Similar to the skimmer, but with a wire base; it is mainly used to remove fried foods from oil and drain them (*photo 4*).
- **Palette knife.** Its flat base is ideal for picking up and spreading products and preparations. It comes in different types, materials and sizes (*photo 5*).
- **Flexible palatte knife.** Rubber palette knife used to collect the last traces of creams, sauces or thick liquids adhering to a container (*photo 6*).

MOULDS

- **Mould.** Container used to shape a preparation under the action of heat or cold. There are an infinite number of varieties, of different shapes and capacities. Silicone moulds are useful, as this flexible and non-stick material allows for uniform cooking in ovens and microwaves (*photo 1*).
- **Dessert ring or mould.** Of different shapes and sizes, used to assemble plates. It is filled with the product and, when removed, the food is formed according to the desired shape (*photo 2*).
- **Biscuit cutters.** Mould used to cut and shape doughs, raw and cooked. It can also be used to cut fruit into attractive shapes. Some biscuit cutters can also function as rings. They come in many shapes and sizes.
- **Cake or tart tin.** Made of metal, smooth or corrugated, of different sizes, and sometimes adjustable; it is placed in the oven to make cakes and tart preparations. It is also used to bake the layers that make up a cake (*photo 3*).

SIEVES

- **Conical sieve.** Cone-shaped sieve with numerous holes, which enables separating the fibres and smaller particles of food from its own juice or liquid. It is normally manufactured in stainless steel. It is widely used to achieve a smooth and silky texture in cold creams or soups.
- **Colander.** It is used to separate food from its draining, soaking or cooking liquid. Colanders are available in different materials and sizes, and with mesh or holes of different diameters.
- **Dredger.** This utensil with small holes is used for sprinkling cocoa, icing sugar or other powdered foodstuffs on the preparations. It is very common in pastry making.
- **Drum sieve.** A wide metal mesh of more or less dense mesh used to lighten or refine products, such as flour or breadcrumbs. You can use it to eliminate lumps and obtain a fine and regular powder. Metal sieves are also used for straining purées.

1

2

3

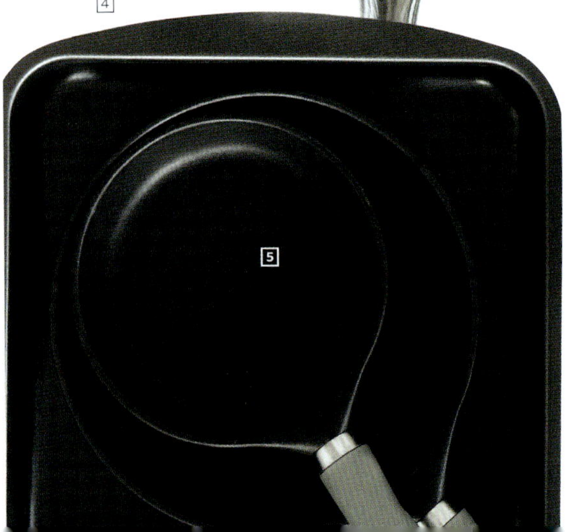

4

5

POTS AND PANS

- **Steamer.** Flat perforated pan that is inserted into a pot for steaming without the product touching the water. There are pans that are stacked on top of each other for the same purpose (*photo 1*).
- **Pot or kettle.** Container with side handles and lid designed to bring liquids to a boil, usually for making broths or boiling pasta and rice. Large capacity pots enable cooking large quantities of food (*photo 2*).
- **Saucepan.** Being circular and small, it is used to boil liquids or to prepare stews in small quantities. It enables long cooking, as most pans have a thick base that distributes the heat evenly and, consequently, achieves a stable cooking (*photo 3*).
- **Bain-marie (water bath).** It is a set of two pans, one large and one smaller, which allows indirect cooking of food through the heat of the water. With an accessory, it can be adapted for steaming.
- **Roasting tray.** Container used for roasting and grilling. It is usually made of metal, rectangular or oval, with a flat base and straight walls (*photo 4*).
- **Pressure cooker.** Hermetically sealed pot for fast cooking of food. The steam pressure makes it possible to increase the temperature inside up to 125°C and accelerate cooking.
- **Frying pan.** With a flat and shallow base, they are available in different sizes. Non-stick pans have a coating that prevents food sticking and allows cooking with less fat. It is ideal for quick sautéing and light cooking (*photo 5*).
- **Griddle/grill.** Usually made of cast iron, ridged (griddle) or flat (grill) pan, it is a heavy utensil, but it transmits heat very well. It is used on high heat and the griddle is excellent for creating charred marks on the product and retaining the flavour of the food.

GRINDING, MIXING, SEPARATING

- **Potato masher.** Its perforated base is used to manually mash boiled potatoes or other food products, such as carrots and parsnips, to obtain a purée of the desired texture (*photo 1*).
- **Potato ricer.** A sieve with a handle used to grind or 'pass' food, it is perfect for smooth purées. In the case of mashed potatoes, the potato ricer achieves a more product-friendly texture than an electric food processor (*photo 2*).
- **Pestle and mortar.** They come in different shapes, materials and sizes and are used to crush and grind food. With their help, you can prepare *picadas*, ground seeds and some sauces (*photo 3*).
- **Juicer.** It facilitates the pressurised extraction of juice from fruit, especially citrus fruit. There are electric and manual juicers (*photo 4*).
- **Manual grinder.** Mechanical mill, with a grinding wheel or wheel, operated by a crank or by a rotational movement of the cover. It enables grinding seeds into particles of a more uniform size than with electric grinders. Although it retains its traditional use for grinding coffee, you can achieve other interesting applications, such as grinding salt and spices in small quantities or reducing to powder certain dried foods, such as some mushrooms. They are available in many sizes and materials.

2

3

1

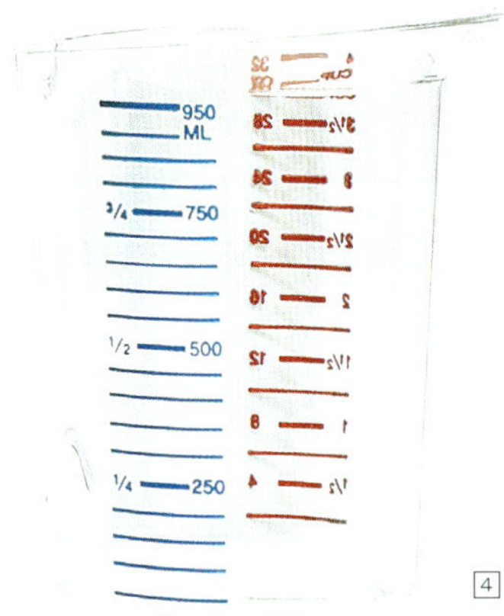

4

5

MEASURES

- **Scales.** Used to weigh the products, there are different types and capacities depending on the food and the quantities to be weighed (*photo 1*).
- **Measuring jug.** This is the appropriate container for measuring liquid volumes. They are available in different sizes and materials (*photo 4*).
- **Timer.** It is a very practical tool for measuring and controlling the times of the different cooking phases of a preparation (*photo 3*).
- **Measuring spoons.** They are used to measure small quantities (volumes) of ingredients. They are also necessary to follow the recipes of certain international cuisines that give measurements in *spoons* — along with measuring cups (*photo 2*).
- **Thermometer.** It is used to cook a product to a precise temperature. There are thermometers for different culinary uses: for frying, for confectionery, a special one for chocolate, etc. (*photo 5*).

KNIVES AND RELATED TOOLS

THERE IS NO KITCHEN WITHOUT KNIVES. THEY ARE AN INDISPENSABLE TOOL THAT WE OFTEN USE INTUITIVELY, ALTHOUGH CERTAIN RULES MUST BE FOLLOWED IF WE WANT TO ACHIEVE MORE PRECISE, FASTER AND SAFER CUTS.

Cutting with knives is relatively simple, although they are not always used properly and it is easy to make mistakes. To begin with, along with the knife, you need a chopping board that stabilises the cutting action properly and is securely held to the work surface. It is also important to use the right knife for each food and each type of preparation, as you will see in the following pages.

Knives should always be clean and dry before starting work. They should also be washed immediately after use. It is better to do so by hand, avoiding abrasive scouring pads and using neutral detergents to preserve the natural shine of the steel. They should not be left submerged in water for a long period of time.

If knives are washed in the dishwasher, they should be placed upside down in the cutlery basket to avoid rubbing against other utensils and, when the cycle is finished, they should be removed immediately and dried thoroughly with a clean, absorbent cloth.

Finally, it is essential that knives are always well sharpened, both to ensure their efficiency and for safety reasons. A good edge allows effortless and controlled cutting, while a dull (or poorly sharpened) knife cuts unpredictably and forces the cook to overexert themselves as they cut.

SHARPENING AT HOME

To properly preserve knives, professional sharpening is the safest, but at home you can keep the cutting edge sharp following some methods.

- **Steel.** A common kitchen practice is to run the steel along the knife's blade, creating maximum friction with the edge. It is not a precise method but helps to maintain the cutting edge (*photo 1*).
- **Mechanical sharpener.** It holds the knife blade at the right angle and thus creates a longer lasting sharp edge (*photo 2*).
- **Stone.** Sharpening with stone is a system widely used in oriental kitchens, which consists of passing the knife over certain types of stone so that it cuts well. It is a very effective method but requires perseverance and practice.

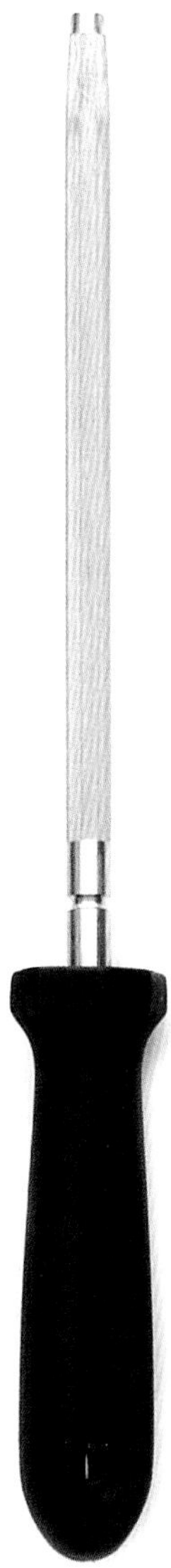

1

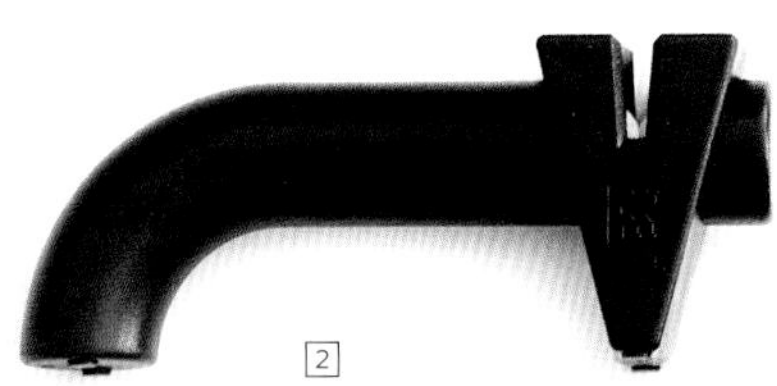

2

TYPES OF KNIVES

- **Paring.** Small knife with a narrow, pointed blade about 7 centimetres long. It is a very versatile and precise cutting instrument used to make small cuts, to peel, turn or shape all types of food (*photo 1*).
- **Cook's.** With a long, triangular blade, it has a strong, stable edge and a slightly curved edge to balance the knife for easy cutting. Used for carving or breaking bones (*photo 2*).
- **Vegetable.** Similar to the cook's knife, but smaller (between 15 and 30 centimetres), it is a multipurpose tool for cutting and chopping all kinds of products.
- **Boner.** Equipped with a thin, pointed blade of about 12 centimetres, it easily accesses narrow crevices, so it is mainly used to remove the bones from all types of meat and fish (*photo 3*).
- **Meat cleaver.** With a very wide and almost square blade, it is used to cut meats and fish and to flatten steaks (*photo 4*).
- **Ham carving knife.** Specific for carving ham, its narrow, flexible blade is about 40 centimetres long (*photo 5*).
- **Bread.** Its serrated, saw-like edge with large teeth tears the fibres of the bread (*photo 6*).
- **Electric.** It has two parallel serrated blades that slide in opposite directions. It is mainly used for cutting, dividing and slicing preparations that have delicate or complex textures and require little pressure (*photo 7*).
- **Cheese.** There is a great variety depending on the type of cheese. A generic classification groups those used for cutting hard cheese, which are large with a flat blade, and those used for soft cheese, with a usually perforated blade (*photo 8*).
- **Filleting.** Thanks to the long, thin, flexible blade and smooth cutting edge of this knife, meat and fish can be filleted with clean cuts.

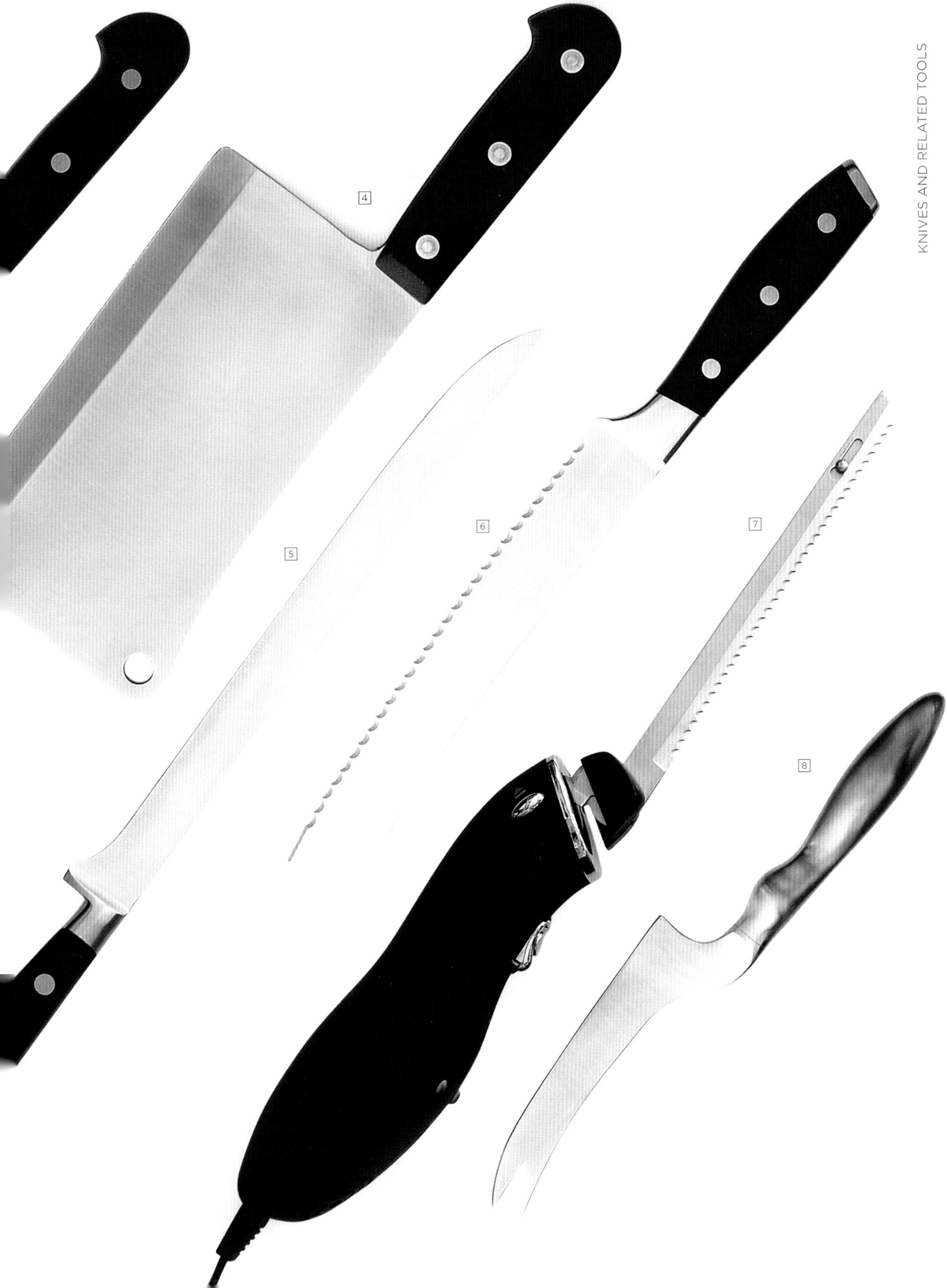
4
5
6
7
8

1

2

3

4

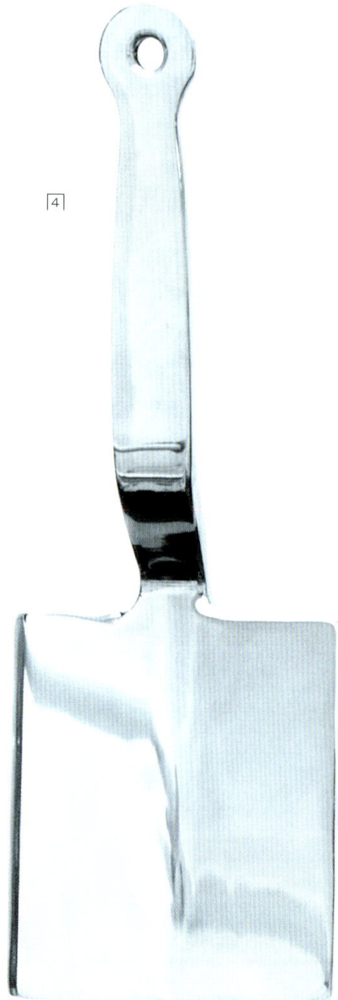

OTHER UTENSILS

WHILE YOU SHOULD MAKE SURE YOU HAVE THE BASIC TOOLS AT YOUR DISPOSAL, THERE IS A WIDE VARIETY OF CLASSIC TOOLS ON THE MARKET, WITH UPDATED DESIGNS, WITH WHICH YOU CAN KEEP YOUR KITCHEN UP TO DATE.

In addition to the basic tools for everyday use, such as scissors and tin openers, there are other more sophisticated tools to help embellish your preparations, such as the zester or melon baller. While the former basic tools are essential at home, it may be interesting to incorporate some of the latter gadgets and have them become part of your regular equipment. Having a good selection of tools will often allow you to introduce more variety to your daily creations and inspire you to tackle new recipes.

OTHER UTENSILS

- **Butter curler.** It has a circular blade with knurled teeth for easy handling of butter (*photo 1*).
- **Zester.** Its small blade makes attractive grooves in fruit and vegetables by removing strips of skin. This provides an interesting contrast of different colour stripes. It is widely used for cocktails, either as a decorative ornament or as an aromatic condiment (*photo 2*).

5

6

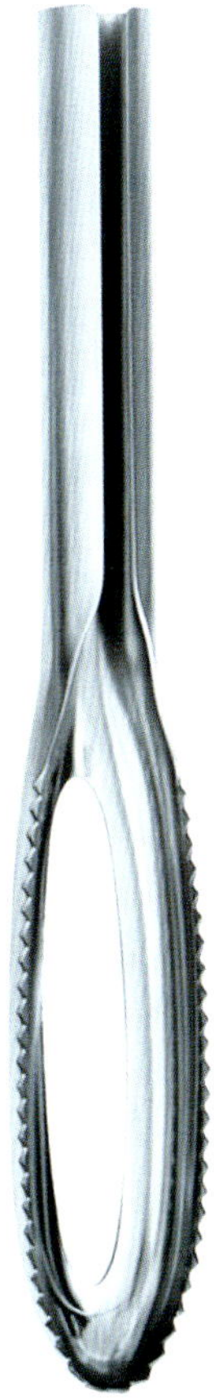

7

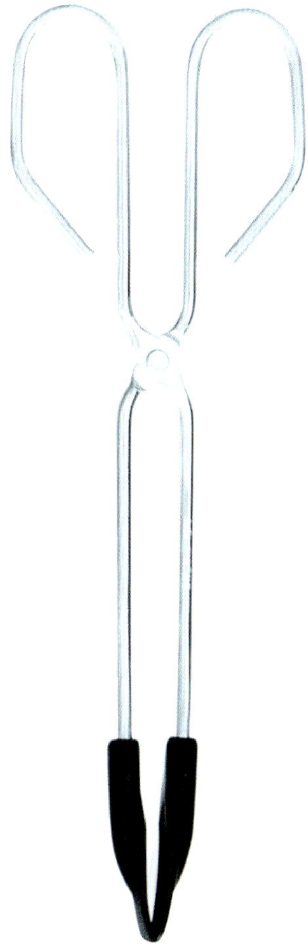

■ **Stainless steel tweezers.** They help to hold products of small dimensions with precision or that require great delicacy (*photo 3*).

■ **Mallet.** Very heavy and made of steel; used to crush raw meat and fish meat (*photo 4*).

■ **Peeler.** Ideal for peeling fruit and vegetables, its blade allows it to superficially cut the product, avoiding the cut to be too thick (*photo 5*).

■ **Larding needle.** Cylindrical and elongated needle used to introduce strips of bacon or some other product inside the raw meat (lard).

■ **Flange needle.** Steel rod used to shape raw poultry by attaching its extremities to the body so that it does not fall apart during cooking.

■ **Stone remover.** It is used to remove the stones from olives or fruits such as cherries.

■ **Scaler.** Thanks to its serrated shape, it can tear off the scales from fish (*photo 6*).

■ **Non-stick kitchen tongs.** The silicone protection allows you to remove ingredients from pots and pans without damaging their coating (*photo 7*).

■ **Ice-cream scoop.** Special spoon to form ice-cream balls. Thanks to its hollow handle, the heat of the hand is used to serve the ice cream more easily. They are available in different sizes.

■ **Oyster knife.** To avoid risks in the arduous task of opening oysters, it is essential to use this specific utensil, which has a hard and sharp blade.

■ **Apple corer.** It is a cylindrical and hollow tool used to extract the core of the fruit (with the seeds and the stalk). Different models are available depending on the type of fruit.

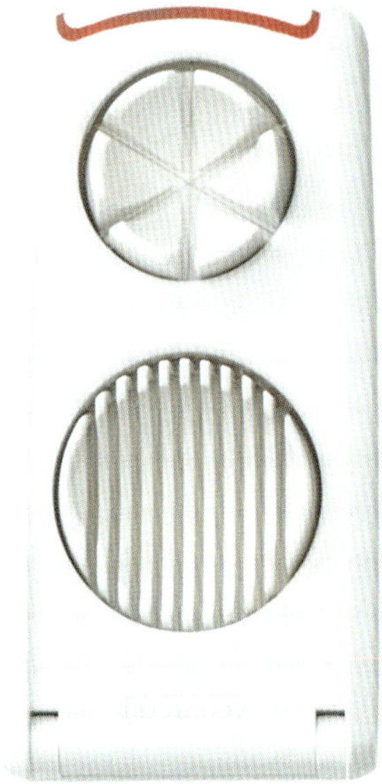

1

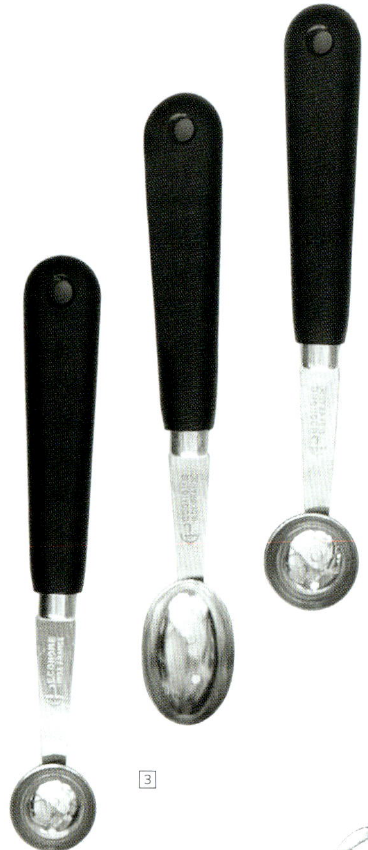

3

2

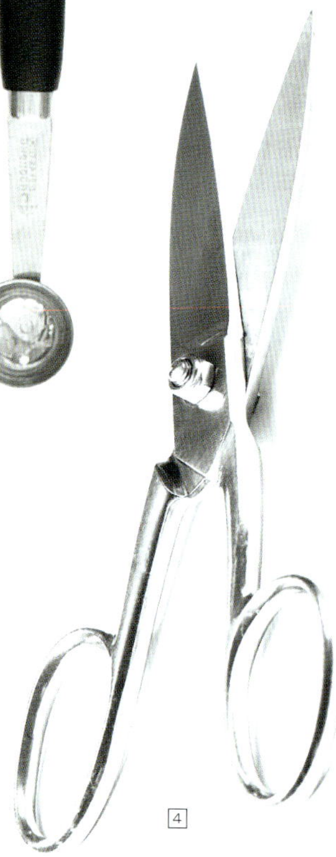

4

■ **Egg cutter.** Allows an egg to be cut into slices of an even thickness with a single movement. It can also be used to cut other ingredients, such as strawberries or mushrooms (*photo 1*).

■ **Egg separator.** It is a simple but very useful tool for separating the egg white from the egg yolk, making sure that the yolk does not spill out.

■ **Tin opener.** A classic and essential utensil for opening tin cans. Today, the most classic models coexist on the market with a thousand and one new designs and materials (*photo 2*).

■ **Melon baller or scoop.** It is used to extract balls from melons and also vegetables, such as potatoes, turnips, carrots, etc., and to present them in a regular and attractive way in garnishes. They come in different sizes and shapes (*photo 3*).

■ **Kitchen scissors.** There are different models with blades adapted for each specific use: for cutting fish, meat tissues, bones, etc. The pivot axis is located away from the handles to make it easier to exert force when cutting. It is one of the indispensable utensils in the kitchen (*photo 4*).

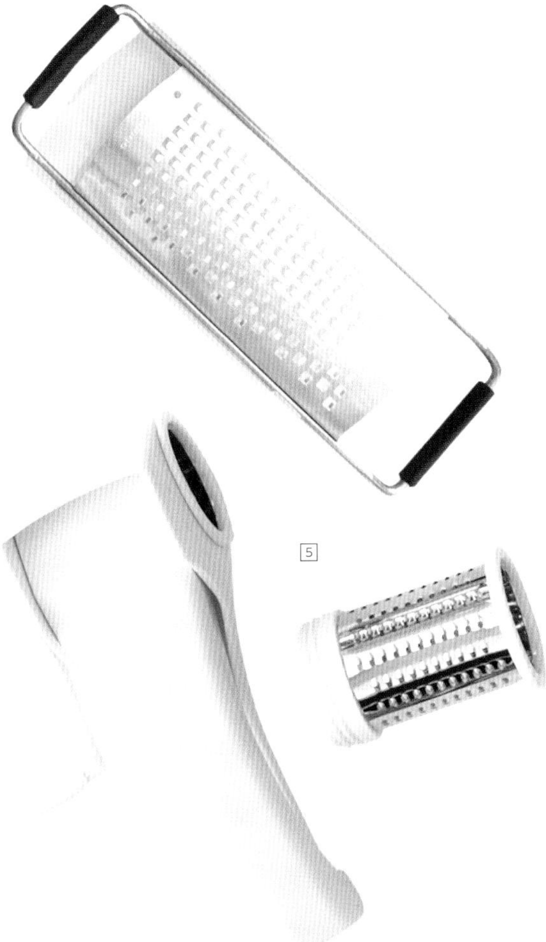

5

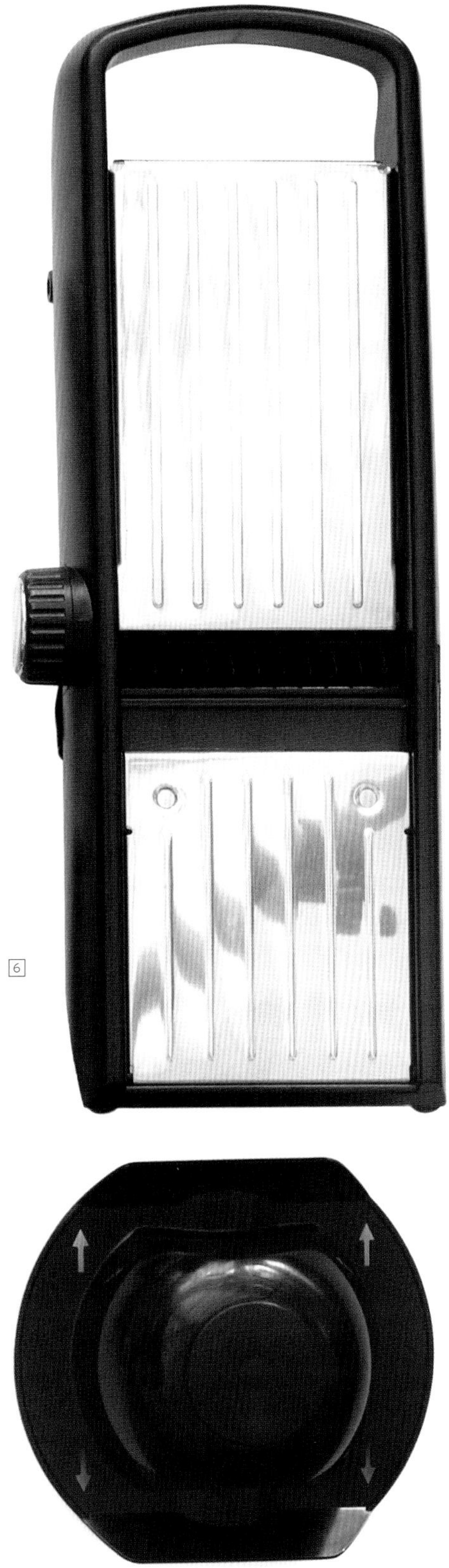

6

■ **Grater.** It is used to grate a wide variety of products (cheese, fruit, citrus peel, vegetables, etc.). Graters are available in various sizes and thicknesses. The Microplane brand, with which you can grate almost effortlessly, are among the most precise ones (*photo 5*).

■ **Mandolin.** Its sharp blades make it possible to make cuts that would be difficult or even impossible to perform with a simple knife. With different accessories, it is possible to make cuts with special shapes: lattice, corrugated, etc. (*photo 6*).

APPLIANCES

MORE AND MORE MACHINERY ARE BEING DEVELOPED FOR NEW CULINARY USES. MANY HAVE ALREADY MADE THE LEAP FROM THE PROFESSIONAL KITCHEN TO HOME USE, ALLOWING HOME COOKS TO ACHIEVE SURPRISING PREPARATIONS.

There are small appliances produced for domestic use that make some tasks much easier. Many of them have already been present in domestic daily lives for some time, such as the electric juicer, stand mixer, blender and grinder; others, such as sous vide cookers, are beginning to gain ground. Some, although more common in professional kitchens, can already be found in domestic format, from ice crushers to small ice-cream makers, flavour distillers or seed germinators. Here's a review of the main ones, some simple and others more sophisticated.

SMALL APPLIANCES

- **Stand mixer.** This is a multi-purpose appliance that is used for whisking, mixing or kneading food. They come with and without a bowl (*photo 1*).
- **Juicer.** It extracts liquids from foods, especially fruit and vegetables, by rapid rotation, then filters them through a sieve that retains the pulp, seeds and skin (*photo 2*).
- **Slicing machine.** It cuts meat and cheeses into equal portions, from thicker to thinner, depending on the selected position (*photo 3*).
- **Kitchen scales.** It weighs a product's mass and gives a measure in grams or kilograms. Due to the introduction of new ingredients, such as texturisers, that are used in very small quantities, another precision type of kitchen scales is attracting more attention (*see p. 88*).
- **Grinding machine.** Generally used for mincing meat, but it can also be used for stuffing sausages or making dried breadcrumbs (*photo 4*).
- **Deep fryer.** It has a basket for holding food that is dipped into a container with hot oil and then draining it. The electric one, besides being safer, provides temperature regulation through a thermostat; some of them have a timer.
- **Grill and sandwich maker.** The upper and lower thermal grill elements of these appliances facilitates cooking, charring, toasting or heating products and preparations without having to turn them over
- **Low-temperature oven.** The heat it generates is distributed by a fan, allowing the products to cook quickly and evenly. It controls the temperature with high accuracy, especially in the low temperature range of 50-120°C. It cooks with dry heat, like a conventional oven, and also allows moist cooking, such as steaming or vacuum cooking.
- **Induction hob.** It cooks food through the heat generated by the induction effect, which is obtained by the action of a magnetic field located under a glass-like surface.
- **Microwave.** It heats or cooks food quickly through electromagnetic waves.
- **Electric griddle or grill.** It cooks food by direct contact with its non-stick, smooth or ribbed surface, using very little fat and transmitting heat in a very uniform way.

1

2

3

4

1

■ **Dehydrator.** Extracts water from food by applying gentle temperatures by means of a consistent, hot air (*photo 1*).

■ **Electric grinder.** Its sharp blades finely grind the products. Nowadays, its use is scarce, since the food processor, which is more versatile, can also assume this function.

■ **Vacuum-packing machine.** There are now several models available for domestic kitchens. Useful for better food preservation, it works by extracting the air that concentrates in the bags or other containers holding the food, creating an almost total vacuum.

■ **Food processor.** This is a multi-purpose appliance, perfect for cutting, chopping and puréeing a wide variety of foods. Most are sold with discs for cutting and chopping, and paddles for kneading.

■ **Food processor-cooker.** Better known by their commercial brand names (Thermomix, Mycook, etc.), this machine performs different functions (shreds, minces, emulsifies, whisks, etc.) with a temperature regulator that allows you to heat or cook food while it is being processed (*photo 2*).

■ **Blender.** At the same time that it grinds the food, it emulsifies it, so that fluffy textures can be obtained. Its most classic use is the preparation of milkshakes (*photo 3*).

■ **Stick blender.** Detachable arm that allows the cook to grind, emulsify, mix and/or whisk products applying different speeds to obtain the desired result (*photo 4*).

■ **Juice extractor.** It obtains juice from food by pressure instead of centrifugation. It is a system that avoids the rapid oxidation of the products and increases the concentration of minerals.

■ **Electric steamer.** Cooks preparations by steam using temperature, time and pressure control.

■ **Frozen food processor.** Both a frozen food processor and emulsifier, it turns frozen food into ice cream or sorbet with perfect texture and temperature.

■ **Probe thermometer.** It measures the temperature of very hot food through contact with or penetration of its probe.

■ **Electric smoker.** For those who wish to delve into special preparations, this utensil smokes small quantities of food by burning wood chips from different woods. It is ideal for cooking meat at low temperature while flavouring it.

2 3 4

- **Ice-cream maker.** This device freezes the products progressively by introducing air into the interior, while constantly stirring the mixture to prevent the formation of ice crystals. It is ideal for achieving frozen ice creams or sorbets with a creamy texture.
- **Sous vide cooker (Roner).** This machine is mainly used to cook vacuum-packed food, as well as to pasteurise already cooked food. These are immersed into a water bath of circulating water, at a controlled and constant temperature of between 30 and 100°C. It has a programming system to cook with maximum precision. It is perfect for low temperature cooking, as it ensures that the temperature is very stable and uniform throughout the container, and preserves the food's nutrients and flavour (*photo* 5).

5

1

2

OTHER KITCHEN ACCESSORIES

FOR SOME RECIPES, ESPECIALLY IN THE WORLD OF PASTRY MAKING, SPECIFIC EQUIPMENT IS REQUIRED. YOU SHOULD ALWAYS MAKE SURE YOU HAVE EVERYTHING YOU NEED TO GUARANTEE YOU HAVE SUCCESS WITH YOUR PREPARATIONS.

In terms of equipment, there is no limit to those used in the culinary universe. As well as the essential utensils for preparing, cooking and storing dishes, there are other kitchen accessories, in some cases specific to certain preparations.

It is not a question of filling the kitchen cupboards with an endless number of tools, but of thinking about whether you have the right one for each preparation. If not, when you do acquire the appropriate equipment, you may discover a big difference.

ACCESSORIES

- **Brush.** This is very practical for brushing, smearing or smoothing preparations, usually with beaten egg. It is often manufactured in plastic (*photo 1*).
- **Pasta-making machine.** Thanks to its adjustable metal rollers, it is possible to roll dough into a fine sheet. In addition to rolling pasta dough, it has accessories to cut the dough into different shapes: noodles, spaghetti, ravioli, dumplings, etc. The domestic version is operated by using a hand crank (*photo 2*).

4

6

5

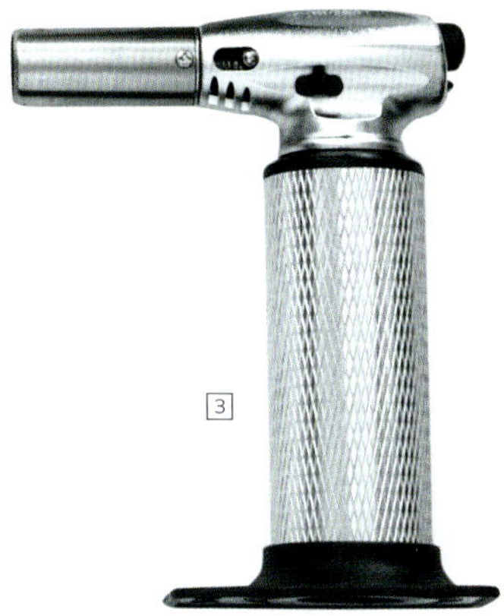

3

- **Cook's blowtorch.** Utensil that gives off a flame to sear or brown food. It is adjustable, so you can work safely and accurately. It is useful for cleaning and removing the remains of feathers on poultry, or to brown the outside of some products, such as tuna tataki. It is refilled with gas cartridges, sold in household goods shops (*photo 3*).
- **Salad spinner.** Container with a plastic grid for draining vegetables well after washing, as it effectively extracts the water that is deposited on the leaves by centrifugal force (*photo 4*).
- **Squeezy bottle.** Cylindrical container with dispenser for precise and controlled application of liquid products such as oils or vinaigrettes (*photo 5*).
- **Piping bag and nozzles.** Widely used in pastry making, the piping bag is a cone-shaped plastic bag fitted with a smooth or star-shaped nozzle attached to the opening. It is used to distribute and shape creams and doughs. There are single-use ones that are very practical and hygienic (*photo 6*).
- **Siphon.** It allows for the creation of light and soft foams without the need to incorporate any ingredient other than air. It is simple to use and works with compressed air cartridges. It achieves very airy and pleasant textures in creams, milkshakes and carbonated beverages.
- **Pipette.** For applying tiny quantities of liquids to decorate dishes with drops or to give them taste notes with oils. It consists of a thin tube that ends in a reservoir that contains the liquid. Graduated pipettes are available.

Joan Roca

PREPARATION METHODS

MASTERING THE VARIOUS PREPARATION TECHNIQUES AND PROCESSES WILL ENSURE A GOOD START IN THE KITCHEN. THEY INCLUDE A WIDE VARIETY OF PROCEDURES, WHETHER BASIC, SUCH AS CLEANING AND CUTTING INGREDIENTS, OR MORE SPECIFIC, SUCH AS CURING.

Culinary techniques comprise three types of processes: the preparation of food before cooking, cooking itself, with its different methods, and storage, both of the products and their preparation. A complete cook should not neglect any of these processes, because if a good product is the basis of a great dish, mastering the techniques will allow you to get the most out of it.

HANDLING FOOD

Various peparation techniques are necessary before cooking a dish. As well as cleaning and handling produce, other tasks include purchasing, storing and sometimes preserving the newly acquired product. The most complex of these are those related to food handling, which differs according to whether the product is processed raw, with water, with salt, heat, for flavouring or for preserving.

In most cases, during preparation, raw foods are kept cold during handling. In professional kitchens, preparation is, therefore, usually carried out in so-called **cold rooms – in other words,** rooms or spaces that have the necessary conditions to maintain the foods' cold chain. Obviously, there is not such space in the domestic home, but that does not mean that you should not pay attention to how and where you handle the products you will be preparing. If, for example, you have to prepare a freshly caught fish to cook it in the oven, you must first clean it, remove the scales, gut it and make a more or less deep cut – and all of this must be done quickly in a clean and cool place.

It is true that nowadays most of these processes can be avoided, because the products are already pre-prepared, or the professionals at the fishmonger's or butcher's can do the preparation for us. However, mastering techniques such as cutting various produce has some advantages: sometimes, buying whole pieces of meat or fish can be more economical, and allows you to cut them to your liking.

CLEANING PRODUCE

AS A GENERAL RULE, IT IS NECESSARY TO CLEAN FRESH PRODUCE BEFORE HANDLING IT, FOLLOWING A SPECIFIC PROCEDURE FOR EACH TYPE, WHICH WILL ENSURE MAXIMUM HYGIENE FOR COOKING.

Washing fruit and vegetables well will ensure that they are free of soil, insects, herbicide residues and bacteria that could be harmful to us. Fish and meat should also be washed or trimmed (the latter, in the case of meat), and the parts that are not suitable or useful for cooking should be removed.

In the course of all these tasks, you must remain rigorous with hygiene so as not to contaminate the food or the work space. You must also keep the products at the correct temperature to avoid breaking the cold chain, especially in the case of perishable foods, such as fish and meat. It is, therefore, important to work as far away as possible from heat sources.

- **Hygiene.** You must work on a clean and well organised surface, with the necessary utensils also clean and dry. You will need a container to place the useless or dirty parts that will be discarded, and another one for the food that will be cleaned and handled.
- **Cold chain.** If you are preparing perishable raw foods, such as meat or fish, you should try not to break the cold chain. Wash the fish or wipe clean the meat without delay and do not remove all the product from the refrigerator at once if it is not necessary.
- **Cleanliness.** When the product has been cleaned, the work area and the utensils or tools used should also be thoroughly scrubbed.

FRUIT AND VEGETABLES

The cleaning process for fruit and vegetables consists of washing them abundantly to remove the remains of soil and dirt that may be clinging to them. Cleaning is also essential to remove the residues of chemical products that are usually used in conventional crops. In addition to cleaning, you should separate the parts of the vegetables that are not edible or that are not necessary for your dish.

THE MAIN PROCESSES

- **Washing.** Simply soak the fruit or vegetable in cold water for a few minutes, rinse it with plenty of water and allow to drain in a colander or similar (*photo 1*).
- **Peeling, trimming or deseeding.** This task consists of removing the parts of the fruit or vegetable to be discarded (the stalk and the core with the seeds) and peeling the skin, usually with a peeler, or sometimes with a paring knife (*photo 2*). In the case of vegetables, such as roasted beets or boiled potatoes with skin, the skin isn't removed until after cooking, while others do not need to be peeled, such as courgette or baby carrots.
- **Supreming.** This technique is mainly used to peel citrus fruit for a beautiful presentation. With a sharp knife, remove all the skin, both the outer and the white parts, and even the membrane that covers the segments, and then separate them cleanly (*photo 3*).
- **Removing stringy parts.** Certain vegetables, such as chard and celery, have filaments in their stalks that can be annoying during processing, which is why it is necessary to remove them.

3

EASILY OXIDISED VEGETABLES

Artichokes, apples and other fruit and vegetables blacken soon after peeling. This is due to the oxidation that occurs when their enzymes come into contact with air. To avoid this, put them into a large bowl of cold water and lemon, vinegar or parsley, which are natural antioxidants, or use preparations such as citric acid.

Alternatively, to avoid the incorporation of other flavours, you could instead cook the vegetables under vacuum, or cook them as soon as possible in boiling water with a little oil.

ARTICHOKE CLEANING

1 Discard the outer leaves up to the third layer. The knife should be parallel to the heart of the artichoke, taking care not to remove the fleshy parts.

2 Peel the stalk to detach the leaves from the base, then cut off the lower, harder part.

3 Remove the fibrous part from the artichoke.

4 Keep in water and parsley to prevent oxidation.

MUSHROOMS

Mushrooms retain many aromas in their most superficial layer, so in general cleaning must be done carefully and gently.

THE MAIN PROCESSES

1 **Cut the stalk.** Cut off the base of the stalk, where there is more embedded soil. If the rest of the stalk is dirty, you can scrape it gently, but if it is a bitter-skinned mushroom — such as the field mushroom — you can peel it superficially. When the mushrooms are already a little old, they blacken; in this case you can also peel them slightly.

2 **Clean.** It is usually sufficient to wipe the mushroom cap with a damp cloth, applying a few light strokes to loosen any soil that may be on the inside of the cap. If you still cannot eliminate it, you can wash the mushrooms with plenty of cold water but drain them immediately.

1

2

CLEANING FISH

Cleaning fish is not always easy and sometimes even a risky task, depending on the species. That's why it's worth asking to have it cleaned at the fishmonger's shop. However, it is useful to know how to prepare the different types of fish, which will also help you to better understand the characteristics of each one.

You should bear in mind that fish is a delicate product in terms of conservation and must be handled as quickly as possible so that it does not lose temperature. It is, therefore, important to clean it in a space away from the hottest areas of the kitchen. Prepare a clean surface near the sink and place a container next to it to dispose of the waste. Finally, make sure that you have the correct tools: a chopping board secured to the surface, the right knives and scissors and, if available, a fish scaler.

STEP-BY-STEP CLEANING OF FISH

- **Deburring.** Start by removing the fins and beards with the help of scissors (*photo 3*).
- **Scaling.** Remove the annoying scales from the fish — if it has them — using a knife or, better yet, a scaler, which you should pass energetically along the body of the fish in the opposite direction to the scales. To prevent the kitchen and yourself being covered with scales, you can perform this operation with the fish and your hands inside a plastic bag (*photo 1*).
- **Gutting.** Remove the fish's viscera: the tripe, liver and roe. To do this you need to make a small incision in the belly of the fish and empty it.
- **Clean.** Rinse the fish under running water to remove the remains of the scales and guts. Cleaning must be done quickly, because excess water can reduce the quality of the product and compromise its freshness.

■ **Remove the skin.** Some fish, such as sole or monkfish, do not have scales, but they do have a hard or thick skin that must be removed. To remove the grey skin of the sole more easily, make a slight cut in the tail part and scald it. Then stretch the skin carefully, so as not to tear off the flesh of the fish at the same time. In the case of monkfish, simply stretch the skin to pull it off. As it is very gelatinous, you can use it to prepare a broth or a base, such as for a fish soup or rice, or to add its gelatine to a casserole with chickpeas or potatoes (*photo 4*).

■ **Deboning.** It is important to follow the same direction of the bones and their arrangement, because if you extract them in the opposite direction you can break the flesh. It is more accurate if you use tweezers (*photo 2*). Certain fish, such as sole, have external bones that surround the fleshy part of the piece; you can use scissors to cut them.

1

2

TRIMMING MEAT

You can usually buy the different types of meat preprepared; however, here is a review of some of the most common preparation techniques you can follow at home without difficulty.

THE MAIN PROCESSES

- **Scorching or singeing.** The legs of chickens or other poultry, as well as some parts of pork, are usually singed to remove the remains of feathers or hairs. For traditional scorching or singeing in the home, meat was exposed directly over the flame of the hob, but nowadays there are more practical, convenient and safer tools, such as the cook's blowtorch (*photo 1*).
- **Deboning.** You will need a suitable knife, called a deboner, and a chopping board. To start deboning, always look for making contact with the bone and following it, scraping and separating the meat. Some precooked products are already deboned and you only need to wait until the piece has cooled down to remove the bone very easily (*photo 2*).
- **Trimming or cleaning.** The term 'trimming' is usually used for most meats, while 'cleaning' is more common for poultry. The operation consists of removing the unnecessary or unwanted parts of the meat, such as the tendons and fat from a whole piece of beef fillet, the bones from a lamb shoulder or the skin from poultry (*photo 3*).
- **Gutting.** This is another part of the cleaning process, generally of poultry, which consists of emptying the inside of the piece of offal: liver, heart and gizzard. You should also get rid of other parts such as the neck and head, from which the crest is traditionally used in some cuisines for preparing dishes or stews, to which it provides a spectacular gelatinous component.

3

CUTS OF FOOD

THE PROCESS OF CUTTING FOOD MAY SEEM TO BE A VERY BASIC TASK THAT WE TEND TO PERFORM INTUITIVELY. HOWEVER, EACH PRODUCT AND EACH PREPARATION REQUIRES A SPECIFIC TYPE OF CUT.

Cutting is simply the act of dividing or separating a food into several parts to prepare it for further processing. It is a common technique in all kitchens, but it should not be overlooked because it is so elementary. There are some basic procedures that will guarantee better food handling and, therefore, greater efficiency, speed and safety.

These procedures are nothing more than the good practices that are basically standard in any task performed in the kitchen before cooking. To begin with, all the utensils you need, as well as the surfaces, must be perfectly clean and dry. You should choose the most suitable knives according to the ingredient and the procedure you will be performing; they must be well sharpened and the chopping boards must be secured well to the work surface. From this point onwards, for the best efficiency, you should also structure your work.

ORGANISING THE CUTTING OPERATION

- **Cut in the right order.** Arranging the utensils and products in the correct order will allow you to move forward in the cutting operation. Position the products to be prepared on your left and always work in a clockwise direction. In this way you will avoid mixing the whole pieces with the ones you have already cut.
- **Use the correct knife.** First, cut off all the tips you want to discard with the appropriate knife, then change knives to tackle the next task, such as peeling or trimming the product.
- **Apply the correct cutting principles.** Each product must be cut with the appropriate tools and by using the required cutting technique, as indicated in the following pages. To apply safe cuts, it is important to hold both the food and the handle of the knife well.
- **Separate the cuttings from the trimmings.** Deposit the fruit and vegetable skins in a specific container for waste. Do the same with the remains from trimming the meat or fish preparation. It is important to clear away the debris from the work surface so you don't soil or contaminate it. Place the peeled or cut product in a clean container.

VEGETABLE CUTS

It is essential to understand the essence of the cut and its function, since there are as many varieties of cuts as there are products, and these cuts often depend on the type of cooking that will be applied to them. Because each cut has its own meaning and its subsequent impact on cooking, sometimes, when cooking several vegetables together – as is often the case in sautéing or steaming, for example – you will need to cut each one in a different way. This is not only because each vegetable needs its own cut to cook well, but also to introduce variety to your dish.

Knives and chopping boards will be the usual tools. A cook's knife, a peeler and also a paring knife will be useful, and perhaps some other knife with a wide blade that is easy to handle and helps to make a quick cut. However, for some cuts you will use other types of utensils such as mandolins, rolling pins or melon ballers.

COMMON STEPS

1 **Make large sections.** First dry the piece well so it does not slip, then place it on the board and cut it into easy-to-handle large pieces (*photo 1*).

2 **Create a base.** Make a cut to create a base so the piece can be seated and you can continue working. In this way you will be able to cut it safely, without it moving (*photo 2*).

3 **Slice.** Cut the vegetables into slices of the desired thickness and size, either with the knife or the mandolin, which will help you to obtain slices of the same thickness at high speed (*photo 3*).

4 **Cut the slices.** Cut the slices into sticks, julienne strips or other desired shapes (*photo 4*).

5 **Cut sticks into cubes.** From sticks you can obtain dice of different thicknesses. These dice will be given different names, as you will see in the following pages (*photo 5*).

2

3

4

5

1

THE MOST COMMON CUTS

- **Slices.** Vertical or horizontal cuts of greater or lesser thickness depending on the intended use. The product can be sliced with a knife, but a mandolin or other slicer is ideal (*photo 1*).
- **Julienne.** Thin and long cuts, of different lengths depending on the product being handled. It is useful in basic preparations such as vegetables to make omelettes or stir-fries. In the latter case, where the cooking is rapid, cut the ingredient very finely so that it cooks quickly (*photo 2*).
- **Mirepoix.** Roughly cut without necessarily trying to obtain regular cubes. Choose the size of the cut depending on the preparation for which it will be used, but in general it is 2-3 centimetres. It is the usual cut for vegetables that are added to a soup, for example (*photo 3*).
- **Brunoise, or small dice.** Cut into very small cubes, 1-3 millimetres thick. This cut is often used for minced meat, for vinaigrettes, for seasoning preparations, or as a base for dishes such as a vegetable stir-fry (*photo 4*).
- **Paysanne, or diced.** This cut produces larger cubes than the brunoise cut and irregular shapes. It is used for salads (*photo 5*).
- **Spaghetti.** Cut very thinly along the vegetable's length to make spaghetti-like pieces. It is difficult to do this with a knife, but a mandolin has sufficiently fine blades to achieve this. With this cut you can obtain colourful vegetable garnishes that, cooked separately, will add freshness and colour to your dishes (*photo 6*).
- **Concassé.** This type of cut is applied to tomatoes, which must first be blanched, peeled, emptied of seeds before the flesh is cut into square pieces of about 1 centimetre (*photo 7*).

2

3

4

5

6

7

1

- **Wedges.** Cut that looks similar to citrus segments, without being exclusive to them (*photo 1*).
- **Score.** Using a scoring tool, you can make incisions on the outside of a vegetable or fruit, usually citrus fruit, to extract strips of peel (*photo 2*).
- **Grate.** Vegetables or other foods are rubbed along the grooves of a grater. Food can be grated in different thicknesses and shapes, usually to prepare sauces or stir-fries, and there is a variety of graters depending on the product, not only for vegetables, but also to grate cheese, wasabi, nutmeg and many others (*photo 3*).
- **Remove the choke.** This cut usually refers to the artichoke. It consists of cleaning and removing the fibrous centre, leaving only the most fleshy part. Nowadays, there is a tendency to keep part of its stalk as well (*photo 4*).
- **Quarter.** Successive cuts, perpendicular to each other, used to cut some vegetables and mushrooms. It is frequently used for mushrooms (*photo 5*).

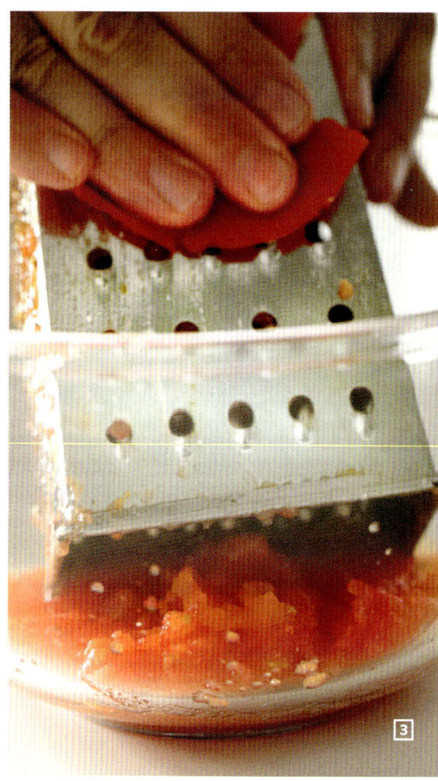

3

2

3

4

5

POTATO CUTS

This tuber deserves a separate mention because of the variety of cuts that can be applied to it. The potato oxidises very easily, so you must keep it in water after peeling, thereby reserving it for being handled.

CLASSIC CUTS

- **Straw.** Potatoes cut into very thin strips from the potato crisp cut (*photo 1*).
- **Matchstick.** Cut into sticks slightly thicker than straw potatoes (*photo 2*).
- **Chip.** Medium-thickness sticks (*photo 3*).
- **Crisp.** Thinly sliced with a mandolin. If you increase the thickness of the cut, you will have sliced potatoes (*photo 4*).
- **Chunky chip.** Cut very thickly to obtain rectangular potato blocks. Potatoes cut in this way need to be precooked before cooking. For example, after cutting it, it is usually precooked in oil over moderate heat, and then fried in a second step (*photo 5*).
- **Irregular chunks.** In this case it is not exactly a cut, since the potatoes are rather irregular, although you can use a knife to help. In this way, the starch in the potatoes is released easily and they cook faster. This type of cut is usually used in stews; the starch gives texture to the sauce, so it is not necessary to add any kind of thickening additive (*photo 6*).

THE TURNING TECHNIQUE

The term '**turning**' refers to shaping vegetables or fruit with a small knife or melon baller. This technique is widely used for potatoes when they complement different preparations, generally as a side, because it achieves a decorative and regular presentation. It is also common for carrots and courgettes.

The process consists of thinning the product with the knife. The vegetable is held by the ends to turn it easily on all sides and give it an oval shape. When turned, the vegetables are usually boiled or sautéed in butter.

By slightly twisting the potato or other ingredient, you can achieve an attractive garlic clove shape. A melon baller will facilitate a spherical turning of different sizes: hazelnut, small balls, olive, etc.

TURNING, STEP BY STEP

1 To make turning easier, first square the potato (or any other vegetable or fruit to be turned). In this way, you will be able to better master the cut.

2 Starting at one end, cut from top to bottom in a curved shape.

3 Repeat this action in successive cuts, making sure that all sides are equally proportionate, until the potato is completely turned.

FISH CUTS

There is a great variety of fish cuts, each of which has its own name. As in the case of vegetables and meats, each of these cuts is suitable for a specific cooking. Sometimes, the cut also responds to the needs of each species: you should not treat a fleshy fish, such as monkfish or hake, in the same way as a species with more bones, such as John Dory, or a small size fish, such as mullet or sardines.

The most common fish cuts are classified according to those that retain the bone or not.

FISH CUTS WITH BONES

- **Darne.** This word, which comes from the French, is usually translated as 'slice'. Culinarily, it usually refers to the steak cut obtained from the centre of a round fish. This cut is equivalent in quality to medallions from beef.
- **Steak.** Cut perpendicular to the backbone of a round fish. Of different thicknesses, it incorporates skin and backbone. Very common in fish such as hake, salmon or monkfish (*photo 3*).
- **Tronçon.** Designates a cut usually of large size (*photo 4*).

FISH CUTS WITHOUT BONES

- **Fillet.** This is the piece that is normally obtained from flat fish, such as sole or turbot, when the bones are removed (*photo 1*).
- **Loin.** These are the two sections that you can obtain from a fish of a certain size (hake, salmon)

when they are filleted. Smaller cuts can be made from the loins (*photo 5*).

- **Paupiette.** Rolled fillet. Often the fish is rolled with some other ingredient, sole with shrimp or other seafood, for example (*photo 2*).
- **Medallion.** The most desirable round cut from the central part of the fish. It is found in large fish, such as monkfish or hake (*photo 6*).
- **Supreme.** Very similar to the fillet, it is obtained once the fish loins are separated, either with or without the skin. This term is used when referring to fish with large-diameter loins, such as hake, cod, tuna, etc.
- **Chunks, cubes or dice.** The usual cut for marinades or fish stews, such as tuna (with which you can prepare a Marmitako), swordfish or mackerel (for escabeche).

PREPARING COD

Although this fish from the cold seas can be bought fresh and prepared using the cutting techniques already mentioned, in some cultures it is part of their culinary tradition to buy it dried and salted. For centuries, before the introduction of refrigerators and freezers, salted cod, and to a lesser extent tuna, have been products that gave inland villages regular access to this extremely valuable source of protein. Today, this ancient tradition has been preserved, thanks to the great gastronomic value that this method of preservation gives to cod.

Dried cod is sold whole or in pieces, and each one has a specific name and gastronomic quality.

COD CUTS

- **Rib, flank or belly.** It is a very tasty and mellow, small piece (*photo 1*).
- **Loin.** One on each side of the fish's backbone, it is generally the most appreciated part of the cod, as it offers generous chunks of flesh. They can be cut with or without the backbone, and in different sizes and shapes (*photos 2 and 5*).
- **Tail.** It has many bones and, therefore, enjoys less gastronomic prestige. However, it is very valuable because it has a lot of gelatine, which is much appreciated for binding preparations such as cod brandade (*photo 3*).
- **Crumbled.** It is not exactly a cut, but cod can be presented crumbled; the flesh is simply pulled apart by hand to form crumbs. Crumbled cod can be prepared for many diverse dishes, from rice to an omelette, or even raw and dressed as a salad (*photo 4*).

1

2

3

PREPARING CRUSTACEANS

The species belonging to the large family of crustaceans vary in size and shape. Cleaning and preparing a lobster is, therefore, not the same as cleaning and preparing a prawn, crab, spider crab or barnacle. With prawns, for example, the meat can be separated from the shell while raw. However, with larger crustaceans, such as a lobster or rock lobster, they must be cooked prior to removing the meat from its shell.

The crustaceans' anatomy must be taken into account when cleaning and preparing them. As a general rule, these extraordinary creatures are protected by a shell, and their body is divided into three parts: head, thorax and abdomen. However, in most of them, the first part of the thorax is attached to the head, forming a cephalothorax. They also often have two antennae and five pairs of appendages, including two forelegs that function as pincers.

Lobsters and rock lobsters are more meaty and, therefore, can be prepared and presented without their shells.

CLEANING A LOBSTER

1 Scald the lobster in boiling water and cool it in water with ice.

2 Separate the cephalothorax from the abdomen.

3 With scissors, cut the soft skin of the lower part of the abdomen on one side to remove the meat in one piece.

4 With the help of a knife, make two transversal cuts in each of the claws to break the shell into two.

5 Extract the meat from the appendages.

6 Use a pair of scissors to open the shell on the upper part of the claws lengthways to remove the meat inside.

2
3
4
5
6

MEAT CUTS

Although we often use the generic term 'slicing' to designate the action of cutting or separating meat into pieces, if you want to choose the most suitable piece for your recipe – and use the correct terminology – you will need to know the names of the different types of meat cuts. Here's a look at some of the most common cuts, focusing on those that we can use more frequently in kitchens. The terms presented here are the common ones for beef, veal, mutton, lamb and pork.

MAIN TYPES OF CUT

- **Dice or cubes.** Cutting the meat into cubes of different sizes is the best cut to use for stews and casseroles.
- **Shank.** Disc-shaped cut. It is the typical cut for osso buco, in which the rear veal shank (part of the leg) is cut horizontally with the bone (*photo 2*).
- **Medallions.** Similar in shape to disc-shaped shank cuts, this is the name given to the cylindrical cuts that are generally made in more tender pieces such as beef tenderloin or lamb loin.
- **Fillets.** Transversal cuts of a piece of meat. This meat must be cut perpendicularly to its muscle fibres so that it can be easily eaten and, therefore, its cut must be precise. There are steaks of different sizes and thicknesses, and depending on these factors, they have different names: from thicker steaks (between 100 and 150 grams, for grilling or pan-frying), to escalopes (100 grams, ideal for breading), to rump steak (50 grams, used in short and fast cooking, such as sautéed dishes, or, if the meat is tougher, in stews such as a Flemish Carbonnade, for example). For a thick steak to be eaten rare, it is better to choose the centre or the lower part of the fillet (tenderloin and fillet steak; see the following page), or the loin (entrecote).
- **T-bone steak.** Bone-in cuts of meats such as pork, beef or lamb. In the case of veal, the T-bone steak, which is often confused with entrecote, refers specifically to a high part of the veal loin with bone (part of the rib), and between 200 grams and 1 kilogram in size (*photo 1*).
- **Entrecot.** French term that refers to the meat between the ribs, although nowadays it has lost its specificity and is used in the same sense as T-bone steak. In the case of veal, the difference between it and the T-bone steak is that entrecote is served without bone, although it comes from the same area of the animal (the loin). The cut ranges from 150-500 grams.

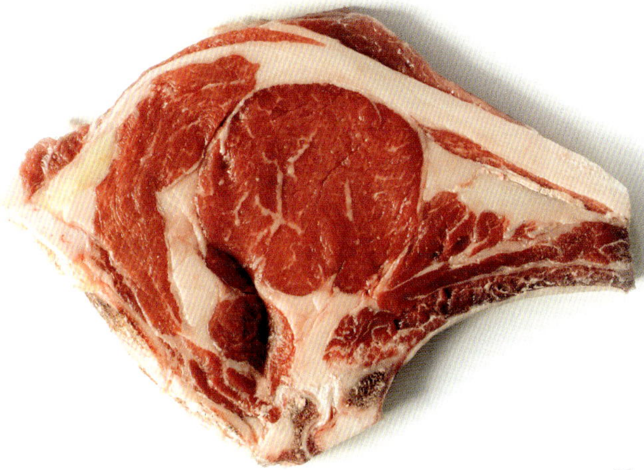

1

2

3 4 5 6

FILLET STEAK CUTS

The fillet is the section of beef or pork meat located in the lower part of the animal's ribs, between the ribs and the spine. It is one of the most appreciated, since it combines flavour, texture and succulence. The fillet can be cooked whole and cut afterwards, basically when grilled, or prepared in chateaubriande, medallions, fillet steak or rounds.

- **Chateaubriande.** Cut from the upper part of the fillet, also known as the sirloin, it is prepared for a minimum of 2 persons. The chateaubriande is usually roasted whole in the oven or on the grill, and cut in front of the guests, to be served slightly bleeding (*photo 5*).
- **Medallion and tournedos.** The medallion is the cross section of the centre of the fillet, weighing between 150 and 200 grams. Since it is the finest cut, it should be prepared right before serving. It is cooked on the griddle or grilled, although this can be followed with a few minutes in the oven to homogenise the cooking. The tournedos also comes from the central part of the fillet, weighs between 100 and 200 grams, and is usually wrapped with a slice of bacon to add juiciness (*photo 4*).
- **Fillet steak.** Cut from the lowest part of the fillet, so that the cuts obtained are small, but extraordinarily tender. They must be cooked quickly (*photo 3*).
- **Round.** Fillet that, trimmed of fat, is used to prepare steak tartare or hamburgers (*photo 6*).

FEATURED LAMB CUTS

- **Leg.** The hind legs can be cooked whole, but once boned, they can be cut into steaks.
- **Shoulder.** This part corresponds to the front legs of the lamb, which are smaller than the hind legs. They are very tender and juicy.
- **Saddle.** Although depending on each region this cut has different characteristics, normally the saddle includes the whole part — without cutting the carcass in half — between the legs and the ribs of the lamb, i.e., the loin.
- **Baron.** This is the rear half of a lamb that includes the two legs joined by the rib or saddle and the entire rib.
- **Kidney chops.** These are the low loin chops, the ones found when cutting the saddle apart. They are very tender, although small.
- **Lamb rack.** This is one of the most appreciated cuts for grilling, because it has a very tasty meat thanks to the fat that covers the skin, and also thanks to the fact that it is cooked on the bone.
- **Rib chops.** They are obtained from the upper part of the ribs, still with some bone, but without fat, since these are located below the shoulder, which when removed leaves them without skin. They are also very tasty, but have more nerves.
- **Noisettes.** The boneless loin is cut into medallions, perfect for frying or grilling.
- **Crown.** Very ornamental preparation of lamb ribs in which, generally, the upper part of each rib is cleaned of meat and fat. Sometimes this cut is also made with rabbit.

POULTRY CUTS

Cutting up a chicken at home is easier than it looks, and you will get a variety of parts for preparing various dishes. Bear in mind that, for food safety reasons, white meat should never be eaten raw, which is one reason why it is useful to cut poultry: it makes it easier for the meat to reach the safe interior temperature of a minimum of 65°C.

- **Supreme.** Boneless chicken breast, with or without skin. It is prepared whole, lending itself to long cooking. It is usually cooked on a griddle, grill or barbecue, combined with a few minutes in the oven or cooking in a sauce.
- **Thighs.** The upper part of the bird's leg, the bone protrudes from the meat. It is usually cooked for a long time in the oven, or with a sauce.
- **Fillet.** Boneless, skinless and filleted chicken breast. They can be cooked for a long time with some kind of sauce. Flattened escalopes are often breaded and fried, and thin slices can also be sautéed quickly, grilled or stir-fried in a *wok*.
- **Quarters and eighths.** When cutting the poultry into quarters, separate the breasts and thighs. Cutting into eighths involves splitting each quarter into two halves, a useful preparation for stewing (*photo 1*).
- **Wings.** Discard the tip, in which there is almost no meat, then divide the wings into two parts: the second phalanx, which has two bones and a very tender meat that can be prepared with quick cooking, and the first phalanx, with a central bone similar to that of the thigh. This inner part of the wing is not as tasty and needs more cooking time.

1

WATER-BASED PROCESSES

REHYDRATION, DESALTING AND BLEEDING ARE PROCEDURES THAT ARE APPLIED TO PULSES, MEAT AND FISH TO MOVE THE FOOD FROM A STATE OF PRESERVATION TO A STATE SUITABLE FOR COOKING.

Some products must be treated with water before they can be handled or cooked. This is the case for dried beans, which need to be soaked for several hours before cooking to rehydrate them and help them to become softer, or salted cod, which often need to be desalted with the help of several changes of water prior to handling. In all these cases, a simple element such as water intervenes as the product's transforming agent, allowing it to pass from a state of preservation to a new state that makes it suitable for preparation and consumption.

Another preparation technique that also requires water is bleeding, which is used to clean products such as pigs' trotters or sardines of blood and odours. In this case, water is used as a cleaning element.

REHYDRATION

Rehydrating a product is a simple process, but it is also essential. Commonly referred to as 'soaking', it simply involves putting a dried food into water so that it is reconstituted – in other words, so that it recovers its lost moisture – before proceeding to cook with it. The product should be placed in a large container and left in water for as long as necessary, depending on its characteristics. Sometimes it will only take a few minutes, but other times the process can take 8-12 hours, or in the case of cod even days.

Depending on the food, once rehydrated, it will be ready for cooking or instant consumption. The following are some of the products that usually undergo this process.

PRODUCTS REQUIRING REHYDRATION

- **Pulses (dried chickpeas, lentils and beans) and nuts.** They must be rehydrated in order to cook them more easily. Each type of pulse requires a specific soaking time. Chickpeas need about 12 hours, while lentils, which are more tender and smaller, need only 2 hours. Some nuts, such as chestnuts, are also processed in the same way (in this case, they require 12 hours of soaking) to be used as a complement for a dish (*photos 1 and 2*).
- **Gelatine.** In order for it to melt properly and perform its function of coagulating a liquid, gelatine must first be soaked in water. It is not necessary to wait a long time, just until it is flexible and transparent. Be aware that with rehydration its volume increases considerably.

- **Rice paper wrappers.** Very common in Asian cuisine to envelope a filling, rice paper wrappers should be soaked until they become transparent. A few seconds in water, no more than 5, is enough to make them malleable (*photos* 3–5).
- **Mushrooms.** To include out-of-season mushrooms in your preparations, you can use their dehydrated version. Dried mushrooms are a very versatile ingredient that need soaking for 30 minutes to 2 hours before cooking to reconstitute them and recover their fleshiness. If you are preparing a soup, stew, rice or even pasta, you can also use their soaking water to add more flavour to your preparation. For mushrooms in powdered form, simply sprinkle the powder over the preparation during cooking to rehydrate them. With the heat, they will release all their aromas.

1

■ **Couscous.** There are varieties of pre-cooked couscous on the market to which you only need to add the same amount of water to rehydrate to the wheat and it's ready to eat. You can simply add hot water, but any type of broth will also do (*photo 1*).

■ **Vegetables.** Certain vegetables, such as dried peppers or tomatoes, should be rehydrated before cooking or adding them to salads. Leave them for 30 minutes-1 hour in warm water to be able to extract their flesh, in the case of the peppers, or to eat the rehydrated product, in the case of the tomato. For preparations such as romesco sauce, the flesh recovered from the peppers is used, which is very tasty. You can also rehydrate onion to prepare sofritos.

DESALTING

For centuries, salt was the only element that could preserve certain highly nutritious foods for consumption. Even today, desalting ingredients that are preserved in salt is still an essential technique. Desalting is understood as the act of introducing a food into water to hydrate it and, at the same time, eliminate the large amount of salt inside due to the drying and salting processes that preserved it.

Without this step, the salted product becomes dry, friable, salty and, in short, unappetising. Cod and other fish preserved in salt are the foodstuffs par excellence that undergo desalting, a process that can be carried out at home.

Anchovies can also be placed in water for a few minutes to handle and debone them more easily. At the same time, this step reduces the salt level to make them more tender.

COD DESALTING PROCESS

- Place the cod in a bowl with plenty of clean water (*photo 2*).
- Change the cod water daily until the desired saltiness is achieved. Depending on the part of the fish used — loin, cuts, crumbled — and its thickness, you will have to wait more or less time.
- Remove it from the water and drain it completely. Once desalted, it can be kept in the refrigerator for 2 to 3 days.

BLEEDING

To clean certain meats and fish from blood, it is best to soak them in water. Bleeding is simply this delicate operation, which cleans certain foods (such as sardines or pig's trotters) of impurities and bad tastes and odours by immersing them in cold water for a certain time (10 minutes in the case of sardines and 2 hours in the case of trotters, depending on the size of the pieces) (*photo 3*). Add ice to prevent microbes from multiplying. It is a similar technique to the blanching process, a process that has the same purpose but is achieved by means of heat.

In some cases, a brine solution of salt and water, which is explained in the following pages, is also used to bleed meat and fish.

SALT-BASED PROCESSES

SALT HAS HISTORICALLY BEEN A PRECIOUS COMMODITY, AN OBJECT OF TRADE AND AN ESSENTIAL ELEMENT FOR THE PRESERVATION OF MANY FOODS. TODAY, IT IS STILL THE BASIS FOR INTERESTING CULINARY TECHNIQUES.

One of the most common acts in the kitchen is seasoning food with salt. This is a prime example of a process based on the use of salt, which is known as salinating.

Salt is also widely used to purify the excess acidity contained in some vegetables, such as courgettes and aubergines. Indeed, sometimes these are a little bitter after cooking, but if you first cut them and allow them to rest uncooked with a little salt, you can avoid this. This operation is known as sweating a food.

As well as enhancing flavours and making foods sweat, salt can also be used to cure them and, as has been done for centuries before refrigeration systems existed, to preserve them. The following pages look in detail at the applications for this extraordinary rock in the kitchen.

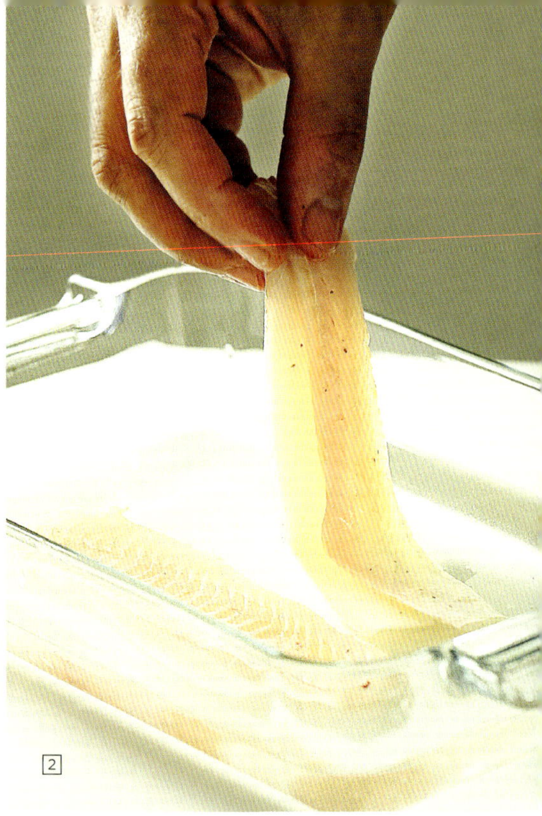

SALINATING

You can add salt, season with salt or soak an ingredient in brine, all of which are an action normally carried out before cooking a food to make a product tastier. But salt has certain properties that provide other valuable functions.

Food can be salinated before cooking and then again at the end of cooking, when the term 'adjust the seasoning' is used. Sometimes the salt adjustment can be done with special salts, such as flavoured or spicy salts, which add a unique flavour.

Although there are no secrets to the salinating technique, bear in mind that it must be done at the correct time, just before you start to cook, because if you salinate too far in advance, the salt can lead to the extraction of water from the product, so that, rather than enhancing its flavour, it acts in the opposite way by extracting its juices.

Nowadays, many professional kitchens tend to salinate using brine – in other words, leaving the food for a certain period of time in a solution of water and salt. This technique ensures uniform salinating of the food and contributes to juicier foods when cooked for long periods of time, as it improves the protein's ability to absorb and release moisture.

SALINATING IN A BRINE SOLUTION

1 Dissolve 7–10 per cent of kitchen table salt in hot water.

2 When the solution has cooled, immerse the product in it for 5 minutes–2 hours, depending on the size of the piece. For example, for sole, about 5 minutes are enough, while a whole suckling pig needs 2 hours.

CURING

Salt causes great transformations in food. Curing is perhaps the most interesting process caused by this edible rock. For centuries, this seasoning has been used to preserve numerous products, usually meat, fish and vegetables, as it prevents the proliferation of microbes. However, it is more than a preservation technique: today, we use it to intensify the flavours of certain ingredients.

Curing modifies the structure of the food, almost as if cooking it without heat, to achieve a texture and composition suitable for consumption. Ham is obtained through curing, for example. The process is simply the extraction of excess water from a product through the action of salt, which enables the modification of its texture so that the food is soft, tender and ready to eat.

Curing is used especially for meat and fish, and as well as the salt, sugar and herbs or spices are often added to flavour the product. It is a very common and tasty way to prepare salmon, for example.

It should be noted that the curing process also includes or combines other techniques such as smoking and food dehydration.

In some Asian cultures, it is very common to cure a wide variety of vegetables, such as cabbages, radishes and mooli, for example, in the same way that Mediterranean countries have traditionally turned a variety of seafood products into salted fish. It is a custom inherited from when there were no refrigeration systems, since curing with salt and the subsequent fermentation to which the vegetables were subjected allowed them to be available and provide a source of vitamins throughout the year.

CARPACCIO OF CEPS WITH PINE NUTS AND PARMESAN CHEESE

Time: 2 hrs| Level: easy

INGREDIENTS FOR 4 PEOPLE

60 g Parmesan cheese

For curing the ceps

1 kg coarse salt

500 g very fresh, tender and small ceps

For the vinaigrette

10 g toasted pine nuts • 2 g fresh chives

60 ml olive oil • Salt and pepper

METHOD

1 Scrupulously clean the mushrooms with a sheet of damp kitchen paper (*see p. 111*).

2 To cure the ceps, add a base layer of salt to a container and place the mushrooms on it. Cover them with more salt and leave to rest for 1 hour.

3 After the curing time has elapsed, remove the mushrooms, clean them and cut them into slices using a mandolin designed for truffles, if you have one, or with any mandolin.

4 Arrange the ceps on the plate. If they won't be eaten straight away, place the ceps in an airtight container arranged with layers of kitchen paper between them so they do not stick together.

5 To prepare the dressing, cut the pine nuts in half, chop the chives into fine julienne strips and mix everything with oil. Add salt and pepper.

6 Finish the dish by dressing the cep carpaccio with the pine nut oil and decorating it with the Parmesan cheese cut in strips.

*This dish is very simple to prepare and at the same time exquisite. It is best preparing only when you have small and tender ceps with compact and healthy flesh. As an alternative, other mushrooms can be used, such as Caesar's mushrooms (*Amanita caesarea*). As well as ceps, the* Boletus edulis *species of mushroom is known by the common names of porcini and penny bun.*

1

3

4

CURED SALMON WITH SPICES, YOGURT AND LEMON SAUCE

Time: 1 hr (+ 12 hrs curing) | Level: easy

INGREDIENTS FOR 15 PEOPLE

Sunflower oil
Frisée endive and purple shiso leaves
For the cured salmon
1.5 kg salmon loin
1 kg coarse salt
1 kg sugar
30 g black pepper
30 g white pepper
30 g Sichuan pepper
30 g pink pepper
30 g Jamaican pepper
30 g coriander seeds
30 g green cardamom
30 g fresh dill, chopped
For the sauce
100 g full-fat yogurt
1 spring onion
10 g fresh dill, chopped
1 lemon - Salt and pepper

METHOD

1 To cure the salmon, mix the salt and sugar in equal parts and add the herbs and spices for flavouring the fish. Cover the salmon with the salt and spice mixture and leave for 12 hours. The curing time depends a little on each cook's or diner's preferences: fewer hours produce a salmon closer to raw fish, while a longer curing time will create more concentrated flavours, but the salmon flesh will be a little drier.

2 After the curing time has elapsed, remove the salmon from the salt and spice mixture covering it.

3 Clean the salmon by using a cloth to remove any remaining salt before cutting it. If the fish will not be eaten immediately, coat it with sunflower oil and wrap in clingfilm. Store it in the refrigerator for no more than 3 days.

4 To make the yogurt and lemon sauce, mix the yogurt with the spring onion cut into fine brunoise. Add a few drops of lemon juice to the mixture and

season with salt and pepper. If desired, add a few pinches of finely grated lemon zest to the sauce.

5 Finally, place some thin slices of salmon interspersed with frisée endive leaves on the plates or platter for serving. Drizzle over the yogurt and lemon dressing, and garnish scattering with some purple shiso leaves and chopped dill.

Shiso leaves can be found in specialist Asian shops, and the flowers and seeds of this plant can also be eaten. They are very typical in Japanese cuisine, where the leaves are used as part of sushi and sashimi, and even prepared in tempura. There are two shiso varieties: green and purple. It is also available in dehydrated flakes for seasoning rice. Anti-inflammatory properties are attributed to it, in addition to being rich in iron and calcium.

The leaves in this recipe have a slight aniseed and mint flavour, and their freshness combine perfectly with unctuous fish such as salmon — the desirable effect in this dish.

KIMCHI

Time: 2 days of processing, minimum 2 weeks resting | Level: moderate

INGREDIENTS FOR 4 PEOPLE

To cure the cabbage

1 kg Chinese cabbage

2 litres water

80 g salt (preferably fleur de sel)

For the sauce

45 g pear

150 g tart apple

7 g garlic

30 g onion

3 litres water, infused with 8 g kombu

9 g salt

For the topping

80 g mooli (Asian radish)

40 g spring onions

40 g leek

3 g salt

50 ml fish sauce or nuoc mam

5 g chilli pepper or Korean paprika specially for kimchi

METHOD

1 To cure the cabbage, mix the 2 litres of water with half of the salt (40 grams). Cut the cabbage into quarters and cut the base so that the salt can penetrate. Place the cabbage leaves in a bowl, season them one by one with the remaining salt and pour the salted water over them so that it penetrates well between the leaves. Allow the cabbage to soak for 8 hours, changing the top leaves for the bottom ones a couple of times. Rinse them 3 times with water.

2 Drain the cabbage leaves and place them on a rack for 12 hours.

3 To prepare the sauce, purée all the ingredients together and strain them.

4 Mix the vegetables (mooli, spring onions, leek) with the fish sauce, to which you have already added the chilli pepper (when soaked, it will swell).

5 After draining the cabbage leaves, add the vegetables on top of each one.

6 Cover the cabbage with the vegetables.

7 After the sauce is incorporated, leave the kimchi for 24 hours at room temperature to start fermentation, then store it in the refrigerator for at least a couple of weeks — but to appreciate the kimchi at its best, wait 2 months, when all its aromas and flavours have completely developed.

Kimchi, one of the most typical dishes of Korean gastronomy, is an example of the vegetable curing process, which is widespread in the East. It is not a complex preparation, but the process is long, since cabbage, its main ingredient, must ferment for at least 2 weeks. It is worth being patient, since, once prepared, the kimchi lasts for a long time: it will keep for up to 6 months.

FLAVOURING PROCESSES

EACH FOOD PRODUCT HAS ITS OWN NATURAL FLAVOUR, HOWEVER, IT CAN BE MODIFIED TO SUIT INDIVIDUAL TASTES BY USING DIFFERENT TECHNIQUES TO ENRICH IT WITH OTHER AROMAS OR FLAVOURS.

Flavour is a fundamental component of food. In gastronomy, you can modify the natural aroma of all kinds of products, flavouring them through different types of techniques. The objective of certain procedures – marinating, macerating, infusing, impregnating and aromatising – is the same: to find a good combination between the natural aroma or flavour of the food or preparation and the supplementary substance that will give it a new aroma and thus enrich it.

This flavouring substance is usually a wine, vinegar, herbs, spices, oil or liquor, as well as many other condiments. The product is immersed in one, or a combination, of them and left to rest for a specified number of hours to impregnate it with the aromatic qualities.

Some techniques, beyond adding flavours and aromas, also transform the product and make it juicier. The specificities of each of these processes are discussed in the following pages.

MACERATE AND MARINATE

These similar techniques consists of immersing certain products into an aromatic liquid for hours. Lemon, oil, wine or vinegar, and condiments – such as herbs, garlic, onions and spices – come into play.

MACERATE

In a way, we can say that macerating is a version of marinating. However, while marinating is often used to modify foods thanks to the acidic action of the liquids that are incorporated into the preparation, maceration is only intended to flavour and soften the product.

Fruits are macerated, usually with the addition of an alcoholic beverage such as muscatel, red wine or others, and sometimes with extra sugar or the juice of other fruit.

MARINATE

Like maceration, marinating consists of immersing a food product into a liquid preparation to flavour it and, at the same time, soften it. The difference lies in the fact that, in the act of marinating, the oil can play a greater role. You can prepare different marinades, always with oil as the main element, along with various aromatic seasonings, to which wines and vinegars can also be added *(photo 2)*.

When marinating a product, the food acquires a certain flavour, is more tender and can lose unpleasant odours – which is what is desired when marinating game meats.

Meats can be marinated with the help of oil, paprika, herbs and spices, and also with wine and lemon, but here it is not so much a question of modifying the product as of softening it and giving it flavour.

COOKING IN A MARINADE

Cured salmon (preprocessed with salt and sometimes sugar and other seasonings) is often confused with salmon marinated in an acidic marinade. However, this form of marinating is substantially different from curing and other processing techniques, since it involves immersing the food in a flavoured acidic liquid (*photo 1*).

The liquids in acidic marinades are usually lemon juice or a similar acid, or wines and vinegars, to which herbs and spices or other plants are often added. The action of the lemon acids, vinegars or wine softens the food tissues and increases their capacity to retain moisture. Thanks to this, they transfer the specific flavours of the liquid while keeping the food very juicy. In certain foods, this action of marinating enables the product to be modified to such an extent that it can even be eaten without cooking with heat, such as fish prepared in this way.

MARINATED SARDINES

Time: 1 hr | Level: easy

INGREDIENTS FOR 4 PEOPLE

20 filleted sardines
200 ml white wine vinegar
60 g tomato
1 spring onion
Chives
Virgin olive oil
Salt and pepper

METHOD

1 Place the sardines in a 10 per cent brine for 5 minutes. The brine bleeds the sardines, eliminates odours and, in turn, provides a hint of salt.

2 Next, marinate the sardine fillets in the vinegar for 30 minutes. Then, remove them from the vinegar and place them on a plate.

3 Drizzle the sardines with olive oil and complement them with diced crushed tomato, freshly ground black pepper, chopped chives and slices of spring onion that have been previously soaked in cold water so that they lose their excess strength.

Simplicity is sometimes exquisite. This is the case for sardines prepared in summer, when they are at their best, since they are fatter and, therefore, more tasty and offer their best texture. In this recipe, the marinating technique simply enhances the freshness of this oily Mediterranean fish.

MARINATED TUNA SALAD WITH GREEN BEANS

Time: 1 hr | Level: easy

INGREDIENTS FOR 4 PEOPLE

400 g fresh tuna - 200 ml soy sauce

400 g fine green beans - 1 tray purple shiso leaves

For the dressing

100 ml soybean oil - 100 ml virgin olive oil

10 ml sesame oil (optional)

10 g toasted sesame seeds

METHOD

1 To prepare the dressing, mix all the ingredients together and set aside.

2 Cut the tuna, which must be very fresh, into regular cubes and marinate it in the soy sauce for 15 minutes. The marination process, however, depends a little on each cook's personal taste: play with the size of the cubes and the time dedicated to the process.

3 Boil the green beans until al dente, having previously topped and tailed the ends and washed them. Prick them with a fork to determine if they are ready, then strain, cool them and set aside.

4 Assemble the dish, interspersing pieces of tuna and beans, then drizzle with the prepared dressing. Finish by scattering with the shiso leaves.

In this simple recipe, the tuna's tender flesh contrasts with the crunchy texture of the al dente cooked green beans. The marination in soy sauce gives the fish an intense taste, while the bean refreshes the dish. In the dessing, the soybean oil serves as a common thread between the sesame, tuna and beans, and the shiso leaves add a slight nuance to the dish's flavours.

RED MULLET CEVICHE

Time: 1 hr (+ 24 hrs maceration) | Level: moderate

INGREDIENTS FOR 4 PEOPLE

8 red mullet (about 80 g each)

Fish brine

For the red mullet broth

750 g red mullet bones

750 ml water

For the tiger milk

750 ml red mullet broth

60 g onion

35 g lime

25 g yellow pepper

20 g red pepper

7 g salt

5 g lime zest

1 ml Tabasco sauce

For the pickled onion

1 red onion

100 ml pomegranate vinegar

To serve

8 cherry tomatoes ▪ 1 avocado ▪ Corn ▪ Samphire

METHOD

1 To prepare the tiger milk, clean the vegetables for the broth and cut them into mirepoix. Then, mix all the ingredients in a container and let them macerate in a cool place for 24 hours.

2 To prepare the red mullet broth, bleed the fish bones by immersing them into cold water for 6 hours. Then strain and brown lightly in a frying pan.

3 Boil the water in a saucepan and infuse the bones for 30 minutes, well covered. Strain and reserve the broth.

4 To prepare the pickled onion, peel and wash the red onion, cut it into julienne strips and blanch it in boiling water for 20 seconds. Cool it immediately in ice water, then remove and drain it. Cover it with pomegranate vinegar or similar, and allow it to marinate for 1 hour.

5 Make a small cross with a knife on the cherry tomatoes to make them easier to peel, then blanch them in a pan of boiling water for only 10 seconds.

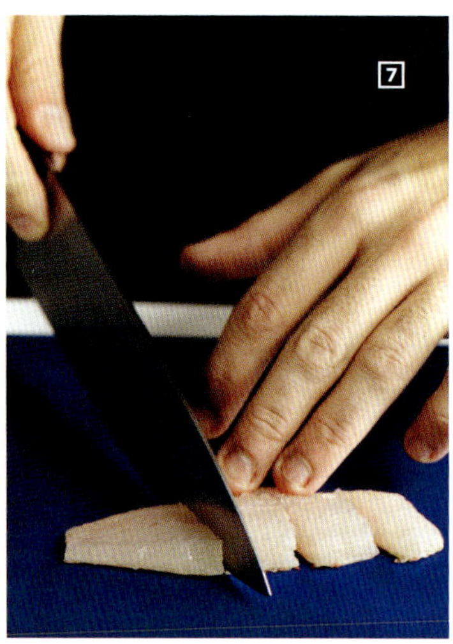

Cool them in plenty of ice water, remove them and peel with the help of a paring knife. Reserve.

6 Scald and debone the red mullet.

7 Cut the fillets into regular pieces and soak them in a brine for 5 minutes.

8 Add the red mullet pieces to the macerated tiger milk and leave them in it for 8 minutes. Remove and reserve them.

9 Blend the vegetables in the tiger milk together with their juice, strain and reserve.

10 Assemble the dish with the red mullet pieces covered with the tiger milk and garnish it with the cherry tomatoes, some avocado cubes, some corn, pickled onion and a a little samphire. You can also add shoots.

INFUSE, SOAK AND AROMATISE

These three techniques allow an ingredient, usually liquid – although not exclusively – to be soaked in the aromas and flavours of another product, which provides the aromatic element. These methods become more effective if heat is applied, since high temperatures produce a more intense reaction in the aromatic ingredient's volatile elements and, therefore, it acquires a greater capacity to transfer its aromas to the liquid. Use these techniques to achieve delicious combinations, either with contrasting or harmonious flavours.

INFUSE

Infusion consists of submerging a product in a hot liquid, without boiling, so that the liquid in question incorporates the aroma or flavour of the infused product. It is important that the liquid does not boil to avoid the destruction of the desired aromas (*photo 1*).

Of course, tea, herbs and coffee are infusions, but the technique can be applied to many other foods. For example, by infusion you can flavour white wine with truffles, milk with vanilla or red wine with cinnamon and cloves.

SOAKING

By using this technique, it is possible to enrich a food product with the flavour of another. It is normally used for porous fruit and vegetables, which are immersed into a liquid so that it penetrates inside. This process is also sometimes referred to as impregnating or perfuming.

Although you can flavour fruit by maceration, the result obtained with soaking is much more intense (the difference can be seen in the image above). The best method for soaking is to use a vacuum-packing machine. Immerse the fruit in the liquid and make a vacuum two or three times; in this way you will have a quick impregnation and the product will not become too soft or lose its own flavour when in contact with the liquid (*photos 2 to 4*).

AROMATISE

In the culinary field, this term is used to designate the act of adding aroma or flavour to a food with the help of another product. For example, you can flavour oils by incorporating some herbs, spices or flowers.

Heat can be applied to the aromatising element to gain aromatic capacity. When working with oils, the recommended temperature for this operation is 65°C for about 30 minutes, because it does not destroy their properties, while reaching the safety limit that keeps microbes at bay.

RED FRUIT INFUSION WITH VANILLA ICE CREAM

Time: 1 hr | Level: easy

INGREDIENTS FOR 4 PEOPLE

400 g assorted berries (strawberries, raspberries, wild strawberries, blackberries, blueberries, etc.)
200 g sugar
200 ml water
Lemon verbena leaves
Vanilla ice cream

METHOD

1 Boil the water and sugar. At the moment of boiling, introduce the lemon verbena leaves and leave them to infuse for 5 minutes.

2 Add the berries, starting with the hardest (e.g. blueberries) and ending with the softest (wild strawberries), so that they all receive different heat intensities according to their texture. This will prevent them falling apart. Leave to infuse for 1 hour.

3 Remove the lemon verbena leaves and place a good portion of red fruit infusion in each glass, accompanied with vanilla ice cream.

Sometimes, simplicity is the most succulent luxury. The secret of this dessert lies mainly in the quality of the berries, which must be very ripe. The syrup, in addition, will sweetly convey their aroma, and the cold and creamy counterpoint of the ice cream will make this pairing a delightful treat.

PINEAPPLE INFUSION WITH FENNEL

Time: 4 hrs | Level: easy

INGREDIENTS FOR 4 PEOPLE

500 ml water

50 g sugar

100 g pineapple

40 g fennel

2 x 2-g gelatine leaves

Ginger ice cream (can also be coconut, lemon verbena or eucalyptus)

METHOD

1 Bring the water to the boil with the sugar. When it boils, remove the saucepan from the heat and add the gelatine leaves, previously soaked in cold water, and stir until they are well dissolved.

2 Infuse the pineapple, cut into 1-cm cubes, and the fennel in the hot syrup.

3 Cover with clingfilm or a lid and refrigerate for at least 3 hours.

4 Place the pineapple infusion with the fresh fennel aroma into a dish and add the ice cream. Ginger ice cream with a few slices of crystallised ginger can be a perfect choice, but it can also be combined with all kinds of fresh flavours, such as coconut, lemon verbena or eucalyptus.

This is a very summery dessert that is all about freshness. The aniseed aroma given off by the fennel accentuates the fresh taste of the pineapple and, thanks to the infusion process, the fruit becomes even more delicious. Combined with ice cream, this infusion is an irresistible dessert.

FLAVOURED CHOCOLATE

Time: 2 hrs | Level: easy

INGREDIENTS FOR 4 PEOPLE

125 g chocolate couverture (70% cocoa fat)

1 bunch mint

Freeze-dried products: mint, raspberry, coconut, passion fruit, yogurt, coffee, etc.

This is a fun project for children. Freeze-dried fruits are a healthy, fun and colourful resource. Along with the simple ingredients for this recipe, you will need some good aprons and a willingness to share.

METHOD

1 Wash the mint leaves. Drain and dry them carefully.

2 Place the chocolate with the mint leaves in a vacuum-seal bag and seal it.

3 Heat the chocolate and mint, still in the bag, in a bowl of water at 65°C for 1 hour. The chocolate will be flavoured with the menthol perfume and acquire a new personality.

4 Strain the mixture while hot and fill a paper cornet or piping bag.

5 Make small chocolate fingers.

6 Before the chocolate solidifies, sprinkle the fingers with different freeze-dried fruits to obtain a cheerful and colourful assortment of chocolates.

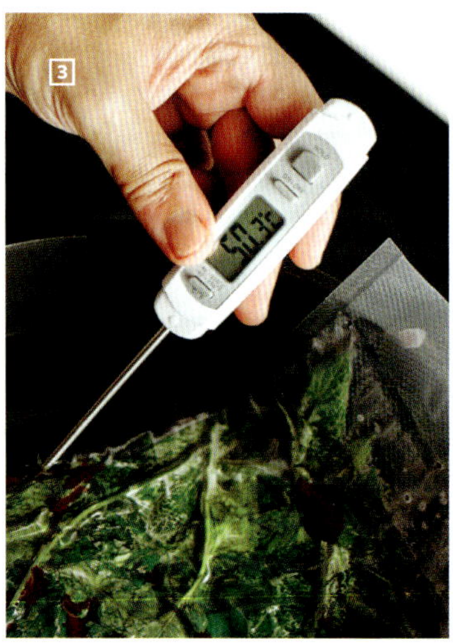

5

6

CHERRY TOMATO BLOODY MARY

Time: 20 mins| Level: easy

INGREDIENTS FOR 4 PEOPLE

20 cherry tomatoes

50 ml vodka

50 ml sugar syrup (equal parts water and sugar)

Celery salt

Tabasco sauce

Young celery leaves

Salt and pepper

METHOD

1 Prepare 50 ml of sugar syrup (made of equal parts of water and sugar boiled for 5 minutes).

2 Mix all the aromatic elements: vodka, salt, pepper, tabasco, celery salt and sugar syrup, and leave to stand for 20 minutes.

3 Make a small cross on the top of the tomatoes, then blanch them in boiling water, cool in ice water and peel them.

4 Place the tomatoes in a jar prepared for vacuuming and pour in the aromatic mixture.

5 Proceed to vacuum 3 times, opening the jar each time.

6 When the tomatoes have been well impregnated with all the aromas, place them in a bowl and garnish with fresh celery leaves. Finally, season with a mixture of salt, celery salt and pepper.

Welcome your guests with fun little treats such as these cherry tomatoes, which explode in the mouth with all the flavour of a classic cocktail.

4

5

FIGS WITH GINGER CHEESE AND GLACÉ KUMQUATS

Time: 2 hrs (+ 12 hrs resting and marinating)
Level: easy

INGREDIENTS FOR 4 PEOPLE

4 ripe figs
2 slices glacé orange peel
12 young almonds
100 g rocket
Fennel flowers and leaves, tarragon tender leaves
For the confit
12 kumquats
100 g sugar
100 ml water
For the ginger oil
100 g soft goat's cheese or similar (not creamy)
50 g ginger
100 ml sunflower oil
For the vinaigrette
Sunflower oil
Modena balsamic vinegar
Salt and pepper

METHOD

1 To confit the kumquats, prick their entire surface with a needle and cook in a mixture of equal parts of water and sugar for 2 hours over a low heat. Then leave to rest for at least overnight in a bowl covered with clingfilm.

2 For the ginger oil, grate the ginger and mix it with the sunflower oil. Incorporate the resulting mixture with the goat's cheese and marinate for at least 8 hours.

3 Peel the figs, taking care not to deform them, and cut into vertical slices.

4 Alternate the fig slices with the goat's cheese mixture and wrap in clingfilm so that the fig's shape is reconstructed. Leave the mixture to rest in the refrigerator for 1 hour until firm.

5 Cut in half or julienne the young almonds and dice the glacé kumquats.

6 To prepare the vinaigrette, mix sunflower oil with the balsamic vinegar, salt and pepper.

7 Assemble each dish by starting with the rocket and some of the complements: the tender almonds, glacé kumquat, and tarragon and fennel flowers and leaves. Cut the figs in half and arrange them on the plate, trying to highlight the layers with the goat's cheese. To finish the dish, drizzle it with the vinaigrette and decorate with the remaining complements.

Simple, versatile and spectacular. It is easy to prepare, so it can be combined with different ingredients to create a surprising result. When in season the sweetness of the fleshy, compact figs is ideal combined with fatty ingredients such as fresh goat's cheese or with foie gras. This is a classic combination of sweet and fatty, which is completed with fresh flavour of ginger.

MISCELLANEOUS COLD PROCESSES

THE TECHNIQUES PRESENTED HERE ARE TYPICAL CLASSIC COOKING METHODS. HOWEVER, THEY ARE STILL USED IN MODERN COOKING, EITHER TO FULFIL THEIR ORIGINAL PURPOSE OR ADAPTED FOR NEW ROLES.

Regarding the art of cooking, the creative capacity of chefs and the food industry itself, there are no limits. Collecting all the processing techniques would, therefore, be an endless task.

The processes mentioned on the following pages, techniques that do not require heat, are well known in our culinary tradition. They have lost none of their relevance or usefulness in today's kitchen.

1

LIQUIFYING

To carry out this technique, you need the help of a liquifier, which will allow you to separate the liquid part from the solid part of a food product. There are two types of liquifiers: those that work by centrifugation (the classic model so far), and those that crush the food (which enables a better utilisation of the food fibre) (*photo 1*).

Nowadays, professional kitchens use this system to prepare the bases for creams and soups with blanched vegetables or to obtain liquids such as tomato water, which is appreciated for preparing cocktails. Herbs can also be liquefied to obtain concentrated and refreshing juices, fruit can be made into sauces, and olives can obtain spherification (*see p. 335*).

The liquefied product provides nutritional and gastronomic advantages, since you obtain a juice with all the nutritional value of the product without being subjected to temperature changes, and it retains all the flavour. When you use sprouts, it becomes a great source of nutritional contributions to health. By liquefying wheat sprouts, for example, you obtain their chlorophyll, which is an exceptional source of vitamin B, is rich in vitamins A and C, and provides calcium, iron, magnesium, phosphorus, potassium, sodium, sulphur, cobalt, zinc, proteins and enzymes.

BREADING AND BATTER

These are surely some of the most popular prepreparations in family homes. We bread and batter a food when we dip it in flour, egg and breadcrumbs to fry it later. This technique protects the breaded product from the high temperature of the oil during frying.

There are many variations. Parmesan cheese can be added to the main base of flour, egg and breadcrumbs, or instead of Parmesan, add garlic and parsley. You can also coat with seasoned breadcrumbs (garlic and parsley, fine herbs, curry, etc.), or with butter. In this latter option, the butter serves as both the flour and the egg, and all that is needed is to coat with breadcrumbs.

In addition, there are different types of breadcrumbs, from fresh to dried breadcrumbs, and sometimes other products are used to make breadcrumbs, such as crumbled potato crisps or panko (Japanese breadcrumbs made from crustless bread) which provide a very crunchy texture.

However, another suggestion is to eliminate the flour, coat the food product with oil and replace the breadcrumbs with bread cut into very thin slices (*photo 1*).

The advantage of breadcrumbs is that they can be made in advance and stored in the refrigerator, or even frozen and thawed directly during cooking.

BINDING

As it's possible to truss, tie and even sew food products, why not be creative in the kitchen? With kitchen string you can give shape to the products that need it, either so that they do not deform during cooking or to handle them better. Sometimes it is convenient to sew the ends of a product well, especially when it has a filling that you do not wish to lose (*photo 2*).

CHERRY GAZPACHO

Time: 1 hr | Level: easy

INGREDIENTS FOR 4 PEOPLE

800 g ripe tomatoes
250 g cherries
4 cherry tomatoes
50 g red pepper
50 g yellow pepper
50 g baby onion
1 chive
Salt and pepper
For the soaked or macerated cherries (optional)
12 cherries
50 ml kirsch or amaretto
For the chive oil (optional)
100 ml olive oil
20 g chives

METHOD

1 Wash the ripe tomatoes, then dry and cut them into large pieces.

2 Wash the cherries and remove the stones. Reserve some cherries for decoration. If you wish to flavour some of the cherries for decoration with liqueur, macerate them (cover them with the chosen liqueur) or impregnate them (place the cherries in a container to make a vacuum, cover them with kirsch and make a vacuum 3 times). If not, put them into a bowl, cover with clingfilm and set aside.

3 Crush the tomato and cherries, then emulsify by adding the oil. Season with salt and pepper, strain the gazpacho and leave it to rest for a couple of hours.

4 Chop the peppers, baby onion and chive into brunoise. Mix together, season with salt and pepper, and set aside.

5 Blanch the cherry tomatoes, then peel and carefully empty them, and stuff them with the chopped peppers, onion and chives.

6 If you wish to prepare a chive oil, blend the chives and oil in a Thermomix for 5 minutes at 70°C. Strain and cool immediately.

7 Assemble the dish with small piles of the chopped mixture interspersed with cherry pieces, place a stuffed cherry tomato in the centre and add a few drops of oil. Fill a small jar with the cherry gazpacho and pour around the tomato.

A light version of a traditional gazpacho, this summer soup, simple and quick, requires cherries to be at their best, at the peak of the summer season, so that they are smooth and fleshy and their flavour is intense. If you wish to impregnate some of them with liqueur, it will add boldness to an already very sensual soup.

MINCING

Synonymous with grinding and very finely chopping, mincing involves passing food through the mincer, although there are some nuances. Depending on the appliance used and its accessories, you will obtain a finer or rougher texture.

You can mince beef or pork – or both mixed – to make beefburgers, meatballs or stuffing. When grinding these meats you should include some fatty parts to make them more tender. You can also mince fish to make terrines, pies or fillings, as well as vegetables for stir-fries or to season elaborate dishes such as lasagne. Another food that can be minced is dried bread, to obtain breadcrumbs. However, when speaking of mincing, it also refers to using a knife to very finely chop; this is how garlic and parsley is normally minced.

Although there are kitchen food processors and other multi-use electric appliances that have a mincing function, the result is not the same as with a mincer, since the electric appliance usually leaves the product smoother, and more pasty in the case of meats, while a manual grinder offers a more chewy texture that gives special characteristics to the final product.

PURÉEING

Food processors and other multi-use electric kitchen appliances can also be used to purée foods. A stick blender is ideal for making fruit purées and puréeing vegetables such as fresh coriander and rocket. Sometimes the purées are further processed by straining through a fine mesh sieve to separate the solids from the juice.

LARDING AND BARDING

Both larding and barding are processes that had better times in the past, when households cooked more and had more time to prepare stews. Both have in common that they use a fatty product to protect the main ingredient, to give it a stronger flavour or both.

For larding, elements such as bacon, sausages, truffles or eggs are introduced into meat, generally beef, mutton or pork, with the help of a larding needle. Beef rounds or larded pork fillet are two common examples of its use *(photo 2)*.

In turn, the technique of barding, by using a fatty product, provides protection for the main ingredient from direct contact with the heat source so that the meat does not dry out. In the case of poultry, the fatty product is usually a thick rasher of bacon and covers the bird for roasting. Its fat also confers flavour and juiciness to the preparation. The tournedos, a cut of beef fillet wrapped in fresh or cured bacon, is another example of this technique *(photo 1)*.

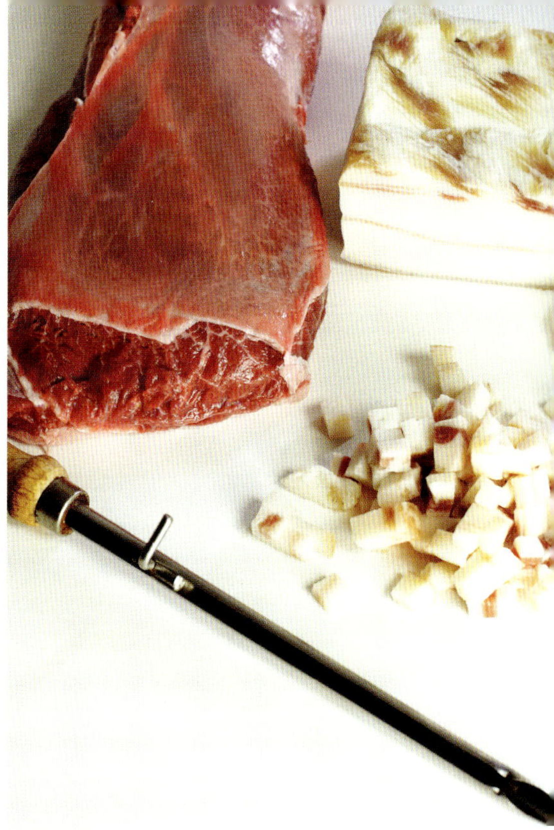

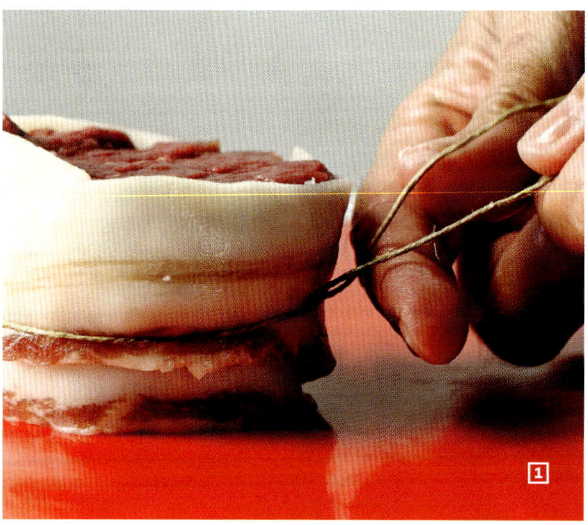

GRINDING

When grinding, or very finely chopping, certain foods, the size of the food is reduced and the mixture is homogenised. For example, grinding nuts, garlic and oil can be achieved quickly with a small electric coffee grinder, or you can grind food in various kinds of food processors or other multi-use kitchen appliances to achieve smooth textures. When grinding solid ingredients, you can obtain a powdered element (soft ingredients with a higher portion of liquids are referred to as purées). Coffee grinders and other electric multi-use kitchen appliances are equipped with specific blades for grinding *(photo 3)*.

3

DEHYDRATING

A very effective way of preserving food is by using the dehydration method. In some cases, this is the aim of using the technique, but in others the goal is to achieve a crunchy texture while preserving the taste and nutritional properties of the food. This is a relatively simple process that consists of extracting the water from the product in order to maintain its organoleptic properties or even intensify them, as occurs when dehydrating mushrooms such as ceps.

This is achieved by using a dehydrating machine that controls the temperature and blows air for rapid dehydration. The process is simple: place the food in it – whole or sliced – and choose the function to dry or dehydrate until the desired texture is achieved. If the product will not be consumed straight away, it should be kept in an airtight container (do not forget to label it with the date of packaging; *photo 4*).

The pleasant crunchy textures achieved by dehydration are widely used for garnishing or decorating dishes.

4

TOMATO TARTARE

Time: 5 hrs | Level: moderate

INGREDIENTS FOR 4 PEOPLE

Slices of bread, toasted

For the mustard emulsion

1 egg yolk

45 ml extra virgin olive oil

8 g mustard seeds

For the tomato tartare

600 g ripe tomatoes

20 g shallot

10 g capers

10 g gherkin

Chilli oil

Salt and pepper

METHOD

1 Blanch the tomatoes, then peel them and remove the seeds and the watery part. Cut the flesh into slices and the cores into equal parts.

2 Place the tomatoes in a dehydrator machine at 55°C for 2 hours. Or dehydrate them in the oven at 70°C, with the fan on and the door slightly open. When the tomatoes obtain a texture similar to that of the meat, remove them and set aside.

3 To make the mustard emulsion, place the egg yolk in a bowl and beat it until it is well aerated. Pour in the olive oil in a drizzle while beating with a whisk to emulsify the mixture. Add the mustard seeds, mix and set aside.

4 To prepare the tomato tartare, place the dehydrated tomatoes in a bowl and add the remaining ingredients: the shallot, capers and chopped gherkin with the mustard emulsion, chilli oil, salt and pepper. Mix well and keep the preparation covered in the refrigerator.

5 Serve the tartare with toast or vegetable chips and add a little more mustard emulsion.

The dehydrated tomatoes, in spite of preserving all the flavour of the tomatoes, resemble meat in texture, making it an ideal dish for fans of playing with textures and a guaranteed success for vegetarians.

MISCELLANEOUS HOT PROCESSES

SOME TECHNIQUES USE TEMPERATURE TO PREPARE PRODUCTS FOR EASIER HANDLING OR COOKING. BLANCHING, CHARRING, SEARING, SCORCHING AND CARMELISING ARE SOME EXAMPLES.

Most of the preparation methods are performed on raw food, but there are several other techniques that require heat to prepare the food and thus facilitate its subsequent cooking or other preparation.

BLANCHING

When a food is immersed into boiling water for a few seconds, the shock from the heat fixes some of its properties, such as colour or texture.

BLANCHING TOMATOES

1 This process facilitates the subsequent peeling of the vegetable. Start by marking a cross with a knife at the base of the tomato so that the skin can be peeled, then blanch it for 5 seconds.

2 Quickly cool the tomato in a container with water and ice so that it does not soften.

3 You can now use a knife to peel the tomato with little effort.

CHARRING AND SEARING

This process involves heating a product quickly, so that it browns and acquires flavour, but it also prevents the heat reaching the product's interior. It is used to seal the product so that the juices do not escape during cooking, and is used as a precooking step in a double cooking process (for example, you can sear a hake before cooking it in the oven, or you can sear a product and then, when it is cold, cook it under vacuum).

BLANCHING

This process can clean or purify a food of its impurities, blood and unpleasant aromas. The technique is similar to bleeding, but bleeding treats food in cold water. Wait until the water starts to boil, then at that moment remove or strain the product and cool it, or continue cooking it in another medium. For an optimal result in offal, such as pig's trotters or tripe, repeat the process.

BLANCHING PIG'S TROTTERS

- Place the trotters in a pot of cold water and bring to the boil (*photo 4*).
- When the water is about to boil, or just when it starts to boil, remove them.
- Cool the trotters in cold water and wash them. The process can be repeated, if necessary.

SCORCHING AND CARAMELISING

Pig's trotters and poultry are singed to remove hair and feather remains (*see p.114*). But you can also scorch certain products to give them a smoky flavour. It is common in tuna tataki. It consists of scorching the outside of the fish loins with the help of a blowtorch – or by quickly exposing them to heat on the grill – while maintaining an almost raw texture on the inside.

COOKING TECHNIQUES

WHEN FOOD IS EXPOSED TO ANY TYPE OF COOKING, A SERIES OF EXTRAORDINARY TRANSFORMATIONS TAKE PLACE: THE PRODUCTS EXPERIENCE A CHANGE IN COLOUR AND TEXTURE, AND THEY ACQUIRE AROMAS AND TAKE ON NEW FLAVOURS.

When we normally talk about cooking, we refer to the different techniques for cooking food. However, in a more academic context, we would speak of modifying or transforming food by means of heat. Indeed, it is the effect of temperature that distinguishes cooking techniques from other food processing techniques that, without the use of heat, can also modify food for consumption, as in the case of maceration or curing.

Cooking causes physical changes in food: its colour, odour, flavour and texture are modified. A chemical transformation also takes place: the food's molecular structure tends to be simplified. Hygienic changes are no less relevant, in the sense that subjecting food to sufficiently high cooking temperatures (from 65°C) stops the proliferation of microorganisms, thus extending its shelf life and guaranteeing food safety.

TYPES OF COOKING

CONCENTRATION COOKING

This encompasses all the techniques used to ensure that the taste of the product remains in its interior, so that it is more palatable. Concentration cooking requires applying high cooking temperatures so that the product can seal in its flavour and juices.

Some of these techniques, such as grilling or roasting, transform the product's colour (it browns), flavour (it becomes more intense and concentrated), and texture (it becomes crunchy on the outside), and envelops it in a characteristic aroma. All these transformations are known as the Maillard reaction.

In addition to grilling and roasting, boiling or vacuum cooking are also examples of cooking by concentration.

EXPANSION COOKING

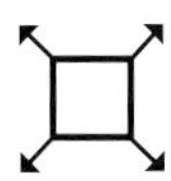

In this type of cooking, which is characteristic of broths and stocks, a product transfers its taste to other products. The food is immersed in cold water and, as it heats up, it releases its flavours into the cooking water. Thus, boiling from cold water, as is done with broth, or blanching — putting into boiling water and cooling straight away — are examples of this type of cooking.

MIXED COOKING

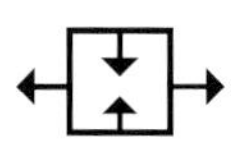

This combination of cooking techniques first requires sealing in the flavour — in other words, cooking by concentration — and then a longer cooking by expansion, generally with the help of a liquid that allows the exchanging of flavours among various products. Stews and casseroles as well as braised and simmered dishes require mixed cooking.

NEW TRENDS

Our technical and scientific knowledge about culinary processes is improving all the time, enabling us to understand more on how the different cooking methods affect the organoleptic and nutritional quality of products. Today, there is a generalised culinary trend to pay particular attention to associated conditions, such as temperature, time and steam, and to apply new cooking techniques with a greater control of these parameters in order to improve the quality of the preparations.

In this sense, one of the techniques that has gained relevance, and will surely gain more in the future, is low-temperature cooking, with the low temperatures being understood to be those between 50°C and 100°C. This technique is usually applied with new instruments and machines, which although still not very common in domestic kitchens, are becoming more widespread in professional kitchens. Their aim is to control the culinary processes and replicate them with precision in order to improve the organoleptic qualities of the preparations and preserve the products' natural flavours, as well as their nutritional properties, to the maximum.

By setting the temperature more accurately, it is possible to cook products very precisely, in a way adapted to the needs of each product and its use. For example, if you prepare a dish at a low temperature – in other words below 65°C (the safe temperature at which microorganisms are kept at bay) – it should be consumed straight away. In contrast, if the product will be cooked at 65°C or above, it can be stored for later. In short, it is important to know about how and why you cook using one method or another.

These are not very complex or sophisticated techniques that cannot be reproduced in the home kitchen. Although you may not yet have the necessary machinery, you can incorporate new habits and simple utensils, such as timers or clocks, thermometers or cooking probes, which will help you to be more aware of cooking times and the importance they have in achieving a delicious and nutritious cuisine.

OPTIMUM COOKING POINT	
FISH	40°C / 55°C
MEATS	50°C / 65°C
VEGETABLES	From 85°C

Take temperatures in the core or interior of the product to achieve the correct texture.

BOILING

THIS IS PERHAPS ONE OF THE SIMPLEST PROCEDURES IN THE KITCHEN AND THE ONE WE USE THE MOST, BUT IT HAS ITS SECRETS! EACH PRODUCT REQUIRES A SPECIFIC PROCEDURE AND COOKING TIME.

TYPE OF COOKING	By concentration
RELATED TECHNIQUES	Blanching - Poaching Pressure Cooking Steaming

Immersing a product into a boiling liquid (at 100°C or above) for a certain period of time is a simple, everyday technique, either for preparing or cooking. Usually, water is used for the boiling liquid, but you can also use broths, stocks or sauces; you should never use oil.

Generally, before the water comes to the boil, you should add salt and introduce the seasonings needed (peppers or other spices, herbs, etc.). Then, at the precise moment of boiling, you can introduce the food you want to cook, whether it is vegetables, pasta, rice, etc. However, there are some exceptions: certain pulses (lentils and beans) or the ingredients to produce a broth are introduced from cold water.

You can also use a pressure cooker for boiling, which will allow you to cook at temperatures above boiling point – at about 125°C – so that the food cooks faster.

BOILING TIPS

- **Use a suitable container.** The products will cook better if they have enough space and the water does not overflow. Use a pot or pan with a size that is appropriate to the amount of water and the ingredients you will be cooking.
- **Use plenty of water.** There should be enough water in the pot so that when the product to be cooked is added, the boiling process does not stop. Even if the temperature drops suddenly at that moment, if there is abundant water, the boil will recover more quickly.
- **Add salt.** Besides enhancing the flavour of the products being boiled, salt contributes to a good boiling. Add 10–15 grams per litre for rice, pasta and vegetables.
- **Efficient energy use.** To avoid wasting energy, the heat source should be no larger than the diameter of the pot. In addition, if you cover the pot at the beginning, the water will be brought to the boil faster, and if you add cut food, it will cook faster.
- **Cool quickly.** When the desired doneness of a boiling food is reached, it should be quickly removed from the water so that it does not overcook. If the boiled product will not be eaten hot straight away, you must also cool it quickly. You can cool the food in a bowl of cold water and ice, or leave it in a cold area of the house or even outdoors, properly protected.

BOILING PULSES

Pulses – or dried beans or legumes – are a staple for classic dishes in many different cultures. They are usually cooked for a long time, perhaps not in accordance with the rush of modern life, and for this reason they are often purchased already cooked, packaged or in bulk at the markets. However, the cooking process is relatively simple.

PROCEDURE

1 Before cooking, soak the dried beans for the time necessary for each one (*see p. 138*); then drain and rinse them, and add them to the pot with the right amount of water (2.5–3 parts of water for each part of beans) to prevent the flavour and nutrients from being diluted more than necessary. The water should be boiled over a high heat and without salt.

To make the beans softer and more digestible, add a portion of kombu seaweed to the beans, which will also add minerals to the preparation.

2 Add the pulses to the water, each one according to its own needs: the beans and lentils, when the water is still cold; the chickpeas, in the boiling water.

3 When the water starts to boil (again in the case of chickpeas, or for the first time in the case of beans and lentils), skim and lower the heat to start a long, slow and steady cooking.

4 Each pulse is particular in terms of cooking time, so you should test if they are ready: this is the best way to get it right. When they are soft, add salt to the water and remove them from the heat.

5 Allow the vegetables to cool in their own water. If you want to make a cream, you can use the cooking water, since it preserves all its flavour.

APPROXIMATE COOKING TIMES

- Chickpeas: 1 hr 30 mins–3 hrs
- Beans: 1 hr 30 mins–2 hrs
- Lentils: 1 hr

2

3

4

BOILING PASTA

You'll need lots of water and high heat to bring it to the boil and cook pasta in the shortest possible time and to perfection. In this matter, each person has their own preferences, although there is a certain consensus that the best way to enjoy pasta is al dente, which means that you should notice a certain hardness when you bite it; if you cut it, you should notice a white spot inside – the heart of the pasta.

PROCEDURE

1 Introduce the pasta to abundantly salted water (15 grams of salt per litre). The salt prevents the starch released by the dough making it sticky. About 1 litre of water is used for each 100 grams of pasta.

2 Stir periodically and carefully to prevent the pasta sticking to the base of the pot and to each other. Allow it to bubble without covering the pot. It is not necessary to add oil to the water; it is only needed for cooking flat pasta.

3 Although each packet of pasta indicates a recommended cooking time, depending on the type and thickness, the right point is always a very personal choice, so the best thing to do is to try it until it suits your taste.

4 Once it is ready, drain the pasta and serve it quickly. If it is cooked or precooked for a preparation, cool it quickly and brush it with oil to keep it covered and prevent it drying out.

APPROXIMATE COOKING TIMES

- Fresh pasta: 2-8 mins
- Fine dried (noodles): 2-5 mins
- Medium dried (macaroni): 5-10 mins
- Coarse dried: 10-20 mins
- Wholewheat, 5 mins more than plain pasta

MEDITERRANEAN MACARONI

Time: 2 hrs | Level: easy

INGREDIENTS FOR 4 PEOPLE

400 g macaroni • 80 g Kalamata olives
20 g olive purée • 12 cherry tomatoes
120 g tomatoes • 70 ml olive oil
40 g sun-dried tomatoes • 8 anchovies
20 g crystallised lemon peel • 1 lemon
20 g capers • Basil • Thyme
Rosemary, thyme or similar flowers
Sugar • Salt • Pepper

METHOD

1 Blanch, peel and cut the tomatoes into concassé. Cover them with oil and season with thyme, salt, pepper and sugar. Confit them in the oven or in a casserole or frying pan for 45 minutes.

2 Stone and cut the olives into large pieces (reserve some whole olives). Cut the sun-dried tomatoes into strips and the cherry tomatoes in half. Cut the anchovies into large pieces and the crystallised lemon peel into cubes. Chop the basil.

3 Allow the capers to soak in water for 10 minutes to lose their excess acidity.

4 Char the cherry tomatoes in a frying pan over high heat, and add the remaining ingredients: the confit and sun-dried tomatoes, the whole olives and olive purée, the anchovies in pieces, the hydrated capers and the crystallised lemon peel. Cook until the tomatoes are soft, but still keep their shape, and until you have a juicy preparation ready to incorporate the macaroni.

5 Boil the macaroni al dente, drain and add to the pan along with the vegetables. Quickly sauté them. Add the basil and serve.

6 Finally, add the grated lemon zest and the chosen flowers.

VEGETABLE RAVIOLI WITH CHANTERELLES

Time: 1 hr | Level: moderate

INGREDIENTS FOR 4 PEOPLE

12 Chinese wonton wrappers
1 chive
Salt
For the sauce
200 g chanterelles
25 g carrots
25 g leeks
25 g onion
50 g unsalted butter
50 ml Chardonnay or similar white wine
200 ml cream
For the filling
125 g onion
125 g carrots
125 g leeks
125 g courgette
125 g unsalted butter
Salt and pepper

METHOD

1 To prepare the sauce, chop the vegetables and some chanterelles into brunoise. Cut the remaining mushrooms into slices.

2 Add the chopped vegetables to a frying pan with a little butter.

3 Cook the hardest vegetables for about 5 minutes, then add the chopped chanterelles and cook everything together for another 3 minutes.

4 Add the wine and allow it to reduce. Add the cream and cook until the sauce has a creamy texture.

5 To prepare the filling, cut the vegetables into jardinière; reserve the courgette, which you should sweat with a little salt.

6 Cook the onion, leek and carrot with the butter over moderate heat for about 15 minutes; when they are almost cooked, add the courgette and cook for a further 7 minutes. Season with salt and pepper and set aside.

7 Cook the Chinese wrappers for 20 seconds in plenty of salted water. Allow them to cool in a cold water bath and spread them over a clean surface or on a tray.

8 Fill the ravioli with the vegetables.

9 Finally, heat the ravioli in the microwave for 1 minute. Place 3 pieces of ravioli in a slightly deep dish and cover them with the mushroom and vegetable sauce. Add the reserved chanterelle slices, sautéed quickly with a little oil, to the dish and finish by sprinkling the chopped chive.

Wonton wrappers, typical of Cantonese cuisine, have a soft and very light texture similar to fresh pasta. They are easy to handle and can be cooked quickly: about 20 seconds are enough, as indicated in this recipe, or 4 minutes if you cook them after filling and you want to steam them. This is a quick and easy alternative for preparing light and tasty ravioli like an oriental dim sum (starters). This recipe provides a vegetable filling combined with a mushroom and vegetable sauce with cream and wine, but you can make an infinite number of variations. Play with these pasta-like wrappers and discover and combine different ingredients.

BOILING VEGETABLES

Boiling is one of the traditional methods for cooking all types of vegetables. Cooking them for just the right amount of time is crucial, both to prevent them losing their nutrients and to achieve pleasant textures.

THE PROCESS

- Add a generous amount of salt to the water (15 grams per litre of water). There should be a sufficient volume of liquid so that, when the vegetables are added, the boiling does not stop.
- When the water boils, add the vegetables.
- Once the vegetables have reached the desired doneness, remove and strain them immediately, so that they do not lose nutrients, flavour and colour (*photo 1*).
- If they will not be eaten immediately, they should be cooled. Adding them to ice water gives them an intense texture, flavour and colour (*photo 2*).

SPECIAL CASES

- **Artichokes.** To prevent them turning black, you can peel and boil them immediately in boiling water with oil, or keep them in water with lemon or parsley before cooking.
- **Potatoes.** They can be boiled with or without their skin. In general, for purées and vegetables, cook them peeled, but for garnishes or salads, cook them with their skin on to retain their moisture. To know if they have been cooked enough, just prick them with a knife or skewer (*photo 3*); if it can be inserted easily and smoothly, they are ready.
- **Asparagus.** Their buds are fragile and can break up during boiling. There are special pots that allow the asparagus to be boiled vertically, so that the water cooks the stalks while the buds are steamed. You can also boil buds and stems separately to give them each their own cooking time.

APPROXIMATE COOKING TIMES

- Artichoke (medium): 15–30 mins
- Asparagus, green: 7–15 mins
- Asparagus, white: 20 mins
- Beetroot (whole): 20–30 mins
- Brussels sprouts: 15 mins
- Cabbage: 10–20 mins
- Carrot: 15–20 mins
- Cauliflower florets: 10–15 mins
- Chard: it is better to cook the stalks separately (10 mins) from the leaves (2 mins)
- Courgette (1-cm slices): 10–15 mins
- Green bean: 5–20 mins
- Mangetout: 7 mins
- Onion: 20 mins
- Peas: 2–5 mins (frozen, up to 20 mins)
- Potato: 20–40 mins (depending on size or cut)
- Pumpkin (1-cm slices): 5 mins
- Spinach: 5–10 mins

TOMATO SALAD WITH VEGETABLES AND SALMOREJO

Time: 1 hr | Level: easy

INGREDIENTS FOR 4 PEOPLE

4 medium tomatoes
1 bunch of thyme, with flowers
Lamb's lettuce or similar
For cooking the vegetables
50 g turnip
50 g carrot
50 g courgette
12 asparagus
50 g chanterelles
Salt
For the salmorejo
500 g tomatoes
40 g farmhouse-style bread
6 ml sherry vinegar
30 ml extra virgin olive oil
1 clove garlic
6 g salt

This dish is as fresh as it is delicious, and very summery, since seasonal vegetables are used. Furthermore, it combines a salad with a soup, providing a two-in-one with a delicious mix of flavours. The tomato is at the epicentre of the dish, and like a good orchestra conductor, it integrates the vegetables and salmorejo to give a symphony of sensations.

METHOD

1 To prepare the salmorejo, cut the tomatoes into pieces and remove the seeds, which can be reserved to decorate the dish at the end. Purée the tomato flesh with the other ingredients. Strain the mixture and reserve it in the refrigerator.

2 To cook the vegetables, cut them all into batons and boil them in water and salt until al dente. Cool and reserve.

3 Dice the chanterelles and sauté lightly with a pinch of salt.

4 Blanch the tomatoes, then peel them and remove the core and seeds. Fill them with the salmorejo and the cooked vegetable batons, the chanterelles and the lamb's lettuce leaves.

5 Pour a base of salmorejo into a soup plate, place a stuffed tomato in the centre and dress with a few drops of virgin olive oil. Finish by decorating with some thyme flowers.

SMOKED SALMON AND POTATO SALAD

Time: 2 hrs | Level: easy

INGREDIENTS FOR 4 PEOPLE

300 g baking potato
300 g purple potato • *200 g smoked salmon*
1 punnet of spicy sprouts
(radish, mustard or onion)
For the tangy sauce
250 g of natural organic yogurt • *50 ml cream*
1 lemon • *1 tablespoon chopped dill*
Wholegrain mustard • *Salt and pepper*

METHOD

1 Wash and boil the potatoes separately, to obtain the desired doneness for each variety. Then cool and set aside.

2 To make the tangy sauce, mix the yogurt with the cream, a few drops of lemon juice (and a few pinches of lemon zest, if desired), 1 tablespoon of chopped dill and 1 small spoonful of mustard, and season with salt and pepper. The objective is to find a slightly acidic taste, but without losing the creaminess of the lactic acid.

3 Cut the smoked salmon into regular cubes and break the potatoes into irregular chunks and fun shapes (*see p. 124*).

4 Alternate the potato chunks and salmon cubes on the plate and dress them with the tangy yogurt sauce. To finish, add some spicy sprouts.

This Nordic-style salad provides a tasty and very attractive combination of smoked salmon, potatoes and tangy sauce. The spicy and refreshing touch of the sprouts rounds out this simple-to-prepare dish that looks great on its own.

CARPET OF CHESTNUTS WITH MUSHROOMS AND ANISEED

Time: 2 h | Level: difficult

INGREDIENTS FOR 8 PEOPLE

500 g chestnuts, peeled • 100 g chestnuts, unpeeled 700 ml water • 60 g butter • 20 g black trumpet mushrooms • 30 g small chanterelles • 30 g saffron milkcaps 1 small pack enokis • 1 pomegranate • 200 g sweet potato 200 g turnip • Chervil oil • Purple shiso leaves • 10 g salt

METHOD

1 To make the chestnut purée, boil the water with the salt in a saucepan and add the peeled chestnuts. Cook for 10 minutes.

2 Strain the chestnuts and purée them.

3 Pass the puréed chestnuts through a sieve and reserve them while hot.

4 Emulsify 300 grams of the still-warm chestnut purée with the diced butter.

5 Pass the chestnut purée through a sieve again to obtain small strands to 'weave' the carpet.

6 Remove the chestnut strands with the help of a palette knife and place on the base of the dish.

7 Cook 100 grams of unpeeled chestnuts until tender. Peel, slice and reserve.

8 Sauté the chanterelles, cut in half, and the black trumpets and saffron milkcaps, cut into small pieces. Cut the enokis into 2-centimetre pieces. Reserve all the mushrooms for assembling the dish.

9 Roast the sweet potato in the oven at 180°C until completely soft. Peel and then purée it. For a creamy texture, add a few drops of broth or water, and pass it through a sieve.

10 Boil the turnip, cut into mirepoix, in water and salt, then mash it, adding any necessary water to obtain a purée. Reserve.

11 Add the sliced chestnuts, the pomegranate seeds and the mushrooms on top of the chestnut carpet. Dress with small dots of sweet potato and turnip purée and chervil oil.

12 Garnish with shiso leaves or other herbs with aniseed nuances, such as fennel or tarragon, or that are earthy, such as beetroot sprouts or liquorice.

1

2

3

4

5

6

11

12

BOILING MEATS

Boiling meats in water is not a common practice, as they are usually cooked in sauces, stocks or some other preparation. This is what happens in stews or casseroles. In this type of cooking, the liquid stabilises the cooking at 100°C, which is more gentle than in an oven; moreover, as it is protected by a liquid, the meat does not dry out and its delicious juices can be combined with other flavours (vegetables, wine, broth, etc.).

Nethertheless, very tough meats, such as pig's trotters, or offal, such as tripe, ear or snout, can be boiled in water, although in this case it is considered more of a first step in preparation.

PREPARING PIG'S TROTTERS

1 Before cooking the pig's trotters, first prepare them by blanching (see p. 177) to remove blood, impurities and bad odours.

2 Once blanched, boil them for 2–3 hours, normally with vegetables, herbs and spices for flavouring, and skim the water as many times as necessary.

3 Once boiled, you can easily debone them and use according to the recipe of your choice.

APPROXIMATE COOKING TIMES

- Pig's trotters: 2–4 hrs
- Veal tongue: 2–4 hrs

STEAMED BUN WITH PANCETTA

Time: 2 hrs | Level: moderate

INGREDIENTS FOR 4 PEOPLE

20 steamed buns

15 g cucumber

Shiso leaves (optional)

For the filling

400 g pancetta or bacon

400 ml water

125 ml soy sauce

75 g brown sugar

40 g leek

75 g onion

½ cinnamon stick

2 g ginger

5 black peppercorns

2

METHOD

1 To prepare the filling, put all the ingredients into a small casserole dish, with the vegetables previously cut into mirepoix (large cubes). Cover it with a circle of greaseproof paper as a lid. Cook for 1 hour, then allow to cool in its own water.

2 Once cold, cut the pancetta or bacon into roughly 50-gram pieces for heating in the oven or microwave.

3 Reduce the remaining sauce in the casserole until thick, then allow to cool.

4 Heat the pancetta and place it, still hot, in the steamed buns (*see p. 218*). Add 2–3 cucumber slices and the meat sauce. Finish by garnishing the buns with shiso leaves.

The key to this dish is combining the fatty taste of pancetta or bacon with the freshness of cucumber. Moreover, thanks to the perfect cooking of the steamed buns and the intensity of the sauce, this simple snack becomes a true gastronomic gem.

CARPACCIO OF PIG'S TROTTERS

Time: 2 hrs (+ 4 hrs of preparation) | Level: moderate

INGREDIENTS FOR 10 PEOPLE

To prepare the pig's trotters
5 pig's trotters, halved
150 g carrots
150 g onions
½ bay leaf
5 black peppercorns
For the cep (Boletus edulis) *confit*
200 g ceps
100 ml extra virgin olive oil
75 g carrot
75 g turnip
Parsley, chopped
For the vinaigrette
100 ml oil used to confit the ceps
25 g ceps and their cooking vegetables
10 ml vinegar - *5 g toasted pine nuts*
Chives, chopped - *Salt and pepper*

METHOD

1 To prepare the pig's trotters, first blanch them to clean them thoroughly (*see p. 177*): boil them in a pot of cold water, then remove it from the heat and change the water. Repeat 2 more times.

2 Add the peeled carrots and onion, the bay leaf and peppercorns to the trotters. Bring to the boil, then turn the heat down to its lowest setting. Leave it for 4 hours or until the trotters are completely tender when checked. Remove and drain them, then debone them while still hot.

3 To confit the ceps, first clean them well (*see p. 111*), then cook them over very low heat (70–80°C) for 1 hour, together with the carrot and turnip cut into medium-sized batons.

4 Once the mushrooms and vegetables are cooked, cool, dice and set aside. Reserve about 25 grams of this preparation for the vinaigrette that will be prepared before serving.

5 Dice a small portion of the trotters and mix with the diced cep confit, carrots, turnips and chopped parsley.

6 Spread out a base of boneless pig's trotters, fill it with the mixture of ceps and diced vegetables, then cover it with another trotter. Form into cylinders with the help of clingfilm. Cool them in the refrigerator, then freeze them.

7 To prepare the vinaigrette, mix the oil from the cep confit, the vinegar, chives, pine nuts and reserved cooked vegetables, and add salt and pepper.

8 Cut the frozen pork trotters into slices 3 millimetres thick — the cut will be easier if you use a slicing machine — and place them on a flat plate.

9 Before serving, heat the whole dish under the oven's grill or in a salamander. Finish the dish by generously dressing it with the vinaigrette.

BOILING FISH AND SHELLFISH

Although boiling fish was a common practice in the past, nowadays gentler cooking methods are used, such as poaching or light blanching. These are procedures that better respect the properties of the product.

However, boiling continues to be widespread for cooking shellfish.

THE SEAFOOD PROCESS

1 Introduce the seafood into boiling water. The water must be salty — it can even be seawater.

2 Boil for as long as necessary depending on the type of seafood (ask at the fishmonger's), although the cooking time also depends on the size of the piece and the desired doneness. Sometimes it is very briefly blanched or boiled if it is then finished off using a different method.

3 Serve or cool quickly.

There is a very special type of cooking for freshwater fish (trout, carp or pike), called 'au bleu' cooking, which requires handling extraordinarily fresh fish. It consists of boiling the fish in a thin broth of vinegar, salt and aromatic herbs, such as bay leaf or thyme. In this way, the skin of the fish turns bluish in colour (hence the name '*bleu*', French for blue, for the process).

APPROXIMATE COOKING TIMES

- Barnacle: 1 min
- Langoustine: 3–4 mins
- Lobster (500 g piece): 6–8 mins
- Octopus: 15 mins–1hr
- Prawn: 2–3 mins
- Rock lobster (500 g piece): 6–8 mins
- Shrimp: 2 mins
- Spider crab: 20 mins
- Velvet crab: 5–6 mins

COCKLES WITH CITRUS

Time: 1 hr | Level: moderate

INGREDIENTS FOR 8 PEOPLE

500 g cockles • Mustard sprouts

Black pepper

For the cockle and lemon juice

200 ml cockle water (from the above preparation)

75 ml lemon juice

For the bergamot gel

125 ml water • 25 g sugar • Bergamot peel

2 g agar agar • 25 ml bergamot juice

For the bergamot emusion

150 g bergamot gel (from the above preparation)

50 ml extra virgin olive oil

METHOD

1 Bring water to the boil in a saucepan and add the cockles, a little at a time, removing them quickly as soon as they open. Depending on their size, they may take 10 to 30 seconds to open.

2 Remove the cockle meat from the shells and reserve the water.

3 To obtain the cockle and lemon juice, squeeze the lemons, strain the juice and mix it with the cockle water. Reserve.

4 To make the bergamot gel, heat the water and sugar. As soon as they boil, remove from the heat and infuse the grated bergamot peel, with the saucepan covered, for 15 minutes. Cool, strain and mix with the agar agar. Bring to the boil and add the bergamot juice. Immediately remove from the heat and allow to set in the refrigerator.

5 For the emulsion, blend the bergamot gel, a little at a time, with the olive oil. Reserve.

6 Place the cockles on a plate. Stir the cockle and lemon juice and season. Add 4 dashes of bergamot emulsion, a little ground black pepper and some mustard sprouts.

OCTOPUS WITH PARMENTIER IN ITS OWN EMULSION

Time: 4 hrs (octopus preparation 1 day before) | Level: moderate

INGREDIENTS FOR 4 PEOPLE

1 medium or large octopus
Sweet paprika
Shiso leaves or some spicy sprouts
Olive oil - *Salt*
For the mashed potatoes
500 g potatoes - *70 g butter*
30 ml extra virgin olive oil - *6 g salt*

METHOD

1 If starting with fresh octopus, to soften the meat well, it is best to freeze and thaw it, then boil it for 1 hour. Strain and allow to cool. If the octopus is already cooked and frozen, simply defrost it the day before.

2 Open the octopus and reserve the gelatinous water that covers the meat. Separate the head from the legs (you can use the head for salads or soups). Season the legs generously with the sweet paprika.

3 Form a cylinder using clingfilm, covering with a second layer of clingfilm so that it is well bound. Freeze the cylinder.

4 Mix the oil with the paprika and salt to obtain a small quantity of paprika oil.

5 Cut the cylinder into thin slices, place them between sheets of baking paper (or clingfilm) and store in the freezer.

6 For the mashed potatoes, follow the baking method (*see p. 277*). You can also prepare the mashed potatoes by vacuum cooking them, along with butter, oil and salt, in the cooking machine at 85°C for 4 hours. Remove from the bag and mash everything. Cool and reserve.

7 Place a dome of mashed potatoes in the centre of the plate with the help of a ring or mould.

8 Cover the potatoes with the octopus slices.

9 Preheat the oven in salamander or grilling mode and place the dish in it for a few moments.

10 Meanwhile, gently heat the octopus jelly, add butter and whip it with the blender so that the sauce is slightly aerated, much thicker than liquid.

11 Place a couple of spoonfuls of sauce around the edges of the dish. Garnish with shiso leaves and a few drops of paprika oil and serve immediately.

This dish is a small nod to the traditional Galician octopus. We prepare it with respect and admiration for traditional cuisine, which always provides us with knowledge and a source for new challenges.

CLAM SOUP WITH MISO

Time: 30 mins (+ 2 hrs previous infusion) | Level: easy

INGREDIENTS FOR 4 PEOPLE

1 litre mineral water
Kombu seaweed (one 5 x 5 cm sheet)
800 g clams
50 g red miso
100 g turnip
Chives
Salt

This recipe is very easy to prepare, as the liquid from the clams provides an almost instantaneous soup, with the warm, unique flavour of miso. It offers a fresh, healthy and uncomplicated style of cooking.

METHOD

1 Place the clams in salt to purge them and reserve them for 1 hour in the refrigerator.

2 Make a series of cuts in the kombu seaweed, then leave it for 2 hours in a bowl with the 1 litre of water to infuse and release all its flavour.

3 Dice the turnip.

4 After the 2 hours of infusing the seaweed, pour the water with the kombu in a small pot and add the clams and turnip.

5 When the water starts to boil, remove the kombu and lower the heat to reduce the boiling.

6 With the help of a sieve, break up the miso paste so that it does not make lumps in the soup.

7 Keep the soup over a low heat for about 3 minutes (without letting the water boil). Add a little chopped chives and serve it immediately, very hot.

4

5

6

BOILING CEREALS

The cooking process for cereals depends on the type and preferred texture. In general, as they are dry products, they need a lot of water, since they must be softened; this is even more so the case for wholegrains, which need longer cooking times, since their outer coating, or bran, is a barrier that controls the passage of moisture.

Thus, the choice of process will depend on the result you want and the product you are working with. You can ask the producer or trader of a particular cereal about its cooking time, but it is also important to experiment until you find the taste and texture that you like the most.

It is worthwhile to try boiling cereals in water enriched with flavours, such as bouquet garni (*see p. 348*), spices, vegetables or citrus peels.

We advise a gentle boiling over low heat. At the end of cooking, drain and cool the product quickly. Before serving, you can brush it lightly with oil and cover it so that it does not dry out.

BOILING RICE

1 Heat a good quantity of salted water over a high heat (4 parts water for each part rice). You must use a sufficiently large saucepan, because the rice increases in size during cooking.

2 When the water starts to boil, add the rice and stir it from time to time.

3 Allow it to cook for 15–20 minutes, depending on the type of rice, or until all the liquid is gone. At the end, leave the rice uncovered for 1 minute to allow the steam to escape, and turn it over with a spoon.

APPROXIMATE COOKING TIMES

- Bulgur wheat: 15–20 mins
- Oats: 10 mins
- Quinoa, white and black: 12–15 mins
- Rice: 15–20 mins

QUINOA SALAD WITH CHERRIES AND STRAWBERRIES

Time: 2 hrs | Level: easy

INGREDIENTS FOR 4 PEOPLE

300 g quinoa
Strawberries
Cherries
Flowers (acacia, thyme, violet, elderberry)
For the dressing
50 g spring onions
50 g red pepper
50 g green pepper
160 ml sunflower oil
30 ml lemon juice
Salt and pepper

METHOD

1 To prepare the dressing, cut the vegetables into dice, mix them with the oil and lemon juice, and add salt and pepper.

2 To prepare the quinoa, boil it according to the instructions on the packet. Normally, 2 parts water are allowed for 1 part quinoa, and it should cook for about 12 minutes. Vegetables or ginger can be added to the water for flavouring and to give it a refreshing touch.

3 Strain and cool in water, or, better yet, by spreading the quinoa on a very cold plate chilled in the refrigerator. Stirring the quinoa will make it cool faster.

4 Once the quinoa is cold, adjust the seasoning, adding salt and pepper if necessary, then serve it in an attractive dish and decorate with quarters or pieces of strawberries and cherries to add acidity and freshness. Finish by adding aromatic flowers.

Quinoa (Chenopodium quinoa) *is a plant with seeds that are edible. Although it is not exactly a cereal, because it does not belong to the grass family, its high starch content allows it to be cooked as such. Widely cultivated in Bolivia and Peru, the native peoples of the Andes revered it as a sacred food due to its nutritional properties. Today, it is considered one of the most complete and healthy foods due to its contribution of essential amino acids, minerals and especially proteins (more than double that of any other cereal). In addition, it is gluten-free.*

It is easy to cook and has a very interesting texture, as well as a mild flavour that makes it very versatile when combined with other foods. For all these characteristics and qualities, it is worth giving it a leading role in your daily preparations.

PARTRIDGE AND CUTTLEFISH RICE

Time: 3 hrs | Level: moderate

INGREDIENTS FOR 4 PEOPLE

2 partridges
300 g pancetta or bacon
400 g rice
2 artichokes
1 ripe tomato, grated (pulp only)
2 onions
1 green pepper
1 red pepper
3 garlic cloves
1 medium cuttlefish
1 teaspoon soy sauce
Salt and pepper
Olive oil
For the stock
Partridge bones and carcasses
1 vegetable stock cube
7 g salt

METHOD

1 To make the partridge stock, using the partridge bones and carcasses and a vegetable stock cube, follow the recipe for the brown stock (*see p. 324*). The stock must be strong, with salt. As it will be further reduced during cooking with the rice, use 7 grams of salt per litre, although this will depend on personal taste.

2 For cooking with the rice, debone the partridge and cut its meat into small cubes, then cut the pancetta or bacon into cubes. Season with salt and pepper, then sauté in a frying pan with a little oil. When the meat is well browned, add the onions, peppers and garlic, chopped into brunoise, and simmer for 1 hour 30 minutes. Then add the tomato and cook for a further 30 minutes.

3 To make the rice, clean the artichokes (*see p. 110*), cut them into quarters and sauté in olive oil.

4 Once the artichokes are browned, add the meat mixture and rice, then fry it all together.

5 Add the very hot partridge stock.

6 Cook the rice over a high heat for 10 minutes, then over low heat for 5 minutes (you can also finish with 5 minutes in the oven at 180°C).

7 Sauté the cuttlefish cut into very thin strips.

8 Season the cuttlefish with salt, oil and a few drops of soy sauce. Arrange the rice on the plate and place the cuttlefish strips on top.

A good rice must be accompanied by exceptional products. Likewise, the broth in which it is cooked must concentrate the ingredients to offer aroma and flavour.

5

6

7

COUSCOUS WITH GRILLED VEGETABLES AND SPICED YOGURT

Time: 30 mins | Level: easy

INGREDIENTS FOR 4 PEOPLE

2 carrots
2 courgettes
1 bunch of young garlic
2 turnips
Beans, cauliflower, cabbage or other vegetables, according to the season
Olive oil
Ras el hanout (Moroccan spice mix)
Salt and pepper

To hydrate the couscous
240 g couscous
240 ml vegetable stock, with salt to taste

For the sauce
250 g Greek yogurt
½ lemon
Fresh mint
Ras el hanout

METHOD

1 To hydrate the couscous, heat the vegetable stock (*see p. 323*) and adjust the salt if necessary. Pour the couscous into a bowl and, once the broth has started to boil, add it to the couscous. Cover and allow it to rest. After 5 minutes, stir the couscous with a fork to loosen and cool.

2 Cut the vegetables into different shapes and cook them in boiling water until al dente. Cool them quickly in water and ice.

3 Once well drained, briefly sear the vegetables and set aside in a bowl. Dress with olive oil.

4 Add the vegetables to the couscous and dress with olive oil and ras el hanout.

5 To prepare the sauce, mix the yogurt with the juice of half a lemon, add some chopped mint and season with ras el hanout.

6 To finish, dress the plate with a base of couscous, add the grilled vegetables and finish the dish by seasoning it with a few touches of the yogurt sauce with mint and spices.

Although the idea of this dish is to obtain a warm first course, it can also be presented as a cold salad or a hot preparation, depending on the season in which you wish to cook it or according to your appetite. The proposed vegetables can be substituted for others, depending on the season.

BOILING UNDER PRESSURE

The pressure cooker allows cooking at temperatures above boiling point so food cooks quickly. These pots are hermetically sealed so steam is trapped inside and increases the temperature, which exceeds 125°C. A device releases the steam before the pressure reaches a safety limit.

It is a useful method for cooking quickly, especially for foods that need a long cooking time. It also makes very concentrated broths (from seafood heads, such as prawns) or purées and creams in which the cooking water is incorporated. Cooking by steam, it does not require adding a lot of water, which allows the maximum flavour to be extracted from the food without dissolving its nutrients in the liquid, which can occur in normal boiling. However, it is not advisable to pressure cook meats because, although it softens their texture, it can also dry them out.

THE PRESSURE COOKING PROCESS

1 Prepare the ingredients to be cooked.

2 Add the water for heating to the pressure cooker (the quantity varies according to the preparation; for a purée, add just enough water to use in blending).

3 Add the food to the hot water and close the pot. The time required for cooking depends on each ingredient and begins counting as soon as steam starts coming out of the device.

4 When you turn off the heat, you must wait until the steam stops coming out of the safety valve.

5 Once you are sure that there is no steam inside the pot, you can open it and remove the ingredients for serving.

APPROXIMATE COOKING TIMES

- Artichokes: 8 mins
- Broths: 1–3 hrs
- Green beans: 5 mins
- Peas: 3 mins

CREAM OF COURGETTE PESTO SOUP

Time: 1 hr | Level: easy

INGREDIENTS FOR 4 PEOPLE

600 g courgettes
100 ml water
200 ml cream
100 g mascarpone cheese
40 g toasted pine nuts
Salt and pepper
For the basil oil
50 ml olive oil
Basil leaves

METHOD

1 To prepare the basil oil, purée some basil leaves (the larger ones, while reserving the small ones for garnishing) with the olive oil using a stick blender.

2 Put the measured water and salt into a pressure cooker, then add the washed courgettes, cut into mirepoix. Boil for 2 minutes from the time the pot releases steam under pressure.

3 Remove the pot from the heat and, as soon as it can be opened, quickly purée the courgettes. Before blending, reserve a little water. It can be added later, if needed, to achieve a creamy texture.

4 Cool the soup in a bain-marie with cold water, so that it does not lose colour or taste.

5 When cold, add salt to the cream and whip it with the mascarpone in a blender until the mixture has the texture of whipped cream. Add salt and pepper.

6 Place 2 tablespoons of warm courgette soup in a soup dish. Add a quenelle or spoonful of mascarpone cream in the centre. Garnish with the basil oil, pine nuts and small basil leaves.

A very simple dish, it has the added value of being cooked quickly in order to take advantage of all the nutrients in the food. The basil and mascarpone add aromas and textures, and give modest distinction to this simple recipe.

COOKING WITH STEAM

CONSIDERED ONE OF THE TECHNIQUES PAR EXCELLENCE FOR HEALTHY NUTRITION, IT ALLOWS FOOD TO BE COOKED QUICKLY WHILE, ABOVE ALL, PRESERVING THEIR ORIGINAL FLAVOUR AND AROMA.

TYPE OF COOKING	By concentration
RELATED TECHNIQUES	Vacuum cooking Boiling Bain-marie

Steaming is a technique that is very respectful of the food, as it preserves all its flavour and safeguards its nutritional properties. In addition, it does not require any type of fat. It consists of cooking food with the steam emanating from a liquid, usually boiling, so it is cooked at a temperature of about 100°C.

Until just a few decades ago, steaming was practically relegated to curative diets, but today it is being revalued, probably because the population is more aware of the benefits of healthy eating, and because the kitchenware industry has also contributed to popularising the technique by putting within our reach a wide range of utensils that are convenient, while providing refinement and variety.

Today, some cooks use this technique to cook certain ingredients, such as vegetables or fish, very gently. Cooking with steam also allows the ingredients to be flavoured with the aromas from the liquid being heated, especially fatty foods, which acquire the aroma more easily than lean foods. For example, oily fish with fatty meat, such as mackerel, absorbs aromas very well.

Many professional kitchens – and increasingly more domestic kitchens – have combi ovens, with convection and steam baking functions, which evenly heat the food with the hot air circulating around it. These can be used for various types of cooking, including steaming, with a lower temperature range than is usual in traditional steaming (between 40 and 130°C).

THE PROCESS

1. Prepare all of the ingredients.
2. Place on the hob a container specific for steaming, with holes or grids, or a steamer. In the lower part, add the water, although it can also be a mild broth, a very spicy broth or even a wine — a Manzanilla or other sherry, for example — to aromatise the preparation.
3. Place the food in the upper part of the steamer, which will keep the food separated from the liquid that will heat it.
4. Finally, cover and cook for the time required for each product.

MACKEREL STEAMED WITH MONTILLA

Time: 1 hr | Level: easy

INGREDIENTS FOR 4 PEOPLE

4 medium mackerel fillets
250 ml Montilla wine
10 g toasted hazelnuts
1 small cep (or 1 small tender mushroom)
1 lemon
Candied orange peel
To prepare the miso
10 g miso
50 ml vegetable broth
Virgin olive oil

METHOD

1 It is important that you first prepare the different elements to be able to assemble and serve the dish very quickly and keep the mackerel warm. Start by breaking the toasted hazelnuts into small pieces and chopping the candied orange peel. Next, prepare a smooth purée by blending the orange peel with the olive oil and adding vegetable broth until the desired texture is achieved.

2 To make the miso, heat the vegetable broth and once it is lukewarm add the miso. Emulsify with a little olive oil.

3 Cut the mushroom into slices.

4 In a steaming pot, add the Montilla wine, place the mackerel fillets in the steamer and cook for 2 minutes.

5 Plate the freshly cooked mackerel and quickly add the complements: the hazelnuts, emulsified miso, some thin slices of cep, the chopped candied orange peel, and the orange purée. Finally, season with olive oil and a few pinches of lemon zest.

This is a recipe full of nuances, thanks to the diversity of aromas of a generous wine, such as Montilla, which manages, with the delicate cooking obtained by steaming, to aromatise the mackerel and harmonise it with the toasted nuts, orange, and earthy notes from the other ingredients.

STEAMED BUNS (CHINESE BREAD)

Time: 1 hr 30 mins | Level: moderate

INGREDIENTS FOR 4 PEOPLE

25 ml water
6 g fresh yeast
2 g baking powder
125 g flour
10 g sugar
45 ml milk
12 ml sunflower oil
1 g salt

METHOD

1 Mix the fresh yeast with the lukewarm water.

2 Form a well with the flour, sugar and salt, and in the centre add the remaining liquids (milk and oil), the yeast dissolved in water and the baking powder.

3 Knead until a smooth ball is formed.

4 Let the dough rest for 1 hour in a bowl covered with clingfilm with a few holes pricked in it so that the dough can breathe and ferment.

5 Knead and form small balls.

6 Roll out the balls with a rolling pin and place them on sheets of baking paper. Brush them with oil and fold (the oil will prevent the two parts of the folded dough sticking together).

7 Steam the buns for 5 minutes and they are ready to be filled.

Steamed buns take us away from the usual references of crusty breads and enter a new world of soft and spongy textures, which can be combined with sauces, giving the bread new flavours and sensations.

They can be available at any time by precooking and freezing them. It is very easy to steam or microwave them again and then fill them with appetising sauces, truffle, ceps, artichokes or any other ingredient you like. Fluffy and delicate, steamed buns offer subtle bites full of flavour.

1

3

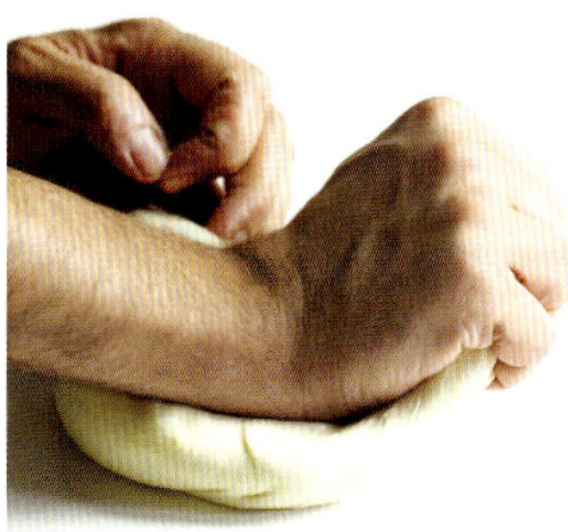

4

5

6

BRIOCHE STEAMED WITH MUSHROOM MAYONNAISE

Time: 2 hrs (+ 6 hrs resting) | Level: moderate

INGREDIENTS FOR 4 PEOPLE

For the brioche

30 g sugar - *25 ml milk* - *2 eggs*

12 g baking powder - *250 g flour*

125 g butter - *3 g salt*

For the mayonnaise

1 egg yolk - *10 ml water* - *100 ml virgin olive oil*

100 g mushrooms - *Salt*

METHOD

1 To make the brioche, mix the milk, eggs, sugar, baking powder and salt with a whisk.

2 Add the flour to the mixture in two batches, to be able to mix it well with a fork or spoon, and then add the butter, which should be smooth. To obtain this soft texture, simply leave the butter out of the refrigerator for 1 hour and cut into cubes, or work it with a fork or whisk until the desired texture.

3 Knead until you have a smooth, elastic dough that comes off easily from the bowl.

4 Place the dough in a bowl and let it rest in the refrigerator for 6 hours.

5 Remove the dough from the refrigerator, then cut small pieces of 6 grams and form into balls. Let them ferment for 40 minutes at 40°C on a baking tray and reserve in the refrigerator.

6 To make the mushroom mayonnaise, follow the instructions in the recipe (*see p. 329*), reserving a couple of mushrooms for garnish.

7 Place the brioches in a steamer and cook for 20 minutes.

8 Once ready, fill them with mayonnaise using a piping bag and garnish them with thin slices of the reserved mushrooms.

In contrast to the creaminess of the mayonnaise, the brioche brings a very special texture. You can adapt the sauce to your taste: truffle sauce, ceps, artichokes, herbs, etc.

5

8

PASSION FRUIT FLANS WITH COCONUT FOAM

Time: 2 hrs (+ 6 hrs resting) | Level: easy

INGREDIENTS FOR 8 PEOPLE

For the passion fruit flans

160 g passion fruit pulp • 475 g sugar • 316 g egg yolks

53 g egg whites

For the base syrup

60 g sugar • 60 ml water

For the coconut foam

250 ml coconut milk • 100 ml cream • 100 ml syrup

For the passion fruit cream

300 g passion fruit purée • 50 g sugar

1 g xantan gum

METHOD

1 To make the passion fruit flans, mix the sugar with the fruit and cook to 120°C to obtain a syrup. Allow it to rest for a few minutes to lower its temperature a little.

2 Beat the egg yolks and egg whites and gradually add the syrup. It should not be too hot, to prevent the eggs curdling.

3 Spread a little syrup in individual ramekins or flan dishes and fill them with the mixture.

4 Steam the flans for 10 minutes. Cover the steamer basket with clingfilm.

5 Check for doneness by pricking with a knife; if it comes out clean, the flans are ready. Once cold, allow them to rest for at least 6 hours in the refrigerator.

6 To prepare the syrup, boil the water with the sugar and set aside.

7 To make the coconut foam, mix the coconut milk, cream and syrup, strain and put the mixture into a siphon. Charge with two gas cartridges and cool it in the refrigerator.

8 To prepare the passion fruit cream, using a stick blender, blend to a purée (which can be bought already prepared) together with the sugar and xanthan gum. Strain the mixture and set aside.

9 To finish, unmould the flans on to a plate, pour over a spoonful of passion fruit cream and add a little coconut foam.

1

2

3

4

5

7

BAIN-MARIE COOKING

USED IN SOFT AND DELICATE BAKING, IT IS THE TECHNIQUE PAR EXCELLENCE FOR DESSERTS AND PASTRIES, AND HAS MANY OTHER USES. IT IS ONE OF THE SOURCES OF INSPIRATION FOR MODERN LOW-TEMPERATURE BAKING.

TYPE OF COOKING	By concentration
RELATED TECHNIQUES	Vacuum cooking Low-temperature cooking

In bain-marie cooking, water once again plays a fundamental role in a water bath. In this case, as with steaming, the food does not come into contact with the water, but is indirectly heated and provided with a stable temperature, no higher than 100°C. In addition, indirect cooking buffers the excess heat, so you can obtain creamy textures, although it will also depend on the intensity of the temperature and the speed with which you stir the product. Finally, as this technique allows the eggs to be cooked without curdling, it is the best way to make custards, scrambled eggs and some creams, such as crème anglaise or hollandaise sauce.

In the case of flans, you must control the oven temperature so that the water does not boil. This will prevent holes on the outside of the flans and stop them drying out too much.

This technique can also be used to heat preparations such as sauces, purées or garnishes, as well as to keep them warm and at a stable temperature that does not dry or curdle them until they are ready to be served.

THE PROCESS

1. Prepare all of the ingredients.
2. Place the food in a cooking container (a saucepan, a bowl or a ramekin).
3. Immerse this container into a larger container (a small pot, casserole or deep baking dish) containing water.
4. Place the containers on the heat or in the oven and cook for the time and at the temperature required for the preparation.

ANISEED SCRAMBLED EGGS WITH TROUT ROE

Time: 20 mins | Level: easy

INGREDIENTS FOR 4 PEOPLE

12 eggs

120 ml cream

90 g trout roe

Rustic bread

Olive oil

Chervil, fennel and tarragon leaves - *Salt* - *Pepper*

METHOD

1 Chop the aniseed-flavoured herbs, but reserve some whole ones for the final garnish.

2 Beat the eggs with the cream, season with salt and pepper, and add the chopped herbs.

3 Cut the bread into thin slices and toast it in the oven with a few drops of oil at 180°C.

4 Place a bowl in a baine-marie (water bath) and add the egg mixture. Cook them while stirring to cook the mixture gradually and thus achieve a creamy preparation.

5 Once the mixture is ready, serve it immediately, together with the toasted bread and the trout roe, and garnish it with the reserved herbs.

A creamy scrambled egg needs a little patience to cook it over very low heat to prevent the egg from curdling. The result deserves such delicacy. This is a simple but very delicious dish.

2

4

CREAMY VANILLA CREAM WITH APRICOT COULIS

Time: 2 hrs (+ 12 hrs of rest) | Level: easy

INGREDIENTS FOR 8 PEOPLE

375 ml cream
125 ml milk
1 whole egg and 5 egg yolks
150 g sugar
2 vanilla pods
Lemon verbena
For the apricot coulis
1 apricot
100 g sugar - 100 ml water

METHOD

1 Heat the milk and cream with the vanilla pod cut in half. When it is about to boil, remove it from the heat.

2 Open the vanilla pod and scrape out its seeds, then add them to the hot milk.

3 Beat the egg and egg yolks with the sugar and add the warm milk.

4 Pour the mixture into flan pans and bake in a bain-marie (water bath) at 120°C for about 45 minutes. The water in the bain-marie must be hot when the pans are placed in it so that the cooking time is correct. In any case, pierce with a knife to check if the internal cooking is ready. If you take out a clean knife, the cream will have set and it will be time to remove it.

5 Allow it to cool and set aside in the refrigerator to rest for 12 hours.

6 To prepare the apricot coulis, cut the apricot into brunoise and cook for 10 minutes with the water and sugar. Cool and reserve.

7 Place the vanilla cream in a soup plate, sprinkle sugar on top and caramelise it with a kitchen blowtorch or over the hob. Finally, add the apricot coulis and decorate with lemon verbena leaves.

Between a custard and a flan, this creamy vanilla custard is the result of baking at a lower temperature than usual. Temperature control is a culinary trend that increasingly more cooks are adopting because of its respect for the products' flavours and also to achieve new textures. This dessert bears some resemblance to the typical French crème brûlée, but instead of using cream and caramelised sauces, it uses a delicious and refreshing apricot coulis.

BRAISING

THIS IS THE RECOMMENDED, ALTHOUGH NOT EXCLUSIVE, COOKING METHOD FOR TOUGH MEATS THAT REQUIRE A COMBINATION OF TWO COOKING METHODS. BRAISING PRESERVES THE FLAVOUR AND PROVIDES A TENDER TEXTURE.

TYPE OF COOKING	Mixed
RELATED TECHNIQUES	Roasting Stewing Simmering

Originating from the French term '*braiser*', the braising technique combines two cooking methods: firstly, browning to seal the food and, secondly, prolonged cooking over a low heat. In the first process, the product – usually meat – is cooked on its own, with only a little fat, while in the second process it is accompanied by prepared vegetables and a liquid, which can be water, broth, wine or even alcohol.

In short, it is a mixed cooking, consisting of a dry-and-quick stage followed by a second wet-and-slow stage in which there is an exchange of flavours between the previously seared piece and the incorporated foods.

THE PROCESS

1 Prepare all of the ingredients.

2 Sear the food in oil at high temperature, season it with salt and pepper (or with a previous brine; *see p. 144*) and truss, if necessary, as in the case of many meats. You can brown it in the oven, in a brazier (slow casserole with a special lid for braising) or any other type of pan.

3 Add the vegetables and cook over a moderate heat until they are cooked.

4 Pour in a young red wine and allow it to reduce over moderate heat.

5 Add the liquid (some type of broth or stock, white or brown, or a vegetable broth, depending on the type of preparation you want to make), cover and cook over a low heat until the meat is tender.

6 Remove the meat and strain the vegetables, although you can also blend them with the juices.

7 Slice the meat when it is cold, as it breaks easily when hot, and add it back to the casserole or baking dish with the sauce to finish cooking over a low heat.

BRAISED VEAL WITH GARDEN VEGETABLES

Time: 4 hrs | Level: easy

INGREDIENTS FOR 4 PEOPLE

1 veal shank
2 onions
2 carrots
½ leek
1 celery stick
6 garlic cloves
3 ripe tomatoes
300 ml red wine
200 ml olive oil
2 litres brown broth or white stock
Salt and pepper
For the garnish
200 g mushrooms • 32 baby onions • 200 g carrots
200 g turnips • 200 g fine beans
For the picada sauce
70 g toasted almonds • 1 bunch of parsley
2 garlic cloves • 10 ml oil • 50 ml water

METHOD

1 Truss the veal shank. If it is very large, you can divide it into two pieces and tie them separately.

2 Season the meat with salt and pepper (or apply a 10 per cent brine for 1 hour; *see p. 144*) and cook until it turns a nice golden colour.

3 Prepare the vegetables by cutting of them into mirepoix (large cubes), then add them when the meat is browned. Continue cooking until the vegetables are also browned.

4 Pour in the wine and allow it to reduce as much as possible.

5 Add the hot broth, cover the casserole and cook for about 1 hour. After this time, check that the meat is sufficiently tender. If so, remove it from the broth and allow it to cool. Strain the broth, skim off the fat and reserve the broth.

6 To prepare the garnish, cut the carrots, turnips and beans into batons, blanch them quickly and set aside.

7 Peel the onions and cook them for 30 minutes with oil, until they are almost cooked.

8 Cut the mushrooms into slices and sauté them, but leave them a little undercooked.

9 To prepare the picada sauce, blend all the ingredients with a stick blender.

10 Cut the cold meat into 1-cm slices and add them to the casserole. Wet them with the cooking broth, add the vegetables and cook for 30 minutes. Season with salt and pepper and add the picada sauce.

Good cuisine is always rooted in classic dishes and cooking that accumulate the knowledge and experience of many generations. We believe it is important to learn the processes of this type of cooking, understanding what happens in each of the steps. By understanding them well, we can prepare the recipes according to the ingredients or containers, an essential task for any good cook.

STEWING

ALWAYS USING LOW HEAT, AND TIGHTLY COVERED SO AS NOT TO ALLOW THE STEAM AND AROMAS TO ESCAPE, STEWING IS THE IDEAL TECHNIQUE FOR MEATS THAT REQUIRE LONG COOKING TIMES.

TYPE OF COOKING	Mixed
RELATED TECHNIQUES	Braising

There are many types of stews, each with its own variations. In theory, the ingredients are cooked raw, but in our gastronomic culture there are many cooks who – in order to seal the meat a little and to bind the liquid and turn it into a smooth sauce – decide to flour the ingredients and brown it before starting to cook it slowly.

Stews should be cooked gently, simmering, and always covered so that the liquids that evaporate condense and fall back into the stew, without losing a single drop of the juices of all the ingredients incorporated.

The stew's garnish can be treated in several ways. If you want it to be a direct part of the dish and its flavours to be mixed in, include it in the cooking. This is the case of the garden stew, in which potatoes, carrots and mushrooms are added, or the Saint Germain-style stew, which includes peas. However, if you prefer the vegetables to complement, refresh and not confuse its flavour, add the almost cooked garnish at the last moment.

In game stews, where the meat is previously marinated, you can take advantage of the liquid from the marination to add it to the cooking.

PROCESS

1. Prepare all of the ingredients.
2. Season the main piece of meat with salt and pepper, flour it and brown it in oil.
3. Add vegetables or a base, such as a sofrito (*see p. 350*), and sauté.
4. Pour in wine and allow it to reduce so that it loses its acidity.
5. Add some liquid, either broth, stock or water, to help cooking.
6. Cook over a low heat and incorporate, if desired, the garnish you want to include. It is important to calculate the right moment to add it, to make sure it is cooked.
7. You can finish the stew by adding some type of seasoning, sauce or other complement to finish the taste and texture, such as a herb or a fatty element that does not need much cooking, such as tender sausages, or vegetables and seafood that require a short cooking time.

CLASSIC STEWS

- **Civet.** Stew made with game meat, such as wild boar or hare, in which the sauce is usually bound with the animal's liver or blood. This method is no longer used, but we continue to call it a civet stew when cooked with this type of meat.
- **Goulash.** Although it was originally a soup, it is usually associated with a stew in which paprika (a type of pepper) is the flavouring.
- **Navarin.** Lamb stew that includes leg meat and seasonal vegetables, and almost always turnip — a vegetable that was originally the main garnish for this stew. Sometimes it follows the conventional stewing process but other times it is combined with cooking in the oven.
- **Ragu.** Of Italian origin, its name generically encompasses all types of stews: red meat, poultry, game, fish or vegetables.

WILD BOAR STEW WITH BABY ONIONS

Time: 5 hrs (marinated for 5 to 7 days) | Level: moderate

INGREDIENTS FOR 4 PEOPLE

For the marinade

1 kg wild boar shoulder • 100 g onion

100 g carrots • 100 g leek

100 g celery • 1 litre red wine • 1 head garlic

Black and white peppercorns • Bay leaf

1 lemon • Cloves • 1 bouquet garni

For sautéing

200 ml oil • 200 g flour

2 litres broth • 40 g baby onions • Salt and pepper

For the picada

2 garlic cloves • 70 g toasted almonds

1 bunch of parsley • 10 ml oil • 50 ml water

PREPARATION

1 To prepare the marinade, cut the shoulder of wild boar into cubes and place them in a container with the wine and the vegetable mixture, cut into mirepoix, the garlic, peppercorns, bay leaf, cloves, lemon and bouquet garni. Allow it to marinate for 1 week (it can be a little less, if the wild boar is tender). Once the marinating time has elapsed, strain and separate into three parts: the liquid, the vegetable mixture and the meat.

2 Sauté the vegetables in oil, and when they are well browned, add the marinade liquid and allow it to reduce.

3 Wet the vegetables with the broth and cook them for a further 20 minutes. Strain and reserve the resulting juice.

4 For the sautéing, season the wild boar meat with salt and pepper, coat it in flour and brown it quickly in a frying pan with plenty of oil.

5 Add the meat to the casserole without the oil, then add the reserved juice and boil for 2 hours over a low heat, although this time will depend on the toughness of the meat.

6 To prepare the picada, while the meat is cooking, crush the garlic, almonds and parsley with a stick blender, and add water and oil.

7 Blanch the baby onions, peel them and sauté before adding them to the stew after 2 hours of cooking.

8 Cook the onions for 30 minutes.

9 Finally, add 2 tablespoons of the almond picada, add salt and pepper and serve.

Preparing a classic stew is a kind of challenge. It requires a long period of rest for the meat to soften and becomes tender. The gentle, constant and patient cooking will give you an extraordinary stew, full of wisdom and tradition. In reality, cooking is neither old nor modern, but good or bad. The legacy received from our teachers is one of extreme generosity. This dish proves it.

FRESH BEAN STEW WITH FRESH GARLIC

Time: 1 hr | Level: low

INGREDIENTS FOR 4 PEOPLE

600 g fresh haricot beans (podded)
1 bunch of fresh garlic cloves
100 g cured bacon
100 ml olive oil
1 large ripe tomato
100 g cooked, boneless pig's trotters
100 g black pudding
1 chive
Salt

METHOD

1 Boil the fresh beans in salted water for 20 minutes, then strain and reserve the beans and cooking water separately.

2 Prepare the base for the stew by sautéing in oil the bacon, cut into julienne strips, with the fresh garlic cloves, cut into strips of about 5 centimetres. Allow to cook for 15 minutes.

3 Add the tomato, cut into concassé, to the casserole and continue stewing for a further 15 minutes.

4 Add the drained beans, black pudding and diced pig's trotters to the stew and sauté for 2 minutes.

5 Wet the whole preparation with the liquid reserved from cooking the beans and continue cooking for 5 minutes.

6 Finish by garnishing with the chopped chive.

We are very used to consuming green beans and dried beans, but it is more unusal to consume podded beans when they are still fresh, before it becomes a dried bean. If you find these little green jewels at a market, don't miss the opportunity to buy and cook them straight away. Simply boil them with a dash of olive oil, or stew them, as in this case, to discover a wonderful product, both in flavour and texture.

FRYING

THIS COOKING TECHNIQUE HAS A HABIT OF PRESENTING NICE SURPRISES. SOMETIMES IT PRODUCES THE PERFECT COMBINATION OF CRUNCHY AND JUICY, BUT OTHER TIMES IT FOCUSES ONLY ON CRISPINESS. THE RESULT IS ALWAYS APPETISING.

TYPE OF COOKING	By concentration
RELATED TECHNIQUES	Poaching Confit Sautéing

Food is fried by submerging it into a fat, usually oil, at high temperatures, between 160 and 180°C, in order to brown and harden the external part of the food while preserving the juiciness of its interior in some cases, or dehydrating it in others.

When frying, it is important that the temperature is high enough to prevent the product absorbing excess oil. Both the type of fats and the cooking system used (deep-fat fryer, frying pan or saucepan) will have an influence on the temperature. To check it with certainty, use a cooking thermometer, which will indicate when the oil has reached the desired temperature and is ready for adding the food.

FRYING WITHOUT PROTECTION

When an ingredient without any protective coating is subjected to oil at high temperature, it is directly and intensely cooked. This is what happens, for example, with fried eggs. Oil is a great conductor of heat and acts by dehydrating the products, and for this reason the cooking times must be well controlled. Oil also has the capacity to produce a crispy layer on the ingredient's exterior, while the interior acquires a soft texture; this is the case with fried potatoes or sweet potatoes. You can also make the whole product crispy, as in vegetable crisps.

FRYING WITH PROTECTION

Foods can also be fried inside a protective coating, for example, by breading or in a batter. These coatings prevent the oil's heat drying out the product, but allow the temperature to penetrate gently so that the food's interior remains juicy.

Using flour, semolina, breadcrumbs and pastry, you can bread everything from Andalusian-style squid to onion rings or any other fried vegetable. In a batter, in addition to flour, you incorporate egg; this is the case of calamari in batter, cod fritters, croquettes and vegetable tempura. There are also wrappings, such as brick pastry, wonton wrappers and filo pastry.

LOW-FAT FRYING

You can fry foods using a minimum amount of fat in shallower pans. This is a gentler cooking method, to cook the product progressively, first on one side and then on the other, without excessive heat.

You can also fry with butter, but so that it does not burn, you must clarify it (heating it to separate its watery part, and decanting it to eliminate it), so that it can withstand the frying point up to 180°C instead of the 140–160°C that it would withstand without clarifying.

THE PROCESS

1. Prepare all of the ingredients.
2. Heat the oil to 160–180°C.
3. Once the oil has reached the minimum temperature, introduce the product. Turn it over if necessary, or stir the pan to achieve uniformity in the frying.
4. When it is ready, remove the product and place it on absorbent kitchen paper to remove the excess oil.

SOME TIPS FOR FRYING

- **Adjust the temperature.** It is essential to fry at the appropriate temperature, between 160 and 180°C, depending on the product, fat and container.
- **Calculate the quantity.** You should not fry too many pieces at the same time: the product should have space when frying. If you introduce a lot of pieces into the pan at once, the temperature of the oil will drop and the food will be impregnated with fat, boiled and softened.
- **Reuse the oil.** While oil from frying can be used for other purposes, bear in mind that the water and impurities released by the food into the oil and the heat itself tend to make the oil rancid and oxidise it. This loss of qualities shortens the oil's useful life.
- **Do not cover.** You should never cover a food when frying it, because the humidity will spoil the oil. Nor should you cover the food once it has been fried, as it will soften.
- **Avoid accidents.** You should never pour water to cool an oil that is too hot or to extinguish a burning frying pan. If this happens, remove it from the fire and cover it to deprive the fire of air.

SARDINES WITH BASIL AND LEMON PEEL

Time: 30 mins | Level: easy

INGREDIENTS FOR 4 PEOPLE

12 sardine fillets

12 basil leaves

4 sheets brick pastry or filo pastry

50 ml sunflower oil

Lemon

Pepper

METHOD

1 Place the sardine fillets for 5 minutes in a cold 10 per cent brine (*see p. 144*).

2 Mix the sunflower oil with a little lemon juice and pepper.

3 Dry the sardines, place them in a tray with the oil and lemon juice mixture and allow to marinate for 30 minutes.

4 Wrap a fillet together with a tender basil leaf in a sheet of brick pastry or filo pastry. Seal the edges with a few drops of water so that it does not open when frying.

5 Heat the oil to 180°C in a frying pan and add the sardines.

6 When the pastry wrapper has a nice golden colour, remove the sardines from the pan and spread them on absorbent kitchen paper to soak up the excess oil. Sprinkle with a few gratings of lemon zest and serve as soon as possible.

This is a crunchy dish for snacking and sharing. It is as easy to prepare as it is delicious, as simple as it is eye-catching. These sardines are ideal as a starter or as part of a tapas menu.

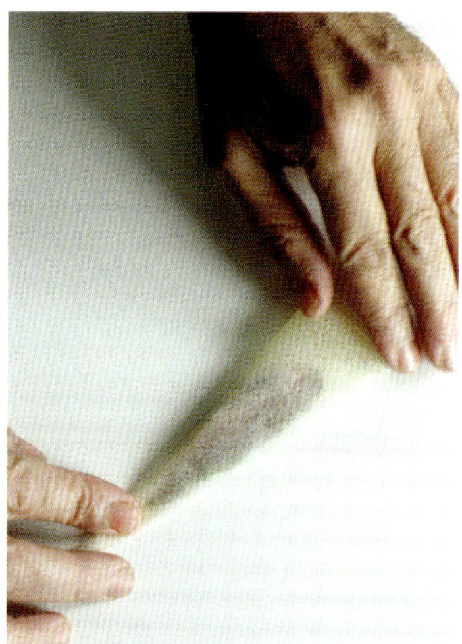

FRIED ONION FLOWER WITH TZATZIKI AND CHILLI SAUCE

Time: 1 hr | Level: moderate

INGREDIENTS FOR 4 PEOPLE

1 large sweet onion - *300 ml sunflower oil*
200 g flour - *10 g paprika*
10 g curry - *5 g pepper*
For the tzatziki
1 creamy Greek yogurt - *10 g mint*
10 g cucumber - *Salt* - *Pepper*
For the chilli mayonnaise
100 g mayonnaise - *15 g chilli sauce*

METHOD

1 To prepare the tzatziki, mix the yogurt with the mint, chopped, and the cucumber, cut into brunoise (*see p. 120*), and season with salt and pepper.

2 To prepare the chilli mayonnaise, mix the mayonnaise with the chilli sauce.

3 Peel the onion taking care not to cut the base, where the layers meet. Make 8 cuts (so that you obtain 16 rows of 'petals'), without reaching the base, so that the petals are united.

4 Place the onion in ice water for 1 hour. Remove from water and drain.

5 Mix the flour with the paprika, curry and pepper to obtain a spiced flour, and cover all the onion layers with it.

6 Fry the onion in a pan large enough to hold it and with enough sunflower oil so that the onion is completely submerged.

7 Remove the onion from the oil and allow it to drain on kitchen paper.

8 Serve the onion together with two bowls with the sauces. To enjoy these appetising sauces, tear off petals from the onion and dip them alternatively into the sauces.

Here is a dish to share that is both delicious and playful. It consists of tearing off, dipping and tasting the onion together with the refreshing flavours offered by the tzatziki and spicy chilli mayonnaise.

5

6

FRIED SWEET POTATOES WITH ROSEMARY SALT AND PEPPER

Time: 30 mins | Level: easy

INGREDIENTS FOR 4 PEOPLE

500 g sweet potatoes

Sunflower oil - Salt and pepper - Fresh rosemary

METHOD

1. Peel the sweet potatoes and cut into batons.
2. Finely chop the rosemary leaves and mix them with the salt and pepper.
3. Fry the sweet potatoes in oil at 180°C until they have a nice golden colour.
4. Remove the sweet potatoes from the pan with a spider and spread them on kitchen paper.
5. Finally, sprinkle them with the rosemary, salt and pepper mix, and serve straight away.

Fried sweet potatoes, cooked as if they were chips, are very tasty and can accompany all kinds of dishes as a side or be a good alternative as a starter. The rosemary-flavoured salt contrasts with the sweetness of this tuber, thus obtaining an excellent balance between sweet and salty. With the same idea of combining contrasting flavours, you could introduce variations with sweet potatoes and curry or ginger mixed with salt.

VEGETABLE CRISPS

Time: 30 mins | Level: easy

INGREDIENTS FOR 4 PEOPLE

1 potato • 2 purple potatoes • 1 sweet potato
1 carrot • 1 turnip • 1 cassava • 1 beetroot
1 banana • 1 apple • 1 pear • Salt

PREPARATION

1 Finely slice the vegetables, then rinse and dry them well before frying them so that they do not splatter or soften.

2 Heat the oil to 160–180°C and fry the vegetables and fruit, in batches, keeping enough space between them so that they do not stick. Monitor the temperature of the oil, because if it is too hot the crisps will acquire a dark colour and if, in contrast, it is not hot enough, they will be soaked in oil, and in neither case will they be crispy.

3 While frying, stir the vegetables and fruit with a skimmer until they take on a nice golden colour and remain on the surface of the oil almost without moving. Then remove them with the same skimmer and place them on absorbent kitchen paper. Season with salt and reserve.

These small bites are very tasty as a snack or to complement dishes as a side. Although this recipe explains how to cook crisps by frying vegetables and fruit, you can also obtain crunchy vegetables by dehydrating them (see p. 349).

VEGETABLE TEMPURA

Time: 30 mins | Level: easy

INGREDIENTS FOR 4 PEOPLE

75 g pepper
75 g asparagus
75 g baby onions
75 g mangetout
75 g aubergine
200 g flour
For the tempura
100 ml ice water
15 g egg yolks
45 g flour
2 g salt

METHOD

1 Cut the vegetables — which could be replaced by others, such as courgette, squash, turnip or cabbage — into different shapes to better adapt to the characteristics of each and to add diversity to the preparation: the asparagus, sliced with a mandolin; the pepper, in julienne; the baby onions, in rings; the mangetout, whole or halved, and the aubergine, sliced leaving one end joined together to achieve a fan-like effect.

2 To prepare the tempura, remove the ice from the water and mix all the ingredients with it. Start by adding the egg yolk to the ice water and add the salt. Stir in the flour and mix gently. It doesn't matter if any lumps remain, caused by the temperature shock with the cold water: in fact, it is important to not over-mix the batter to obtain a crispy tempura.

3 Flour the vegetables.

4 In a frying pan or deep saucepan heat the oil to about 180°C.

5 Dredge the vegetables through the tempura batter and put them into the oil until they are golden brown and have a crunchy texture. Drain on absorbent kitchen paper and serve with soy sauce or lemon sauce and salt.

3

4

5

ASPARAGUS WITH SQUID INK AND ROMESCO SAUCE

Time: 30 mins | Level: easy

INGREDIENTS FOR 4 PEOPLE

24 green asparagus
100 g flour
2.5 g baking powder
1 egg
25 ml water
1 bag of cuttlefish ink or squid ink
Sunflower oil
Salt
Romesco sauce (see p. 250)

METHOD

1 Prepare the batter by mixing the flour, egg, baking powder, water, salt and cuttlefish or squid ink, using a whisk. The mixture should be completely smooth; if possible, allow it to rest for a few hours for the baking powder to act and turn it into a spongy batter: this is the secret for a crunchy batter when fried.

2 Peel the asparagus stalks and lightly flour them.

3 Dredge the asparagus in the batter.

4 Carefully fry the asparagus in oil at a moderate temperature, about 170°C, until the batter is crispy. Remove from heat and place on absorbent kitchen paper.

5 Transfer the asparagus to a bowl and serve with the romesco sauce.

This recipe creates the false illusion of eating a calçot (a young onion) fresh from the embers of the fire, thanks to the burnt skin effect from the batter stained by the cuttlefish ink. However, there is no disappointment when you discover that what you are actually tasting is a delicious and tender asparagus that combines perfectly with the romesco sauce. Although it is somewhat laborious to prepare, it is extremely tasty.

2

3

4

ROMESCO SAUCE *(see previous page)*

Time: 3 hrs | Level: easy

INGREDIENTS

1 kg ripe tomatoes ▪ 6 garlic cloves ▪ 1 ñora pepper or romesco (goat horn) pepper ▪ 400 ml olive oil
50 g toasted hazelnuts ▪ 50 g toasted almonds
15 ml sherry vinegar ▪ Salt ▪ Pepper

METHOD

1 If possible, prepare the romesco sauce the day before, as it will be tastier. Place the tomatoes and peeled garlic into a tightly packed container and cover with all the oil. Put it into the oven to confit tomatoes and garlic at a moderate temperature (160°C) for 2 hours.

2 Meanwhile, rehydrate the ñora or romesco pepper in a container. When the flesh is hydrated, separate it from the skin by scraping it with the help of a knife.

3 When the tomatoes are cooked and warm, peel them and use only the flesh. Reserve the oil and garlic.

4 Blend the tomato and pepper flesh with the garlic and nuts, previously skinned. Gradually add the confit oil until the sauce is completely blended. Season with salt and pepper and add the vinegar.

5 Strain the sauce, if necessary — you should have a smooth texture — and reserve it in the refrigerator.

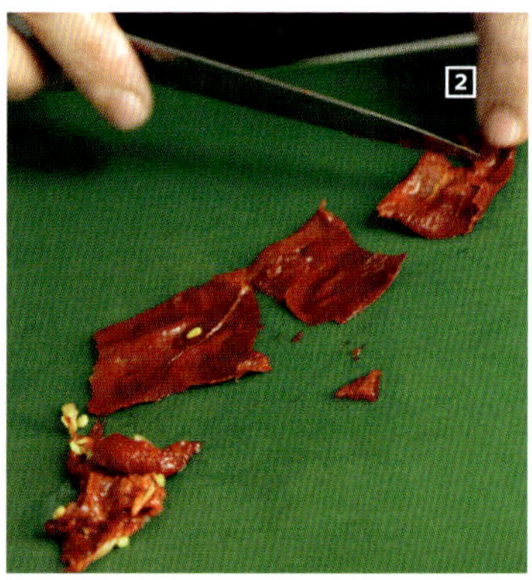

CHICKEN WITH CHILLI MAYONNAISE AND POTATO RÖSTI

Time: 30 mins (+ 2 hrs marinating) | Level: easy

INGREDIENTS FOR 4 PEOPLE

2 chicken breasts

For the marinade

10 g paprika (sweet or hot, according to taste)

200 ml sunflower oil, for frying ▪ Salt ▪ Pepper

For the potato rösti

250 g potatoes

100 g clarified butter

For the chilli mayonnaise

50 g chilli sauce ▪ 50 g mayonnaise

250 ml sunflower oil ▪ 1 spring onion

METHOD

1 To prepare the marinade, cut the chicken breasts into strips and leave them in the paprika, oil, salt and pepper mixture for 2 hours.

2 To prepare the rösti, peel the potatoes and, without washing them (just wipe them with a damp cloth, in case they got dirty during peeling), slice them in the mandoline as if they were potato crisps. Then stack the slices and cut them into thin batons.

3 Melt the butter. Add the thin potato batons to the pan of melted butter and mix.

4 Cook the potatoes in a frying pan slowly, inside a ring so that it looks like an omelette.

5 To prepare the chilli mayonnaise, mix the mayonnaise with the chilli sauce.

6 Fry the chicken in a frying pan with oil at 170°C for 2–3 minutes, depending on the thickness, and remove it with the help of the spider. Transfer to absorbent kitchen paper.

7 Place the chicken strips on the rösti base, add the chilli mayonnaise and garnish with the chopped spring onion.

Different culinary traditions come together in this dish, in which the mildly fried chicken is enhanced by the spiciness of the mayonnaise mixed with the Latin American sauce, and at the same time offset by the garnish of potato rösti, typical of Switzerland, although it is already a classic in all cuisines.

MARINATED CHICKEN WITH CURRY

Time: 1 hr 30 mins | Level: easy

INGREDIENTS FOR 4 PEOPLE

For the marinade
2 chicken breasts ▪ ½ onion
1 Granny Smith apple ▪ 50 ml sunflower oil ▪ Salt ▪ Pepper
For the chicken
10 g coconut powder or 30 g grated coconut
250 ml sunflower oil
For the curry mayonnaise
1 baby onion ▪ 1 Granny Smith apple
5 g curry powder ▪ 100 g pineapple ▪ Butter
100 ml cream ▪ 100 g mayonnaise ▪ Salt
For the garnish
200 g pumpkin ▪ 30 ml sunflower oil
5 g thyme ▪ 5 g rosemary ▪ Salt ▪ Pepper

METHOD

1 To prepare the marinade, cut the chicken breasts into thick strips and marinate them in 50 ml of sunflower oil with the onion, diced apple, salt and pepper for 2 hours.

2 To prepare the mayonnaise, cut all the pieces into small cubes (between brunoise and jardinière) of about 5 millimetres. Fry the onion in butter for 10 minutes, add the apple and pineapple, and cook for a further 5 minutes. Add the cream, 5 grams of curry powder and salt and continue cooking for 10 minutes. Cool and mix with the mayonnaise.

1

3 To prepare the garnish, cut the pumpkin into large wedges (irregular cuts) and roast it in the oven at 180°C with the rosemary, thyme, salt, pepper and oil for 45 minutes.

4 Prepare a flour by mixing the coconut powder or shredded coconut with the 5 grams of curry powder. Flour the chicken and fry it immediately in sunflower oil at 170°C. Cook until the coating is golden brown, then remove the chicken strips with a spider. Dry on absorbent kitchen paper.

5 Place the fried chicken on a plate or serving platter and serve with the curry mayonnaise and roasted pumpkin.

This is a dish with lots of spice, with curry as the main character. However, you could also prepare it in garam masala or tandoori style (aromatic spice mixtures typical of India and other Asian countries).

MARINATED CHICKEN WITH ASPARAGUS AND SOY MAYONNAISE

Time: 1 hr | Level: easy

INGREDIENTS FOR 4 PEOPLE

250 ml virgin olive oil

150 g flour

12 green asparagus

Sunflower oil

Shiso and purple shiso leaves

For the marinade

2 chicken breasts

100 ml soy sauce

Fresh ginger

For the soy mayonnaise

100 g mayonnaise • 15 ml soy sauce

1 g ground ginger (or grated fresh ginger)

1 g wasabi paste

METHOD

1 For the marinade, leave the chicken breasts, cut into goujons, in the soy sauce and a little grated ginger for 1 hour.

2 To make the mayonnaise, follow the instructions in the recipe (*see p. 328*). Mix the mayonnaise with the soy, ginger and wasabi paste (previously diluted with a few drops of soy sauce).

3 Using a peeler, peel the asparagus stalks, then boil them for 1 minute in water and salt. Allow to cool, drain and set aside.

4 Remove the chicken from the marinade. Drain by placing on absorbent kitchen paper, then dredge in flour and fry in virgin olive oil at 170°C. Remove and dry by placing them on kitchen paper.

5 Heat the asparagus slightly in the microwave or sauté briefly in a frying pan with sunflower oil.

6 Arrange the chicken goujons on a plate and serve with the soy mayonnaise, asparagus and shiso leaves.

A dish defined by the umami taste of soy sauce, it is a powerful dish that is refreshingly combined with ginger, asparagus and shiso leaves.

POACHING, CONFIT AND PICKLING

THESE THREE RELATED COOKING TECHNIQUES SHARE THREE CHARACTERISTICS: COOKING IN A LIQUID, AT A LOW TEMPERATURE AND BY CONCENTRATION, TO RETAIN ALL THE FOOD'S JUICES. LET'S SEE WHAT DISTINGUISHES THEM.

POACHING

TYPE OF COOKING	By concentration
RELATED TECHNIQUES	Confit Pickling

When poaching, food is cooked or precooked in a liquid, but without reaching boiling point. There are three types of poached products. One of them consists of a gentle precooking at low temperature, usually of vegetables (e.g. potatoes), which are then subjected to a second cooking at a higher temperature. Another type of poaching is cooking by immersion in a liquid without exceeding 100°C, as in the case of Basque-style hake, in which the fish is cooked in its sauce. And finally, it basically refers to poached eggs, which are cooked at a temperature close to 100°C but without boiling, in order to cook the whites and prevent the yolk curdling.

THE PRECOOKING PROCESS

1 Prepare all of the ingredients.

2 Cut all the vegetables to the desired shape and size.

3 Introduce the vegetables to the oil at a temperature between 80 and 120°C. Sometimes it is necessary to exceed 100°C (boiling temperature) because some vegetables have a lot of water, and if the temperature is too low, they become soft and may even fall apart, such as potatoes (where it is known as parboiling). Unlike when frying — where you want the food to be crispy — here, you can introduce all the vegetables at the same time, because the objective is to make them soft.

4 Drain and reserve for further cooking (baking, frying, sautéing, etc.).

THE COOKING PROCESS

1 Prepare the cooking liquid, which is usually a broth or sauce, and heat it to a temperature close to 100°C.

2 Introduce the previously seasoned food. In some traditional recipes, the food is covered only halfway and covered with a lid or greaseproof paper so that part of the food cooks with the steam and the broth or sauce concentrates. In other cases, cooking is done in the sauce itself with the idea that it stabilises the cooking at a temperature that does not exceed 100°C.

3 Remove the product and, if necessary, in the case of cooking with a base liquid, finish reducing and binding the sauce with the help of a roux (a mixture of fat — usually butter — and flour, *see p. 334*) before serving.

CONFIT

TYPE OF COOKING	By concentration
RELATED TECHNIQUES	Poaching Pickling Vacuum cooking

It consists of gentle cooking at low temperature (between 50 and 90°C), in order to retain the food's interior juiciness (cooking by concentration), with the singularity that the liquid in which the products are immersed is usually a fatty or sweet medium. The fatty medium can range from duck or goose fat (generally used for poultry or game recipes) to neutral oils, such as olive oil, or flavoured oils. The sweet medium contains sugar for candying fruits in syrups, which can be spiced if desired. Sugar, in these cases, also functions as a preserving element. Candying has traditionally been used to preserve foods by exposing them to long cooking to reach the safety temperature (65°C). Today, cooking times are shorter in order to preserve as much as possible of the product's original flavour.

THE PROCESS

1. Prepare all of the ingredients.
2. Prepare the fatty medium — oil, as a general rule — at the appropriate temperature (between 50 and 90°C, depending on the product).
3. Incorporate the food (already preprepared: clean, seasoned, cured, etc.) and cook it for the necessary time according to its characteristics (if it is a meat, it will depend on its toughness).
4. Remove and serve, or cool and store. If you will be storing it, it is better to allow it to cool in the same fat, as it serves as protection.

PICKLING

TYPE OF COOKING	By concentration
RELATED TECHNIQUES	Poaching Confit

It is a technique almost identical to confit, with the difference that pickling introduces an acidic element (usually vinegar) in the fatty medium, which adds taste and at the same time can act as a preservative.

Pickling has been a popular method in many regional cuisines in order to prepare certain dishes for later preservation (tuna, sardines, mussels, mackerel, game such as partridge, mushrooms, poultry, pickled veal tongue, etc.). However, it has required cooking food at temperatures close to, or even higher than, 100°C, and long cooking times with abundant acid. Today, there is a tendency to use pickling as a cooking technique in which the process allows the use of lower temperatures, shorter cooking times and less vinegar, although as a consequence the shelf life of the preparation is much shorter.

THE PROCESS

1. Prepare all of the ingredients.
2. Brown the product, with or without flour.
3. Add sautéed vegetables and cook over low heat with oil, vinegar and some liquid to reduce the strength of the vinegar. It can be water, broth or even wine. Incorporate any herbs and spices.
4. Reserve the pickled ingredients in the refrigerator. This type of preparation improves after a few days, even after a week, for tough meat products such as game birds.

POACHED VEGETABLES

Time: 20 mins | Level: easy

INGREDIENTS FOR 4 PEOPLE

For poaching the potatoes and onions

400 g potatoes

200 g baby onions

300 ml olive oil

4 garlic cloves

1 bunch of rosemary

Peppercorns

To poach the sweet potatoes

400 g sweet potatoes

200 ml olive oil

METHOD

1 Peel the potatoes and cut them into slices. Peel the onions without cutting the base so that they remain whole.

2 For poaching the potatoes and onions, put the aromatic elements — garlic, rosemary and peppercorns — into a saucepan with enough olive oil to cover the potatoes and onions. Cook over low heat until soft and reserve in the oil.

3 To poach the sweet potatoes, cut them into batons (you could also use yucca or pumpkin) and cook them in oil at a low temperature until soft. Drain and reserve.

4 Finish the preparation with a second cooking at high temperature so that the vegetables take on a more intense flavour. The potatoes and onions can be baked until golden brown and served as a garnish for meat dishes. The sweet potatoes can be fried using the poaching oil, but with very hot oil and for a short time, just enough to brown on the outside.

Although poached vegetables can accompany different preparations as a garnish, they normally function as a preparation for a later cooking over high heat. These two cooking steps make it possible to speed up the preparation of products that require considerable cooking time and that can be quickly finished in a second step. That is, you can carry out the first step in advance and the second step just before the service. The recipe suggested here can also serve as a starter.

COD WITH SPINACH, RAISINS, PINE NUTS AND IDIAZABAL CHEESE

Time: 1 hr | Level: easy

INGREDIENTS FOR 4 PEOPLE

600 g cod
200 ml virgin olive oil
400 g fresh spinach
60 g raisins
20 g pine nuts
25 g Idiazabal cheese
25 ml single cream
50 ml Pedro Ximénez sherry
Fresh chives

METHOD

1 Reduce the Pedro Ximénez over a low heat so that it does not burn. When hot, it will seem liquid, but the liquor will thicken when cold.

2 Meanwhile, melt the cheese with the cream over a low heat and set aside.

3 Chop the chives and mix with a few drops of virgin olive oil. Reserve.

4 Sauté the pine nuts and raisins in a frying pan, then add the tender spinach leaves and sauté for a further few seconds.

5 Heat the oil to 50°C and add the cod. Cook it for 15 minutes, checking that the temperature remains constant.

6 Place the spinach in the centre of the plate, add a piece of cod confit and complement with the cheese sauce, Pedro Ximénez reduction and a few drops of chive oil.

Cooking at low temperature allows the flavour and texture of the fish to be maintained. This preparation respects the gelatinous texture of the cod and makes the most of it.

4

5

CHICKEN CURRY TOAST

Time: 1 hr | Level: easy

INGREDIENTS FOR 4 PEOPLE

400 g chicken breasts
200 ml sunflower oil
3 g cardamom
For the sauce
300 ml cream
75 g baby onions
75 g pineapple
75 g apple
7 g curry powder
30 g unsalted butter
Salt and pepper
For the garnish
200 g rice
1 baby onion
50 g pineapple
50 g apple
65 g unsalted butter
Sliced bread
Chives
Salt and curry powder

METHOD

1 To prepare the sauce, dice the baby onions, apple and pineapple. Sauté the onion in butter until tender. Add the apple and cook for 5 minutes, add the pineapple and continue cooking for a further 5 minutes. Pour in the cream and season with salt, pepper and curry powder. Cook for 5 minutes and set aside.

2 Season the chicken breasts with salt and pepper or preferably place them in a 10 per cent brine for 15 minutes (*see p. 144*).

3 Put the chicken into a saucepan with the cardamom and sunflower oil at 65°C — the chicken should be well covered with the oil. Leave it to confit for 40 minutes; check with a thermometer that the centre of the meat has reached 63-65°C.

4 Remove from the heat and cool by placing the pan in a bain-marie with cold water to stop the cooking.

5 To prepare the garnish, boil the rice in 2 different waters, half with salt only and the other with salt and curry powder, for 18 minutes, so that you obtain rice of 2 different colours. Once cooked, allow to cool.

6 Sauté the halved baby onion and diced apple and pineapple in a frying pan with the butter. Then add the rice and sauté briefly.

7 Toast a slice of bread.

8 Cut the chicken into slices and place them on the toast. Drizzle with the hot curry sauce and glaze it in the salamander or with the oven grill.

9 Serve the chicken with the rice garnished with the chargrilled onion halves and chopped chives.

Toast is a perfect resource for light dinners and informal meals. The ingredients can be as varied as our tastes, and it is easy to have bread at home to improvise an appetising toast at any time and with hardly any work.

VEGETABLE SALAD WITH PEACH VINAIGRETTE

Time: 2 hrs | Level: easy

INGREDIENTS FOR 4 PEOPLE

100 g green beans - *1 baby onion* - *4 anchovies*
4 garlic cloves - *25 g black olive purée* - *20 ml olive oil*
60 g Kalamata olives - *Flowers*

For the potato confit

200 g small potatoes - *200 ml olive oil*

For the peach oil

40 ml olive oil - *40 g peach*
5 g chopped chives - *Salt and pepper*

For the peach vinaigrette

80 g peach - *40 ml light olive oil*
Salt and pepper

For the tomato confit

2 tomatoes - *25 g sugar* - *Basil*
20 ml olive oil - *Salt*

The oil and peach emulsion replaces a classic vinaigrette to give the salad a mix of acidity and sweetness. Placing the dressing at the base of the dish guarantees that this refreshing dressing will be in every bite.

METHOD

1 To confit the potatoes, place them, unpeeled, in a saucepan with the garlic, then cover them with 200 ml of olive oil and cook over a low heat, at about 90°C, for 1 hour or until they are soft. Remove from the heat and reserve.

2 Boil the beans until al dente and set aside.

3 Cut the onion into fine julienne strips and cool it in water and ice.

4 For the peach oil, cut the peach into regular cubes and mix with the olive oil, chopped chives, salt and pepper.

5 For the peach vinaigrette, blend the peach flesh with the 40 ml of light olive oil, salt and pepper.

6 To confit the tomatoes, blanch and peel them, then cut them in half and separate the core (the tomato 'caviar') from the flesh. Cut the rest of the tomato into wedges and bake them with salt, sugar, basil and a teaspoon of olive oil in the oven, at 120°C, for 1 hour. It is a gentle way to confit and concentrate tastes, even if the product is not totally covered with oil.

7 Mix 25 grams of the olive purée with 20 ml of oil. Add a few drops of water so that it is well emulsified.

8 Cut the olives into thick pieces. Cut the tomato confit and anchovies into strips.

9 Assemble the dish with a base of peach vinaigrette and add the remaining ingredients: the potato chunks, the beans, the tomato caviar and tomato confit, the olives and olive purée, and the julienned onion. Dress with peach oil and chives. Finish by garnishing the salad with flowers.

VEGETARIAN TRILOGY I: PICKLED VEGETABLES WITH PEPPERS

Time: 2 hrs | Level: easy

INGREDIENTS FOR 4 PEOPLE

1 frisée endive - Aromatic herbs and seasonal sprouts (cumin, coriander, mustard sprouts, mooli/daikon or onion sprouts)

For the boiled or blanched vegetables

100 g carrot (in batons) - 100 g turnip (in strips)
3 asparagus spears (in strips) - 75 g pumpkin (diced)

For the candied vegetables

100 g small potatoes (halved)
12 baby onions (halved)
12 fresh garlic cloves (in batons)

For the raw vegetables

8 radishes (cut in half) - 12 cherry tomatoes

For the marinade

25 g red onion - 25 g green pepper
25 g red pepper - 25 g courgette - 25 g onion
200 ml olive oil - 80 ml white wine vinegar - 15 g spices (cardamom, black and white peppercorns, Sichuan and pink peppercorns)

For the roasted vegetables

150 g onions - 3 peppers: red, green and yellow - 60 ml sunflower oil

METHOD

1 Clean all the vegetables for the marinade and put the courgette into a little salt to sweat. Cut them in brunoise.

2 Sauté the vegetables for the marinade (fry without browning) with a little oil.

3 When the hardest vegetables are cooked, add the courgette and cook for a further 1 minute.

4 Lower the heat to the lowest setting and add the remaining oil, vinegar, salt and spices. Cook over a very low heat for 1 minute.

5 Add the precooked and raw vegetables and cook over a low heat for 20 minutes. You could also use raw vegetables; in this case, cook them for 1 hour over a low heat (or until tender).

1

2

3

6 Once the vegetables are cooked and tender, remove the casserole from the heat and set aside.

7 Clean the endive, drain it and place it on the base of the plate. Add the pickled vegetables on top and dress with the marinade. Finish the dish by garnishing with aromatic herbs and sprouts.

Like the recipes for sautéed vegetables (see p. 272) and roasted vegetables (see p. 280), this marinade offers a play with vegetables. The selection of vegetables depends on the season. Provide variety in the cut and precooking you choose for each vegetable, as well as in the final cooking. Here, the marinade gives them freshness and intensifies their flavour.

SAUTÉING AND CARAMELISING

BOTH METHODS ARE SIMILAR: THEY ARE COOKING TECHNIQUES THAT USE FATTY ELEMENTS, SUCH AS OIL OR BUTTER; THEY ARE CARRIED OUT AT A LOW TEMPERATURE, AND CAN BE A PRELIMINARY STEP BEFORE ANOTHER COOKING TECHNIQUE.

TYPE OF COOKING	By concentration
RELATED TECHNIQUES	Poaching Confit

In spite of the similarities between both techniques in terms of the cooking medium – as a general rule, in oil or butter – they are both usually used to prepare vegetables, although not exclusively: there are also some differences between the sautéing and caramelising cooking processes. The latter requires slow and very long cooking times, while sautéing requires only short cooking times. However, both procedures can be a preliminary step to another cooking.

SAUTÉING

Diced or sliced vegetables are usually sautéed over a low heat, with oil or butter, as a preliminary step to a preparation in which these vegetables will serve as a base or complement. You can, for example, sauté some leeks for a soft texture as a complement to a salmon toast.

A small variation on this technique is braising, which consists of covering the preparation. In this way the water in the vegetables is prevented from evaporating and you can ensure that the cooking temperature does not exceed 100°C, so that the vegetables, or the preparation in general, do not acquire colour.

CARAMELISING

This is a long cooking technique in which the product is gently cooked in a little fat until it is fully cooked and roasted, sometimes very dark, almost black in colour. The most common example is the sofrito made with tomato and onion, with or without garlic, which serves as a base for a multitude of preparations *(see p. 350)*.

Sometimes, in addition to vegetables, the sofrito includes other elements – meat, poultry or fish – as a base or brand for paellas, rice dishes and other types of casserole preparations.

Occasionally, a short cooking at a higher temperature, known as gratinising, is used to finish a dish. In this case, it is a basic preparation for which long cooking is not necessary. This happens, for example, when we want to brown the ingredients at the end of sautéing them.

STIR-FRYING

ENERGETIC HEATING AND GOOD REFLEXES ARE ALL THAT STIR-FRYING REQUIRES. THE PRIZE IS A MEAT, FISH OR VEGETABLE THAT IS CRISPY ON THE OUTSIDE, TENDER ON THE INSIDE AND VERY DELICIOUS.

TYPE OF COOKING	By concentration
RELATED TECHNIQUES	Poaching Confit

Stir-frying is a quick cooking method that requires high heat, little fat and small quantities of products cut into regular pieces. This is a technique that can work as a precooking when you want to seal the product to brown it so that it does not lose its juices before cooking, or as a cooking of tender products that do not need too much cooking time.

The technique must be very balanced in terms of cooking temperature. If you stir-fry with a low heat, the food will lose its juices and become dry or tasteless. However, if the temperature is too high, the heat quickly dehydrates them and burns or hardens them. Nothing could be further from the reason for stir-frying, which is intended to make the food juicy.

In some cases, the food may be flambéed with liquor. In addition, you can use the cooking juices to prepare a sauce or glaze. It is a matter of adding a liquid, which can be wine, cava or any type of stock, so that it mixes with the caramelised juices of the pan and you end up obtaining a tasty and aromatic sauce.

THE PROCESS

1. Prepare all of the ingredients.
2. Heat a frying pan, or frying pans, prepared for stir-frying, such as a sauté pan or wok, with a small amount of fat — which can be oil or butter — and wait for it to reach the right temperature (find a balance, neither too little heat nor too high).
3. Add the food, previously cut into not very large pieces. The amount of product that you add to the pan should be in batches, so that the food has enough space and you can control the temperature.
4. Season with condiments and serve immediately.

STIR-FRIED VEGETABLES WITH JANG SAUCE

Time: 30 mins | Level: easy

INGREDIENTS FOR 4 PEOPLE

100 ml sunflower oil
75 g asparagus
50 g leeks
75 g courgette
75 g mangetout
75 g carrots
75 g cabbage
75 g green and red peppers
75 g spring onions
50 g green beans
50 g turnip
Jang sauce (Korean fermented soy sauce)
Green and purple shiso leaves

METHOD

1 Cut all the vegetables into julienne strips. Keeping all the vegetables of equal sizes means it will not be necessary to precook them.

2 Heat the oil in a wok and add all the vegetables. If you do not have a wok, use a wide frying pan to quickly stir-fry all the vegetables at the same time.

3 Stir-fry for a few minutes until the vegetables lose their firmness.

4 Season with the jang sauce. This sauce can be replaced with another type of soy sauce. Spices or aromatic herbs can also be incorporated.

5 Cook for a further few seconds.

6 Serve and garnish with the shiso leaves.

As with all vegetable preparations, the variety of vegetables in this stir-fry will depend on the seasonality of each one — and, to be practical, also on what is at hand, since quick cooking in a wok can give an outlet for vegetables in the fridge that have no planned use. Combined with the jang sauce, which adds power and intensity to the dish, you can present an eye-catching and appealing dish full of vitamins and flavour.

VEGETARIAN TRILOGY II: STIR-FRIED VEGETABLES WITH GINGER

Time: 15 mins | Level: easy

INGREDIENTS FOR 4 PEOPLE

Vegetable cooking broth
10 g fresh ginger
70 ml olive oil
60 ml sunflower oil
Seasonal herbs and sprouts
Salt and pepper

For the boiled or blanched vegetables
100 g carrot (in batons)
75 g turnip (in strips) ▪ 100 g courgette
(irregularly cut, as if they were irregular potatoes)
75 g mangetout
6 asparagus (in strips)

For the candied vegetables
12 small potatoes ▪ 12 small onions ▪ 12 fresh garlic cloves

For the raw vegetables
100 g of assorted mushrooms (chanterelles, wild mushrooms, etc.) ▪ 12 cherry tomatoes ▪ 8 radishes

For the roasted vegetables
100 g onions

METHOD

1. Peel and chop the ginger.
2. Heat sunflower oil in a wide frying pan and add the chopped ginger.
3. When the ginger is transparent, add all the well-drained precooked vegetables and the mushrooms and stir-fry for 1 minute.
4. Add a little of the cooking water from the vegetables, stir-fry for another 30 seconds, remove from the heat and add the radishes, cherry tomatoes and a tablespoon of olive oil. Move the pan to obtain a small emulsion between the cooking liquid and the oil.
5. Serve the stir-fry straight away, complementing it with the herbs and sprouts.

This is the second version, along with the pickled vegetables on p. 264 and the roasted vegetables on p. 280, of how to cook various cut and precooked vegetables in different ways. It's a simple dish but very expressive.

4

5

ROASTING AND GRILLING

DIRECTLY OVEN ROASTED, GRILLED OR BARBECUED, BUT ALWAYS AT HIGH TEMPERATURES, AND WITH NO OTHER COMPANY THAN A LITTLE FAT, A ROASTED INGREDIENT ACQUIRES A CLEAR, CLEAN TASTE, WITHOUT CONFUSION OR MIXTURE WITH OTHER FLAVOURS.

TYPE OF COOKING	By concentration
RELATED TECHNIQUES	Gratin Glazing

A food is roasted or grilled when it is exposed directly to a heat source, at a high temperature and in a dry environment. Food can be roasted in an oven, on a barbecue or on a spit, but it can also be roasted when cooking on a grill or griddle.

It is a type of cooking in which time and temperature factors are crucial and must be adjusted to the type of product, and its cut and size. It is important to always preserve the food's juice and prevent it drying out. Although the food is cooked in a dry medium, without liquids, sometimes a little fat can be added.

GRILLING

Like oven grilling or roasting, grilling on the hob or countertop griddle is a type of cooking at high temperature and in a dry environment, i.e. without any liquids involved in the cooking process. It allows the food to be cooked quickly so that it can keep its juices inside, in addition to acquiring a characteristic texture, flavour and aroma on the outside. It is ideal for tender products that do not need moisture or long cooking to soften.

The name of the technique refers to the utensil where the food is cooked. It should be noted that there are different types of pans depending on the foods we cook on them. For meats, unlike griddles, grill pans normally have grooves that allow collecting the fat released by the product, while charring or browning it in the parts where the piece has direct contact with the surface.

THE PROCESS

1 Prepare all of the ingredients.

2 Heat the griddle or grill before cooking, first ensuring that it is very clean so that no fat or food residues are burnt.

3 Add a small amount of oil — just a few drops — to prevent the food sticking.

4 Add the food.

5 Turn the piece once and serve it. If the piece is very large, as it could be a chop of 500 grams or a rather wide fillet, the cooking can be finished in the oven so that its uniform heat cooks the whole product. In this case, as in the case of oven roasts, allow the piece to rest in a warm place, so that the juices stabilise and the meat becomes more tender.

BARBECUING

This is a very special way to cook, thanks to the flavour and aroma that the wood or charcoal gives the product exposed directly to the heat of its embers. The high temperatures seal the outside of the food and give it an intense taste with smoky notes and woody nuances. The temperature of the embers can be controlled by moving the grill closer to or further away from the fire.

THE PROCESS

1. Prepare all of the ingredients.
2. Prepare the barbecue and wait for the fire to turn the wood or charcoal into embers.
3. Heat the barbecue grill rack so that the product does not stick. It must be very clean.
4. Place the food on the grill rack, but depending on the product, you can brush it with a little oil beforehand.
5. When the product is cooked as desired, remove and serve it immediately.

TIPS

- **Do not allow it to rest.** This type of cooking does not require resting, unless the pieces are very large; for example, a whole fillet of veal that is cooked to bleeding or very rare, so that its juices are reabsorbed as when it is roasted in the oven.
- **Seasoning and enriching.** Although meats are seasoned with salt and pepper before cooking, when you remove them from the barbecue you can finish seasoning them with fleur de sel and freshly ground pepper, or enrich them with virgin or flavoured oil, or barbecue sauces, including chimichurri, picadas or majados. It is ideal for cooking meats marinated in aromatic oils.
- **Bringing to room temperature.** If the piece is very large, such as a beef fillet or a pork rib, bring the meat to room temperature by taking it out of the refrigerator 1 hour before cooking so that the product is not too cold and the heat can penetrate gradually; otherwise, it will cook very slowly and the meat's exterior may be dry, or, if cooking is too quick, the meat's interior may be cold. Start with a strong heat to char the meat and continue with moderate heat so that the interior cooks gradually.
- **Do not remove the skin.** The skin should not be removed from foods such as chicken, because it serves as protection and prevents the meat burning or drying out.
- **Do not peel before cooking.** Some foods, such as aubergines, peppers or young onions, are exposed to the flames of the fire directly, and their outer layer burns and is discarded later, so you do not have to peel them before cooking, but after.
- **Protecting food.** To protect certain foods from the intensity of the dry heat, bread them, as is the case with pig's trotters, which are very gelatinous and, without protection, would stick to the grill.

OVEN ROASTING

This type of cooking is intended to give the cooked product a clear and clean taste, without confusing or mixing with other flavours, which is why we often roast in the oven with only a little fat.

THE PROCESS

- Preheat the oven to between 180 and 220°C. Prepare the ingredient, if necessary; put it into a roasting tin or dish with a little fat — generally oil — and place it in the oven.
- At first, cook the product at a high temperature to seal it, so that it retains the juices inside, and then lower the temperature to continue with a gentler cooking or with a stable temperature, so that it cooks gradually.
- Throughout the cooking process, turn the piece. Brush it with the fat, so that the meat or external skin does not dry out and split. For the cooking of certain meats, fatty parts of the animal are placed on the base of the pan so that they do not stick together.
- When roasting meats, once the piece is cooked, remove it and allow it to rest in a warm place. It is best to place it on a wire rack so that the juices can be collected and do not remain concentrated in the centre of the meat, making the meat more tender and juicy. This operation is not necessary for fish or vegetables.

THE PROCESS FOR POTATOES

1. Bake the potatoes whole and in their skins in the oven at 180°C for 45 minutes. When they are soft, remove, cool and peel.
2. Pass them through a potato ricer or sieve.
3. Add the oil, diced butter and salt and mix.

ROAST PORK FILLET WITH POTATOES

Time: 2 hrs | Level: easy

INGREDIENTS FOR 4 PEOPLE

600 g pork fillet

75 ml olive oil

200 g small potatoes

100 ml red wine (or brown stock)

Salt and pepper

For the Béarnaise sauce

50 g butter - 1 egg yolk - 1 shallot

Tarragon vinegar - 2 g fresh tarragon

Salt and pepper

METHOD

1 Turn the potatoes (*see p. 125*), cut them in half and boil them in salted water for 5 minutes.

2 Trim the pork fillet and sear it on both sides in a frying pan with hot oil. Add the prepared potatoes and brown them.

3 Preheat the oven to 140°C and place the fillet and potatoes in a roasting tray.

4 Cook the meat and potatoes for about 40 minutes or until the meat reaches 55°C at the centre of the fillet.

5 To prepare the Béarnaise sauce, follow the recipe for Hollandaise sauce (*see p. 331*), adding shallots, tarragon vinegar and chopped tarragon.

6 Remove the fillet from the oven and leave it covered with an inverted plate or a lid, in a warm place, for example, in an open oven, so that it rests and its juices are fixed and it is tender.

7 If you want to deglaze the roasting tray to take advantage of the cooking juices, remove the potatoes, degrease the baking tray (i.e., with the help of a spoon, remove the surface fat) and place it over a low heat, adding a few tablespoons of red wine (or brown stock; *see p. 324*). Reduce the liquid and mix it well with the juices settled on the base of the tray. Strain the reduction and bind it with a dash of olive oil.

8 Slice the fillet, place it hot on the plate, dress it with the reduction of cooking juices and accompany it with a spoonful of Béarnaise sauce and a few pinches of black pepper.

Pork fillet is a tasty meat, but you must pay close attention to it because it can quickly become overcooked. With the deglazing, take advantage of all the preparation juices and complement it with the unctuousness of the Béarnaise sauce.

AUBERGINE WITH GOAT'S CHEESE AND ROSEMARY OIL

Time: 30 mins | Level: easy

INGREDIENTS FOR 4 PEOPLE

1 large aubergine

160 g goat's cheese

Salt

For the rosemary oil

Olive oil - *Fresh rosemary*

Salt and pepper

METHOD

1 Slice the aubergine with a thickness of more or less 5 millimetres and sweat it for a few minutes by seasoning it with salt.

2 Once drained, grill or roast at a moderate temperature, then remove.

3 Roll goat's cheese slices with the grilled aubergine and set aside.

4 To prepare the rosemary oil, chop the fresh rosemary, mix it with the olive oil, and season it with salt and pepper.

5 Finally, heat the aubergine in the oven or microwave for a few moments so that the cheese melts slightly, and place it on a plate, seasoned with the rosemary oil.

Warm salad or fresh starter, this simple recipe can be varied by adding spices and nuts to the filling, or changing the seasoning for pepper or spice oil, or another choice to your liking.

VEGETARIAN TRILOGY III: ROASTED VEGETABLES

Time: 30 mins | Level: easy

INGREDIENTS FOR 4 PEOPLE

60 ml virgin olive oil
Thyme, rosemary, basil leaves
Salt and pepper
For the boiled or blanched vegetables
75 g purple potatoes (cooked whole)
75 g celeriac (in strips)
75 g carrot (in batons)
75 g sweet potato or pumpkin (diced)
For the candied vegetables
12 small potatoes (halved)
12 baby onions
12 fresh garlic cloves (sliced)
4 artichokes (quartered)
For the sautéed vegetables
100 g mushrooms (chanterelles, ceps and wild mushrooms)
Raw vegetables
8 radishes (halved)
100 g beetroot

METHOD

1 Place all the cut and prepared vegetables, as well as the sautéed mushrooms, in an oven-proof dish. Season with the chopped herbs, virgin olive oil, salt and freshly ground pepper.

2 Roast in the oven at a moderate temperature, at 180°C, for 40 minutes. At the end of cooking, cut the beetroot into wedges.

3 Add the radishes, dress with a little virgin olive oil and serve immediately.

For this third version of the vegetarian trilogy (see the first, pickled vegetables, on p. 264, and the second, stir-fried vegetables, on p. 272), cool-season vegetables have been chosen. With intense earthy nuances, you only need to add a touch of aromatic herbs, with the idea of respecting the original flavours as much as possible. For the same reason, a cooking method such as oven roasting is best, adding only a dash of virgin olive oil.

1

2

COURGETTE FRITTATA WITH MASCARPONE AND DILL

Time: 2 hrs | Level: easy

INGREDIENTS FOR 4 PEOPLE

12 eggs
120 g mascarpone cheese
800 g courgettes
Rustic bread
Rocket
Butter
Chopped dill
Blend of peppercorns (black, white, pink, Sichuan and allspice)
Salt

For the dill oil

Sunflower oil - *Chopped dill* - *Ground coriander*
Salt and pepper

For the sauce

100 g fresh cheese (quark or ricotta) - *4 radishes*
15 g wholegrain mustard - *1 lime* - *Salt*

METHOD

1 To prepare the dill oil, mix all the ingredients together.

2 To prepare the sauce, reserve some of the fresh cheese to spread on the toasted bread. Mix the remaining cheese with a little lime juice, salt, julienned radishes and mustard. You can also add a pinch of lime zest. Reserve.

3 To prepare the frittata, cut the courgettes with a mandoline into thin julienne strips or a spaghetti shape, sprinkle salt over them and allow to sweat to reduce their acidity. Sauté in butter over a high heat, remove and set aside.

4 Mix the eggs with the mascarpone cheese, season with salt and pepper and add chopped dill.

5 Combine the mascarpone mixture with the courgettes and place in an oven-proof dish lined with cling film.

2

3

5

6 Preheat the oven to 160°C, put the tray with the courgette and mascarpone mixture into the oven and bake for about 30 minutes (check that the mixture sets).

7 It can be served hot or cold. If you choose the second option, cool and reserve.

8 Prepare the toast by cutting the rustic bread into slices. Toast it, spread with the fresh cheese and sprinkle it with the mixture of peppers (preferably freshly ground).

9 Cut the frittata into rectangles and serve with a cheese toast, rocket, some sauce and a few drops of dill oil.

The frittata, a traditional Italian dish, is usually a good choice as an everyday dish, soft and creamy. Halfway between an omelette and a quiche, it is a simple and delicate dish. In this recipe we have given our own interpretation.

ROSSEJAT OF COUSCOUS WITH PRAWNS AND AIOLI

Time: 2 hr 30 mins | Level: easy

INGREDIENTS FOR 4 PEOPLE

400 g couscous
800 ml seafood fumet
16 medium prawns
Olive oil
For the aioli
Mayonnaise ▪ Sunflower oil ▪ Garlic

METHOD

1 Before starting, prepare a seafood fumet *(see p. 327)*.

2 To prepare the aioli, crush the garlic with a little sunflower oil in a mortar or with a blender and gradually add the mayonnaise. You can also prepare an aioli without mayonnaise, just with garlic, salt and oil in a mortar, or adding, once the garlic has been crushed, a yolk to help emulsify it better with the oil, which should be poured in gradually.

3 Brown the couscous in a paella pan over a low heat with a few drops of olive oil until well toasted. You can also toast it in the oven at 180°C, stirring it occasionally.

4 Add the seafood fumet seasoned with salt and fat removed, and cook for 4 minutes.

5 Add the prawns and finish cooking in the oven at 180°C until the couscous is dry.

6 Serve with the aioli.

Noodles or rice are the typical ingredients for rossejats, which are characterised by being cooked with a strong fish or seafood fumet, or both. Both the pasta and the rice — or in this case, the couscous — should be browned, almost toasted, before adding the fumet, to achieve a crunchy texture and an intense flavour.

RAZOR CLAMS AND SEAWEED EMPANADILLA

Time: 2 hrs (+ 1 hr resting) | Level: easy

INGREDIENTS FOR 4 PEOPLE

For the pastry
500 g strong flour • 240 ml water
20 g fresh yeast • 2 tablespoons
olive oil • 9 g salt • Flour (optional)
Egg (optional)
For the filling
8 razor clams
400 g assorted fresh seaweeds: pistle weed
(Gigartina pistillata), *sea spaghetti* (Himanthalia elongata), *velvet horn (Codium tomentosum)*
3 garlic cloves
Soy sauce

METHOD

1 To make the pastry, knead all the ingredients until you have a smooth, elastic dough. Leave it to rise until it doubles in size.
2 To prepare the stuffing, steam the razor clams until they open, then separate them from the shells and cut them into pieces of about 1 centimetre.
3 Blanch the seaweeds for 1 minute in boiling water and chop them so that they are the same size as the razor clams.
4 Sauté the garlic. Add the seaweed and razor clams, sauté over a high heat and season with a few drops of soy sauce. Reserve.
5 Roll out the dough and cut it into 6 or 8 cm circles. Fill the circles with the sautéed seaweed and razor clams, then seal them by pinching the edges.
6 If desired, you can brush the outside of the empanadillas with oil or egg, or simply sprinkle them with flour.
7 Preheat the oven to 180°C and bake the empanadillas for 20-25 minutes.

This empanadilla is a very simple interpretation of the classic Galician empanada. Old family recipes and traditional recipe books offer inexhaustible resources for new dishes. All you need to do is tinker with cooking methods or vary ingredients to suit your taste, or apply the latest techniques and know-how to constantly enrich your culinary repertoire.

HAKE WITH YOUNG GARLIC VINAIGRETTE

Time: 30 mins | Level: easy

INGREDIENTS FOR 4 PEOPLE

4 x 125 g hake supreme fillets
2 potatoes
2 onions
200 ml sunflower oil
Spring onion
For the vinaigrette
80 ml olive oil
6 garlic cloves
15 ml red wine vinegar or balsamic vinegar from Modena
Fresh rosemary
Salt and pepper

METHOD

1 To prepare the rosemary vinaigrette, put the garlic into a frying pan with the olive oil. As soon as the garlic begins to brown, add the rosemary and remove from the heat straight away. When the oil is warm, add the vinegar, salt and pepper.

2 Cook the julienned onions in a casserole over a low heat with 50 ml of sunflower oil until they have a caramelised appearance.

3 Peel and slice the potatoes and confit them with the remaining sunflower oil in the oven or in a saucepan over a low heat until soft.

4 In a frying pan over a high heat, sear the hake supremes, previously seasoned with salt and pepper, so that they are only browned on the outside.

5 Place them on the baking tray with a spoonful of the vinaigrette and cook them at 180°C for 7-10 minutes. To detect if it is cooked, press the hake, which should be somewhat hard, or check with a thermometer that the centre of the fish is 50-55°C.

6 Heat the potato slices in a frying pan with a little oil over a low heat and add the onion confit.

7 Arrange the potatoes and onions on the plate as a side, add the piece of hake, season with garlic and rosemary vinaigrette, and garnish with slices of spring onion and fresh rosemary.

In the repertoire of traditional cuisine, you can always find an inexhaustible source of good recipes, which, revised with modern techniques, more precise in terms of cooking times and more nutritionally balanced, can offer us dishes as affordable and exquisite as this one.

TWICE-COOKED PORK RIBS

Time: 3 hrs or 18 hrs (depending on the type of cooking)
Level: moderate

INGREDIENTS FOR 4 PEOPLE

1 pork rib
Olive oil
3 garlic cloves
Bouquet garni

METHOD

1 For the first cooking, confit the ribs in a casserole with the oil, garlic and bouquet garni. Cook it gently, without exceeding 100°C, for 3-6 hours, depending on the meat (the type of meat, the size of the piece and its thickness). To test for doneness, pierce the meat with a skewer or a small knife; when it penetrates easily into the meat, it means that it is cooked.

If you prefer to first vacuum cook, pack the meat into a sous vide bag with the other ingredients and cook it in the sous vide cooker at 65°C for 18 hours or at 85°C for 6 hours.

2 Allow the pork ribs to cool in the oil if they have been confit, or in water at 65°C, if they have been cooked under vacuum.

3 Continue with a second cooking by roasting in the oven at 180°C, basting the ribs with the cooking oil, until they are completely browned and crispy (about 15 minutes).

You can also finish the dish on a barbecue. In this case, oak wood is preferable, as it provides smoked nuances to the meat.

Although two cooking techniques are used with different times and temperatures, it is not a complicated recipe. In the first step, the ribs are cooked at a low temperature so that the meat is very tender and mellow, either gently by the confit process or by cooking it under vacuum. In the second step, it is roasted or grilled at a high temperature, in the oven or on the barbecue, to achieve a crispy texture on the outside and enhance the meat's flavour.

SOLE WITH AN OLIVE EMULSION

Time: 30 mins | Level: easy

INGREDIENTS FOR 4 PEOPLE

4 soles
200 g green olives
100 ml virgin olive oil
50 ml black olive oil (see p. 313)
48 capers
Salt

METHOD

1 Stone the green olives, crush them with a little of their liquid and add the olive oil, a little at a time, as if you were emulsifying a mayonnaise, until you obtain a sauce.

2 Fry the capers in hot oil for 1 minute. Once cold, they should be crispy.

3 Clean the sole of skin and bones and leave it in a 10 per cent brine (*see p. 144*) for 10 minutes. Dry the fish and grill it.

4 Serve the sole with the olive emulsion, seasoned with black olive oil and garnished with the fried capers.

The sole flesh, soft and tender, only needs to be cooked quickly to enhance its flavour. Combined with olives and capers, the fish in this dish acquires strength and aroma.

AUBERGINE, TOMATO AND ENDIVE SALAD WITH PIG'S TROTTER VINAIGRETTE

Time: 1 hr | Level: easy

INGREDIENTS FOR 4 PEOPLE

1 frisée endive ▪ *1 aubergine* ▪ *12 cherry tomatoes*

For the vinaigrette

1 boiled pig's trotter ▪ *100 ml virgin olive oil*

25 ml Cabernet Sauvignon vinegar

100 g tomato confit ▪ *25 g toasted pine nuts (or toasted hazelnuts)* ▪ *Chives* ▪ *Salt and pepper*

METHOD

1 To prepare the vinaigrette, dice the pig's trotter — which has first been boiled, allowed to cool and boned — and mix it with the tomato, cut into concassé (*see p. 120*), the chopped pine nuts and chopped chives. Add the oil, vinegar, salt and pepper.

2 Clean the endive and set aside.

3 Cut the aubergine into batons, cut the cherry tomatoes in half and grill everything. Reserve.

4 Assemble the salad with a base of endive and add the warm, grilled vegetables. Finally, dress generously with the pig's trotter vinaigrette.

A salad does not necessarily have to be cold; sometimes warm or hot vegetables or vinaigrettes can be added that will intensify the flavours and achieve different textures than usual. A variation for this dish could be an endive salad with ham or sautéed pancetta or bacon, finished with a warm vinaigrette.

CHICKEN PAILLARD WITH VEGETABLES AND LEMON BUTTER

Time: 30 mins | Level: easy

INGREDIENTS FOR 4 PEOPLE

4 medium-sized chicken breasts
10 cherry tomatoes
100 g aubergine
100 g courgettes
150 g chanterelle
100 g citrus butter (see pp. 346-347)
Rosemary or other aromatic herbs to taste
Sprouts (optional)
Salt and pepper
For the citrus herb oil
100 ml olive oil
Lemon thyme
Fresh lemon verbena
Salt and pepper

METHOD

1 To prepare the citrus herb oil, chop, together with the oil, the lemon thyme, the tender lemon verbena leaves (although they could also be lemon balm or similar), and salt and pepper.

2 Season the breasts with salt and pepper or place them in a 10 per cent brine for 30 minutes (*see p. 144*). If you opt for the latter procedure, you will then have to dry them. Then, with a knife, cut them open in half.

3 Spread a tablespoon of citrus oil on a sheet of baking paper and place the opened chicken breasts on top. Next, dress the top with a little more flavoured oil.

4 Cover the preparation with the paper and flatten the breasts so that they are of uniform thickness. You can use a rolling pin, a mallet or even place them between two chopping boards.

5 Cook the breasts still in the baking paper on a very hot griddle or grill for 1 minute. In addition to uniforming the thickness of the meat, the paper will prevent it from sticking to the griddle.

6 Cut the vegetables into batons and the cherry tomatoes in halves, and grill them together with the chanterelles.

7 Open the paper and place the chicken on the plate with the vegetables. Dress with citrus oil and citrus butter cubes, and garnish with rosemary or other herbs, or with sprouts.

The oil and butter round out the dish and make a simple grilled chicken a different experience.

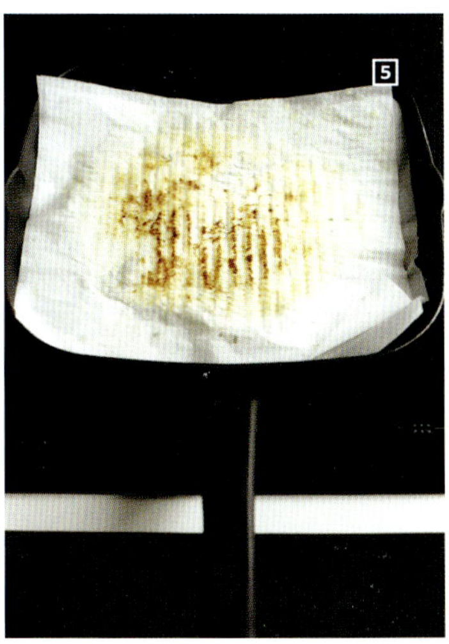

5

7

BREADED SARDINES

Time: 30 mins | Level: easy

INGREDIENTS FOR 4 PEOPLE

Frozen prebaked bread
16 sardines, filleted
100 ml olive oil
75 g ripe tomatoes
50 g aubergine
50 g courgette
75 g onion
75 g green pepper
75 g red pepper
Chervil
Salt and pepper

METHOD

1 Cut the precooked bread into very thin slices. Alternatively, if you do not have a machine to cut it, flatten the slices of bread between two sheets of greaseproof paper.

2 To clean them of blood and season them, place the sardine fillets in a 10 per cent brine (*see p. 144*) for 5 minutes. Then, dry them and set aside.

3 Blanch, peel and remove the seeds from the tomato, and cut it into brunoise. Do the same with the other vegetables. Cover the courgette and aubergine with salt so that they lose their acidity.

4 Cook the onion in a frying pan with olive oil for 5 minutes over a moderate heat. Add the peppers and cook for a further 3 minutes. Then add the drained courgette and aubergine and cook for 4 minutes. Then add the tomato and cook for a further 5 minutes. Add salt and pepper and reserve.

5 Place the sardines on the slices of bread and cut the latter so that they are just a little larger than the sardines.

6 Sear the assembly in a frying pan over a low heat so that the bread is toasted and the sardine is gently cooked. Cook the bread side only.

4

5

6

7 Serve the breaded sardines on a base of vegetables and dress them with the chervil-flavoured oil and salt. Garnish the dish with some chervil leaves.

This breading has the advantage of protecting the soft sardine flesh from direct contact with the griddle, while providing a crunchy texture, without masking the properties of the main ingredient. This is an interesting type of breading that you can consider for many other dishes.

COATING AND GRATINATING

BOTH TECHNIQUES WILL GIVE YOUR DISHES THE FINAL TOUCH: A CRUNCHY AND TASTY TEXTURE, WITH AN INTENSE GOLDEN OR EVEN A SHINY FINISH THAT WILL MAKE THEM MORE DECORATIVE AND APPETISING.

TYPE OF COOKING	By concentration
RELATED TECHNIQUES	Browning (To cook over a high heat with fat an already cooked product, such as boiled potatoes that are later fried.)

Coating and gratinating are two techniques that work as complementary cooking techniques to each other, because they are more like a final step. Both need the dry heat of an oven grill or salamander to achieve their purpose.

The difference between coating and gratinating is that coating starts with an egg base to obtain a thin, shiny and slightly golden layer, while gratinating seeks a crispy result, usually with the help of a cheese or breadcrumb base. In both cases, the final objective is that the upper part of a food, through the direct contribution of heat, acquires greater intensity of colour, flavour, aroma and texture, or to carry out a quick cooking, basically to give a touch of heat and obtain a crunchy texture.

Coating can be interpreted in other ways, too. Referred to as glazing, it can be understood as the process of caramelising a food, generally vegetables, to coat them, with the help of some type of sugar or glaze – a concentrated juice containing gelatines and sugars that provide density and a typical colour to the glaze. A glaze, such as a mixture of honey and soy sauce or other dense sauces, usually with some kind of sweet element, can be applied with a brush over the food to coat it. Another way to finish a dish is to, for example, coat it with a sprinkling or dusting of icing sugar on any type of sweet preparation.

GLAZED SALMON TOAST WITH A MUSTARD AND DILL HOLLANDAISE

Time: 30 mins | Level: easy

INGREDIENTS FOR 4 PEOPLE

600 g fresh salmon - *100 g leek*
30 g butter - *100 g turnip*
100 g courgette - *100 g carrot*
1 slice of sliced bread - *Salt and pepper*
For the hollandaise sauce
300 g clarified butter - *3 egg yolks*
10 g mustard - *5 g fresh dill*

METHOD

1 Cut the turnip and carrot with a mandoline into the shape of vegetable spaghetti.

2 Boil each vegetable separately to reach the ideal doneness for each one. Cool and set aside. Cut the leek into slices and sauté it slowly in butter until completely soft, ensuring that it does not take caramelised nuances.

3 Prepare the hollandaise sauce (*see p. 331*) with the butter and 3 egg yolks, adding the dill and mustard. Keep the sauce warm in a bain-marie, at about 60°C.

4 Toast the slice of bread.

5 Cut the salmon into ½ centimetre-thick slices as uniform as possible. Season with salt and pepper.

6 Place a spoonful of hot leek on the toast and add the salmon slices on top. Coat with the sauce and glaze in the oven.

7 Serve immediately with the vegetable spaghetti and decorate with fresh dill leaves.

TUNA WITH HUMMUS, SOYA BEANS AND SPROUTS

Time: 30 mins | Level: moderate

INGREDIENTS FOR 4 PEOPLE

1 x 400 g tuna piece
Toasted sesame seeds
Shiso and purple shiso leaves
(or onion sprouts, bean sprouts,
radish or mustard sprouts, or chopped chives)
For the hummus
200 g cooked chickpeas
30 ml liquid from cooked chickpeas
25 ml olive oil
2 g tahini (or sesame oil)
1 g garlic
1 g ground cumin
Salt and pepper
Lemon
For the soy sauce
60 g soya beans
60 ml olive oil

METHOD

1 To prepare the hummus, drain the chickpeas and reserve some of the cooking liquid. If you have bought them packaged, use the liquid that comes in the jar or a white stock or vegetable stock. Place them in a blender together with the garlic, lemon juice, cumin, some of the cooking liquid and the tahini or sesame oil. Blend, incorporating olive oil. Add more liquid, if necessary, until a smooth but thick texture is obtained (more like purée than cream). Add salt and pepper and reserve.

2 Sear the tuna quickly and briefly in the frying pan, so that it is browned but not cooked on the inside. Cool it, then cut it into thin slices of ½ centimetre and reserve it protected with clingfilm.

3 To prepare the sauce, mix 60 ml of olive oil with 60 grams of soya beans.

4 Gently heat the hummus in a bain-marie (water bath) or in the microwave.

5 Place 2 tablespoons of hummus in the base of a soup plate, cover with tuna slices, season with soy sauce and glaze (or gratinate) the preparation briefly in the oven grill or in the salamander.

6 When you take the dish out of the oven, add the toasted sesame seeds and the shiso leaves or sprouts, and serve straight away.

By glazing the preparation in the final process of the dish, you give the tuna the ideal temperature, without cooking it, at the same time that you heat the hummus to provide warmth and flavour. The soy sauce, in addition, complements the two main flavours while binding them together.

VACUUM COOKING

THIS TYPE OF COOKING IS THE SYNTHESIS OF TWO OF THE PRINCIPLES THAT PROFESSIONAL CULINARY TRENDS ARE BASED ON: TEMPERATURE CONTROL AND GENTLE COOKING.

TYPE OF COOKING	By concentration
RELATED TECHNIQUES	Steaming Poaching Confit

Vacuum cooking, also called sous vide cooking, is simple. However, you need a specific machine – a sous vide cooker – as well as other utensils. It is essential that you have previous training to know the characteristics of these elements and, above all, the basics of the technique.

This cooking method is based on vacuum packing the products to be cooked, so you will need a vacuum-packing machine and vacuum-seal bags (available from specialised kitchenware suppliers; they are not the same bags used to preserve food).

The sealed product is cooked in the sous vide cooker, a type of water bath cooking machine with temperature controls and constant water circulation. It is important to carefully read the instructions of each model, which will indicate the type of vacuum suitable for each food, as well as the time and temperature required, since they are very different for this technique than for conventional ones. There are also specific recipe books for vacuum cooking that will give you important information to help you become familiar with this revolutionary way of cooking.

There are two main types of vacuum cooking: direct cooking and indirect cooking, depending on whether the dish is to be consumed straight away or whether it is intended to be preserved.

THE PROCESS

1. Prepare all the ingredients.
2. Make the necessary preparations as indicated in the recipe (in some cases, browning or searing; in others, seasoning or blanching, etc.).
3. Vacuum pack the product and its complements (always cold).
4. Cook the product inside the sous vide bag at a controlled temperature in steam convection ovens or thermostatic water baths. In some cases, you can also use this procedure by introducing the bag into boiling or very hot water (for cooking vegetables), or even in the microwave.

65.4
SELECT
START STOP
ICC
International Cooking Concepts
RONER DOMO

3

4

DIRECT COOKING

The objective of direct cooking is, as with most modern cooking techniques, to obtain the highest quality from the finished product and give it its best flavour and texture potential. When they are made to be served straight away, cooking times can be short and temperatures low. Normally products with soft textures are cooked easily and quickly, such as fish, which require between 10 and 20 minutes at a temperature of between 50 and 55°C.

The product must be very fresh, since cooking will probably not reach the safe 65°C necessary to destroy microorganisms. But this should not worry you, as the same applies to a multitude of dishes cooked with traditional techniques: a beefburger, roast beef, grilled prawns, etc. Simply take the same hygienic measures as usual when handling the product. If it is fresh and of high quality, you can eat it without worrying about it.

DIRECT COOKING TEMPERATURES

	COOKING TEMPERATURE	COOKING TIME	CORE TEMPERATURE
TUNA, COD, SALMON, MACKEREL	45°C / 50°C	10 mins / 15 mins	40°C / 45°C
SEA BREAM, SEA BASS, MONKFISH, HAKE	50°C / 55°C	10 mins / 20 mins	45°C / 52°C
RARE RED MEAT (fillet, entrecôte)	50°C / 65°C	10 mins / 30 mins	50°C / 55°C
MEDIUM-COOKED MEAT	60°C / 65°C	10 mins / 30 mins	58°C / 62°C
WELL-DONE MEAT	65°C / 70°C	20 mins / 30 mins	65°C / 70°C

LOW-TEMPERATURE SALMON WITH CITRUS EMULSION

Time: 1 hr | Level: moderate

INGREDIENTS FOR 4 PEOPLE

4 x 150 g salmon supremes • 300 g mangetout

Butter • Salt

For the citrus gel

125 ml water • 25 g sugar • Lime, lemon and grapefruit peel • 2 g agar agar • 25 ml juice from the citrus fruits

For the citrus emulsion

150 g citrus gel (see above)

50 ml extra virgin olive oil

For the citrus oil

5 g citrus peel • 80 ml sunflower oil • Salt

METHOD

1 To prepare the citrus gel, boil the water and sugar in a saucepan, remove from the heat and infuse the grated peels for 15 minutes with the container covered. Cool and strain. Mix the infusion with the agar agar, bring it to the boil and add 25 ml of citrus juice. Remove from the heat and allow the preparation to set in the refrigerator.

2 To make the citrus emulsion, purée the citrus gel with a stick blender and emulsify it, a little at a time, with the olive oil. Reserve.

3 To prepare the citrus oil, grate the citrus peel and mix it with sunflower oil and salt.

4 Cook the mangetout in water and salt and cool.

5 Place the salmon in a 10 per cent brine for 15 minutes (*see p. 144*).

6 Dry the salmon and place it in a vacuum-seal bag with a few drops of citrus oil.

7 Pack at maximum vacuum and cook in a sous vide cooker at 50°C for 15 minutes.

8 Sauté the mangetout for 30 seconds with a knob of butter and a few drops of water.

9 Remove the salmon from the bag, place it warm on the plate and accompany it with the citrus emulsion and mangetout. Finish by seasoning the preparation with the citrus oil.

5

6

7

INDIRECT COOKING

To date, indirect cooking has been the most widely used process in vacuum cooking. The food industry has been using this method for many years as a preservation system for numerous preparation and processing operations.

These are cooking processes in which the value of food safety takes precedence over gastronomic value, but at the same time still seeks maximum quality. Its main principle is clear: cook always to reach above 65°C in the centre of the product, for a minimum of 30 minutes to ensure health safety, and rapidly cool to reach 4°C in less than 2 hours.

Although indirect cooking is also carried out at low temperatures – but always above 65°C – unlike direct cooking, the cooking times are long, which makes it an ideal cooking method for tough meats that need a long time to tenderise. In contrast, it is not a good cooking process for fish, as it leaves them very dry.

This system usually requires a double process: after the first vacuum cooking, of a gentle nature, with which a tender and juicy texture is achieved, a second cooking at a higher temperature is carried out, to provide firmness and a crunchy texture, intense aroma and golden colour typical of grilled, roasted or barbecued cooking.

Indirect cooking allows us to cook at different temperatures starting at 65°C; the higher the temperature, the shorter the cooking time required. The ratio is different depending on the characteristics of the product (whether it is more or less tender, for example) and the size of the piece (or whether it is whole or cut). Since indirect cooking is used to ensure the preservation of the product, it is sometimes more practical to cook at a slightly higher temperature – at 80°C, for example – for faster cooking without making a great difference in terms of taste preservation and loss of the food's juiciness. However, when cooking for preservation purposes, it is important not to stop cooking, as this would result in the loss of the guarantee of food hygiene safety.

One way to determine the ideal length of cooking time for vacuum-packed vegetables is to introduce a piece of the same vegetable in the cooking medium without packaging it. As soon as it is cooked, you will know that the vacuum preparation will also be cooked, and, therefore, that you should remove the bag.

THE PROCESS

1 Prepare all of the ingredients.

2 Make the necessary preparations.

3 After cooling the preparations, pack the main food with its complements.

4 Cook for the time and at the temperature indicated according to the recipe and the machinery.

5 Cool the product quickly (ice water, cold water) and keep it in the refrigerator or freezer until you're ready to use it.

6 Bring the food to the food's cooking temperature according to the requirements of the recipe. At this point a second cooking may be necessary.

INDIRECT COOKING TEMPERATURES

MEATS	AT 65°C	AT 80°C
Beef, steak	22 hrs	6 hrs
Chicken, breast 2	5 mins	16 mins
Chicken, drumstick	3 hrs	1 hr 30mins
Chicken, whole	10 hrs	3 hrs
Duck, breast	50 mins	20 mins
Duck, leg	16 hrs	8 hrs
Goat, shoulder	20 hrs	12 hrs
Lamb, shoulder	24 hrs	18 hrs
Pork, belly	18 hrs	12 hrs
Pork, cheeks and jowls	24 hrs	12 hrs
Pork, ribs	18 hrs	10 hrs
Pork, snout, ear and feet	36 hrs	18 hrs
Veal, cheeks	34 hrs	18 hrs
Veal, shin and knuckle	24 hrs	10 hrs
Veal, tongue	36 hrs	18 hrs

VEGETABLES	AT 85°C	AT 100°C
Artichoke	45 mins	27 mins
Asparagus, green	24 mins	8 mins
Asparagus, white	40 mins	18 mins
Beans, frozen	20 mins	15 mins
Cabbage	35 mins	20 mins
Cauliflower	40 mins	12 mins
Chard	15 mins	8 mins
Celery/radish	30 mins	9 mins
Courgette (cut 1 cm thick)	15 mins	4 mins
Courgette, baby	20 mins	7 mins
Fennel	50 mins	24 mins
Garlic, young	25 mins	10 mins
Mushrooms	16 mins	7 mins
Potato, sliced (1 cm thick)	25 mins	10 mins
Pumpkin	15 mins	6 mins
Turnip	15 mins	12 mins
Turnip, black	25 mins	14 mins

VACUUM-PACKED LAMB SHOULDER WITH CONFIT VEGETABLES

Time: 12 hrs or 24 hrs (depending on the cooking method chosen) | Level: moderate

INGREDIENTS FOR 4 PEOPLE

1.5 kg lamb shoulder
100 ml olive oil
12 g cardamom
3 garlic cloves
Fresh rosemary
Fresh thyme
Pink, black and white peppercorns
Salt

For the confit vegetables

400 g potatoes
200 ml olive oil
60 ml concentrated meat stock (optional)
24 baby onions
3 garlic cloves
1 tomato
Black peppercorns

METHOD

1 Cut the shoulder into 3 pieces of about 350 grams each and place them in a 10 per cent brine for 1 hour (*see p. 144*).

2 Put the lamb in a vacuum-seal bag with the peppers, cardamom, 3 cloves of garlic, rosemary and a spoonful of olive oil, and pack it in the maximum possible vacuum.

3 Cook the lamb in a sous vide cooker at 65°C for 24 hours, or at 80°C for 12 hours.

4 Cool the preparation in cold water and reserve it cold, without removing it from the cooking bag.

5 To confit the vegetables, cut the potatoes into slices and peel the onions. Confit them in a casserole covered with oil, with 3 cloves of garlic and the peppercorns. Blanch, peel and cut the tomato into concassé (*see p. 120*), and lightly confit it in light oil.

6 Heat the lamb in warm water in the same cooking bag. Do not exceed the temperature in which you have cooked it.

7 Open the bag and sear the meat in a frying pan, griddle or grill, only on the skin side. It should be a quick searing, to brown and intensify the flavour of the lamb without cooking the inside of the meat, since it is already tender and mellow when removed from the bag. At the same time, also cook the garnish (the tomato in concassé, the potatoes and onions) on the grill or in a hot oven.

8 If you want to use the juices left in the bag, bind it with a meat stock (*see p. 324*) to obtain a small amount of sauce.

9 Plate the garnish and lamb, and add rosemary, thyme and a few drops of the meat sauce.

VEGETABLE DIPS

Time: 1 hr | Level: easy

INGREDIENTS FOR 4 PEOPLE

50 g courgette • 50 g carrot
20 g celery (the tenderest leaves)
50 g turnip • 50 g pumpkin
For the hummus
100 g cooked chickpeas • 15 ml juice from cooking the chickpeas • 15 ml olive oil • 2 ml tahini (or sesame oil)
1 garlic clove • Salt • Pepper • Lemon • Ground cumin
For the tzatziki
1 Greek yogurt • Mint • 15 g cucumber
5 ml lemon juice • Salt • Pepper
For the guacamole
1 avocado • 25 ml olive oil • 1 ripe tomato
1 spring onion • Tabasco sauce • Lemon juice • Salt • Pepper

METHOD

1 Wash the most tender celery leaves and reserve them for garnishing. Clean the remaining vegetables and vacuum pack them. Cook at 85°C if you have a thermostatic bath or a steam oven, or at 100°C you immerse them packed in a pot of boiling water (*see table on p. 303*). Cool and reserve.

2 To prepare the hummus, if you cook the chickpeas at home, drain them and reserve some of the cooking liquid. In the case of tinned chickpeas, you can use their packing liquid or a white or vegetable stock (*see pp. 322 and 323*).

3 Place the chickpeas, garlic, lemon juice, cumin, some of the chickpea cooking liquid and tahini (or sesame oil) in a blender, and blend, adding the olive oil a little at a time. If necessary, add more cooking liquid until a smooth but thick texture is obtained (more like purée than cream). Add salt and pepper and reserve.

4 To prepare the tzatziki, mix the yogurt with the chopped mint, the cucumber cut into brunoise and the lemon juice. Season with salt and pepper.

5 To prepare the guacamole, briefly blanch the tomato, peel it, remove the seeds and cut it into concassé. Cut the spring onion into brunoise.

6 Remove the flesh of the avocado, which must be ripe, and mash it with a fork together with the lemon juice and olive oil. Mix the purée with the chopped vegetables, season with salt and pepper, and add a touch of Tabasco.

7 Serve the three sauces in glasses or bowls, and the vegetables in another bowl, so that the diners can choose the vegetables and combine them with the sauces.

A dish for sharing and snacking, it allows, thanks to the vacuum cooking, serving the vegetables with a very pleasant texture, very al dente, almost raw. They can be presented with the suggested sauces or other seasonings, according to the taste of the cook and the guests.

VACUUM-PACKED VEGETABLE STOCK

Time: 3 hrs | Level: easy

INGREDIENTS FOR 4 PEOPLE

200 g carrots ▪ 100 g leek
10 g celery ▪ 80 g turnip
200 g onions ▪ 1 sprig parsley
8 chives ▪ 40 g salsify
500 g ice cubes

METHOD

1 Wash all the vegetables well, then peel and cut them into mirepoix.

2 Put the vegetables into a vacuum-seal bag, together with the ice cubes, and pack them in a 100 per cent vacuum.

3 Cook in a sous vide cooker or steam oven at 85°C for 3 hours, although the range of possible temperatures can vary between 65 and 100°C, creating different nuances and gustatory results. You can experiment to find which temperature range you prefer.

4 Once the cooking time has elapsed, open the bag, strain and cool the stock.

Stocks cooked under vacuum and at low temperature have many advantages: firstly, they better preserve the nutrients of the vegetables, which can also be reused to prepare purées or creams, since they conserve their organoleptic properties; secondly, the broth has milder aromas than those of a boiled broth, but at the same time is more authentic; and finally, there is no evaporation, so you will obtain almost the same amount of liquid that you introduced, with a crystalline appearance. The stock can be used as a soup or consommé, enriched with more ingredients, or as a base for more complex preparations, to which it will provide flavour and consistency.

VACUUM-PACKED VEGETABLES WITH ANISEED-FLAVOURED HERBS

Time: 2 hrs | Level: moderate

INGREDIENTS FOR 4 PEOPLE

60 ml olive oil
75 g potato • 75 g sweet potato
75 g carrot • 75 g turnip
4 artichokes • 12 asparagus
75 g parsnips • 12 young garlic cloves
100 g mangetout or green beans
15 g ginger
Pepper
For the aniseed oil
Aniseed-flavoured herbs (fennel, tarragon, chervil)
60 ml olive oil • Salt

METHOD

1 Clean all the vegetables and cut them in different ways: turnip, carrot, asparagus and garlic, in batons; sweet potato and potato, in slices or half slices; parsnips, in slices, and artichokes, in quarters. Leave the mangetout whole.

2 Vacuum-pack the vegetables separately and cook them according to the temperatures in the cooking tables: at 85°C if you have a thermostatic bath or steam oven, or at 100°C if you put them packed in a pot of boiling water (*see table on p. 303*).

3 Once the time indicated on the tables has elapsed, remove the bags, cool and set aside.

4 Open all the bags and reserve the water they contain, no matter how little.

5 To prepare the aniseed oil, chop and mix the herbs with the olive oil and salt.

6 Grate or chop the ginger and sauté it in a frying pan with a little oil. Add the vegetables and sauté for 2 minutes.

7 Add the reserved vegetable cooking water. Cook for a further 2 minutes.

8 Remove the vegetables from the heat, drizzle with the olive oil, season with a little ground pepper and serve.

Vacuum cooking, besides being simple — once you have the necessary tools and master the temperature control — has the advantage that it respects the product's original taste to the maximum and takes advantage of all its nutritional properties. In the case of cooked vegetables, don't even add salt, because when they are cooked in their own juices, they retain their own mineral salts. Therefore, it is very suitable cooking for people who cannot take salt or who must follow low-fat diets. But it is also an attractive alternative for everyone, since it provides refined and authentic flavours.

MICROWAVE COOKING

THE ABILITY OF THIS PRACTICAL APPLIANCE TO COOK FOOD IN ITS OWN JUICES, WITH ALMOST NO NEED FOR WATER OR FAT, OFFERS A WIDE RANGE OF POSSIBILITIES AND INTERESTING COOKING OPTIONS.

The microwave oven is an appliance that is as indispensable in most homes as it is disputed by others. Its method of cooking or heating food is different from all the methods invented by humankind since the discovery of fire. Perhaps for this reason, even today its existence is still divided between faithful lovers and staunch detractors.

Recent studies, however, have confirmed the safety of cooking with the aid of this type of oven and have found that the loss of nutrients is lower than using techniques such as boiling and similar to that of steaming. The World Health Organization published a report in February 2005, stating that microwave ovens are safe and convenient appliances for heating and cooking food, and that it is sufficient to follow each manufacturer's instructions for their proper use. This organisation periodically evaluates, together with the International Commission on Non-Ionising Radiation Protection, the safety of microwaves, as it does with mobile phones.

The main difference between a conventional oven and a microwave oven is that the heat of the traditional oven, as well as the rest of the cooking methods we generally use, is provided by an external temperature and always in the same direction: from the outside to the inside of the food. In contrast, the microwave generates electromagnetic energy which, through waves, causes friction in the water molecules inside the food. This friction produces heat, which is transmitted to the rest of the molecules by contact. Another great differential factor of microwaves is the speed in which this process occurs, since the heating speed is four times faster than that of gas or electric ovens.

In most households, microwave use is still restricted to simple tasks, such as heating or defrosting food. But the truth is that it offers very interesting cooking with certain products (stir-fries, sauces, soups, stocks), since, as the food is cooked in its own juice, it retains its nutrients and all its flavour. Meat, rice, vegetables and fish can also be cooked in the microwave with very good results. In addition, you can use it to dehydrate or dry products or bake cakes very easily.

There are more and more products and utensils to cook specifically with this appliance and that help us to refine its handling. However, it is important to study the characteristics and possibilities of each model carefully in order to get the most out of it, since, as it produces such fast cooking, it requires precise temperature control and programmes, depending on the microwave, the product and the type of processing that you wish to obtain.

RECOMMENDATIONS FOR USE

▪ **Introduce small or medium-sized pieces.** For better cooking, it is best to avoid whole and large pieces, since microwaves penetrate 1–2 centimetres deep into the food and then the heat spreads by the friction of the molecules. It is also better to arrange the food evenly on the plate or container.

▪ **Stir during cooking.** You should stop cooking once or twice to stir the food for even cooking. Stir from the outside to the inside of the container, as it cooks on the edges sooner. This also allows you to maintain the heat of the food longer.

▪ **Use little water.** To cook most foods, little liquid is needed, because their own liquid is used.

▪ **Cover.** Cover the food with clingfilm or a lid, without allowing the food to touch the protection.

▪ **Use appropriate materials.** Use glass, ceramic, porcelain or earthenware containers. Metal materials and aluminium foil should never be placed in microwave ovens, as the waves bounce off them and can damage the oven. You should also avoid paper or cardboard, since they can catch fire, and plastics that are not suitable for this type of appliance, since some of them release toxic substances. There is usually a symbol on the packaging indicating whether they can be microwaved.

▪ **Fill the moulds halfway.** In the microwave, the cake mixture tends to expand more than in the conventional oven; therefore, it is not advisable to fill the moulds completely.

DEHYDRATED OLIVE OIL

Time: 10 mins (microwave) or 12 hrs (dehydrator)
Level: easy

INGREDIENTS FOR 4 PEOPLE

300 g black olives
(Cacereña or Aragonesa varieties, etc.)
80 ml virgin olive oil

METHOD

1 Choose between the two possible options to dehydrate the olives: in the microwave or with a dehydrator. The microwave allows a fast drying process, while the dehydrator is slow, but it also better maintains the food's aromatic properties.

If you choose the microwave, dehydrate the olives with a medium programme. Cook in 3-minute intervals, until the olives are completely dry.

If you decide to use a dehydrator, place the olives in it and heat it at 80°C for 12 hours so that the olives are completely dehydrated.

2 Once dried, blend them with the olive oil with a blender or food processor, until you extract a fine and totally black liquid. Reserve in an airtight jar.

To obtain a good olive oil it is essential to dehydrate the olives beforehand. This is the way to get them to mix well with the oil. If you do not dehydrate them, a thick sauce will form, and not the flavoured liquid that you want from this recipe.

RED MULLET WITH LEMON TREE LEAVES

Time: 1 hr | Level: easy

INGREDIENTS FOR 4 PEOPLE

4 red mullets - *Lemon tree leaves (or similar: grapevine leaves, lemon verbena leaves, etc.)* - *1 lemon* - *1 shallot 200 g butter* - *Chives* - *Sunflower oil - Pink and black peppercorns* - *Cardamom* - *Salt*

ELABORATION

1 Prepare a flavoured oil by mixing the sunflower oil, the peppercorns, a little cardamom and the peel or zest of 1 lemon. Reserve some of the zest to assemble the dish at the end.

2 Debone the red mullet and reserve the bones. Season the fish with salt or place it in 10 per cent brine solution for 5 minutes (*see p. 144*).

3 Brush the skin of the red mullets with the spiced oil and place them on the lemon leaf.

4 Wrap the red mullet and the leaves in greaseproof paper and reserve in the refrigerator.

5 To prepare the red mullet broth, bleed the bones in cold water for 6 hours. Strain them, then lightly brown in a frying pan. Boil water in a saucepan and infuse the bones for 30 minutes, covered. Strain and reserve the broth.

6 To prepare the citrus sauce, fry the shallot cut into brunoise with a little butter. Add 50 ml of lemon juice and reduce it until it is almost dry. Then add 100 ml of red mullet broth and reduce it by half.

7 Remove from the heat and add some butter cubes and emulsify.

8 Reserve the sauce while hot, making sure that it does not boil or cool down.

9 Cook the red mullet in the microwave for 20 seconds (or slightly longer, if they are large pieces) at 800 W. Cooking should be brief, so that the fish is tender and almost raw.

10 Place the citrus sauce at the base of the dish and add the cooked red mullet.

11 Season with a few drops of the spiced oil and garnish the dish with a little lemon zest and chopped chives.

3

4

6

7

8

9

10

11

BASE RECIPES

SAUCES, BROTHS, PICADAS, SOFRITOS, CROÛTONS, VINAIGRETTES AND OTHER PREPARATIONS ARE CONSIDERED TO BE COMPLEMENTARY ELEMENTS IN MANY RECIPES. HOWEVER, THEY ARE OFTEN ESSENTIAL FOR PREPARING OR FINISHING THE DISHES PROPERLY, AND SOMETIMES THEY ARE EVEN THE KEY TO SUCCESS.

A tasty fish rice requires a good broth or fumet (a concentrated stock), just as stocks, sofritos (*see p. 350*) or picadas (ingredients ground in a mortar, used to thicken sauces) are essential for certain stews; a fresh and spectacular salad will require a vinaigrette to match; traditional cannelloni, a smooth, exquisite béchamel sauce. The list is endless. These bases are complementary preparations that enrich any type of dish, that structure it, harmonise it or give it unique nuances to distinguish it.

These basic preparations are part of the routines of any professional kitchen. Stocks, sauces, marinades and various other complements should always be ready to use as a base for many recipes and to finish or provide a special touch for many others. There are also more sophisticated base preparations that provide dishes with surprising textures and turn them into creative and novel recipes, thanks to certain complements traditionally used in the food industry, and now adapted for the most restless gastronomy. We are referring to texturisers that can aerate, emulsify, thicken, gel or spherify your preparations, processes that are now possible in the home kitchen.

Deepening your knowledge of these techniques will help you to perfect and round out your dishes, and will allow you to experiment and encourage our creativity.

BASIC STOCKS

MANY RICE DISHES, STEWS, BRAISES, CASSEROLES AND SAUCES ARE BASED ON STOCKS, WHETHER SOUPS, BROTHS OR STOCKS THEMSELVES. THESE ARE SIMPLE, BUT ESSENTIAL PREPARATIONS.

There are different types of stocks or broths and they can be customised as much as desired, but the ones that are commonly prepared and are versatile for many dishes and sauces are considered the classic or basic stocks. They are classified here into these groups: white and vegetable stocks, brown stocks and fish fumets.

RECOMMENDATIONS

- **Carry out the necessary preparation.** Clean all the ingredients before cooking; including blanching meats (*see p. 177*), if necessary. Cut all the products to a suitable size. Vegetables, in mirepoix (large cubes), and meat or fish, in medium-sized pieces.
- **Start with cold water.** The bases are always prepared starting with cold water, so that the flavours can develop. The cooking starts over a high heat and, when the liquid begins to boil, the heat is reduced so that the boiling is gentle and the broth does not become cloudy.
- **Cook without salt.** As a general rule, these bases are not seasoned with salt until the moment they will be used, so you do not add salt during cooking. As it is a base or complement, it should be seasoned afterwards, taking into account the characteristics of the preparation it will accompany. The proportion ranges between 7 and 10 grams of salt per litre. If it is a stock for rice, 7 grams will be enough, because boiling and evaporation concentrate the broth.
- **Skimming and degreasing.** At the beginning of cooking, you must skim a broth — that is, eliminate the scum that forms on the surface — to avoid unpleasant flavours. If necessary, you can skim the fat several times throughout the process, as well as once the broth has been strained, when the fat has solidified.
- **Time control.** The cooking time differs depending on the desired result and the ingredients incorporated. Fish fumets need little time, while tough meat stocks need several hours. In any case, the cooking times indicated in the recipes are calculated from the moment the stock begins to boil.
- **Incorporate the aromatic elements.** You can add aromatic elements to aromatise the stock, or sometimes to deodorise it — neutralise the excess of aromas — with spices such as cloves or peppercorns. A bouquet of aromatic herbs (bouquet garni, *see p. 348*) may be a good choice.
- **Strain and cool.** At the end of cooking, a broth should be strained and cooled by placing it in a cool place or in a bain-marie of cold water. Many of the vegetables and meats removed from the broth can be used to make croquettes and similar dishes.
- **Storing.** As they are the base or complement of other preparations, broths are often frozen to use on different occasions.
- **Use sous vide bags.** By cooking solid foods in this special bag, you prevent them from clouding the preparation. In addition, the sous vide bags facilitate subsequent straining.

WHITE STOCKS

All white bases are characterised by the fact that their raw ingredients are added directly to the cooking liquid.

The quick stock, as its name indicates, is a very simple or plain stock. In fact, it is nothing more than a base that is prepared with a certain improvisation to enrich the cooking of some products that only need little more than water.

The white, or basic, stock itself is also a very simple stock that is used to help cook some dishes. It is similar to a soup, but milder, since it does not have the consistency and flavour of soup.

And, finally, the homemade stock is no longer simply a base or complement, but is, in itself, a preparation, a soup. Its process is very similar to that of the white stock but includes a greater variety and quantity of ingredients (more meat and potato or pulses, such as beans and chickpeas), which provide thickness. In addition, its cooking time is longer.

QUICK STOCK Time: 20 mins

INGREDIENTS FOR 2 LITRES OF STOCK

2 litres water

Ingredients to cook in the stock

1 onion • 1 stick celery • ½ turnip • 1 leek

1 carrot • Bouquet garni (optional)

METHOD

1 Clean and cut all the vegetables into large cubes (mirepoix).

2 Cook the ingredients in a pot with cold water for 20 minutes and skim.

3 Season with salt and add the ingredients you wish to cook in the stock, often fish and seafood (such as prawns).

4 After the necessary time for cooking the ingredients, remove the stock from the heat, strain it and, if it is not going to be used straight away, cool it.

BASIC WHITE STOCK Time: 2 hrs

INGREDIENTS FOR 3 LITRES OF STOCK

4 litres water • 1 kg of chicken bones or carcasses

1 onion • 1 stick celery • 1 leek • 2 carrots

Bouquet garni (optional)

METHOD

1 Clean the vegetables, cut them into mirepoix (large cubes) and set aside.

2 Chop the chicken carcasses. If necessary, first blanch the bones to clean them of impurities (*see p. 177*).

3 Put the meat and vegetables into a pot with cold water and cook them.

4 Skim at the beginning of cooking and degrease throughout the process, if necessary. As it is not a very concentrated stock, it is not necessary to allow it to reduce too much, so cook it, half covered, for 2 hours.

5 Strain and cool. It can be stored in the refrigerator or freezer, properly labelled.

HOMEMADE STOCK Time: 4–5 hrs

INGREDIENTS FOR 4 LITRES OF STOCK

5 litres water • ¼ chicken (thigh) • 200 g veal shin

200 g of veal bones or chicken carcasses • 1 onion

1 peeled potato • 2 carrots • 100 g beans or chickpeas

1 stick celery • 1 leek • Bouquet garni

METHOD

1 Clean and cut the vegetables into mirepoix.

2 Chop the bones. If necessary, blanch them to remove their impurities (*see p. 177*).

3 Put all the ingredients into a pot with cold water and cook them.

4 Skim at the beginning of cooking and degrease throughout the process, if necessary. Cook, with the pot covered (to avoid excessive reduction of the stock), for 4–5 hours.

5 Strain, cool and reserve.

VEGETABLE STOCK

It is a light, fat-free base that adds freshness to preparations. If you have vegetables that are about to spoil, you can use them to make a stock to enrich other dishes.

Vegetable stocks can be perfectly prepared under vacuum and, in this way, have the advantage of retaining more nutritional properties due to the gentle cooking temperature.

VEGETABLE STOCK Time: 1–2 hrs

INGREDIENTS FOR 3 LITRES OF STOCK

4 litres water
1 turnip
1 carrot
1 stick celery
1 onion
1 leek
1 bay leaf
Bouquet garni

METHOD

1 Clean all the vegetables and cut them into mirepoix (large cubes).

2 Bring a pot of water to the boil; when it boils, add the vegetables and allow them to cook for 1–2 hours.

3 Strain and cool.

4 Store the stock in the refrigerator or freezer, labelled with the date of preparation.

1

BROWN STOCK

Brown stocks are based on first cooking, generally in the oven, certain products (especially meats). In this way, more flavoursome stocks are obtained. In addition, the cooking time is considerably prolonged to reduce the stock and to obtain a concentration of flavours. After 5 hours on the heat, the stock is reduced by 20 per cent and is ideal as a cooking liquid for stews; if you reduce it to the maximum, it is considered a sauce; this is the case of the demi-glace sauce (8 hours of cooking, 50 per cent reduction) or a *glace de viande* (24 hours of cooking, 80 per cent reduction), typical of French cuisine and used to coat meats.

BROWN STOCK Time: 5–24 hrs

INGREDIENTS FOR 4 LITRES OF STOCK

5 litres water • 1 kg beef bones, tendons and trimmings
1 carrot • 2 tomatoes • 1 onion • 1 leek • 1 stick celery
5 garlic cloves • 500 ml red wine • 70 ml oil

METHOD

1 Preheat the oven to 180°C. Add the meat and roast until browned. Meanwhile, clean and cut the vegetables into mirepoix.

2 You can cook the vegetables in three ways: in the water for the stock, in the oven with the meats, or sautéed in oil, and then put them into the pot together with the roasted meats.

3 Add the roasted meat.

4 Pour in the wine and cook until reduced.

5 Add the deglazed juice from the baking tray.

6 Pour in the water and boil, slowly, uncovered.

7 Degrease and skim.

8 Strain and cool the stock, which will have almost set due to the reduction.

2

3

4

5

6

7

8
6 L
6 qt.
4 L
4 qt.
2 L
2 qt.

FISH STOCK

Fish stock or fumet is a very simple stock, essential for all types of rice and fish stews. Its process is similar to the white or quick stock, and the cooking time is usually, as in the latter, quick: 20-30 minutes are sufficient to obtain a good fish base. If you want a more concentrated stock, you must reduce it after straining it. But we can also obtain a more concentrated fumet by preparing it in a similar way to the brown stock – in other words, by first cooking the fish to brown it beforehand and intensify its flavour. This type of stock is common in recipes containing seafood.

FISH STOCK Time: 20-30 mins

INGREDIENTS FOR 3 LITRES OF STOCK

4 litres water

1 kg fish bones, heads or fish for soup

1 carrot

1 stick celery

1 onion

1 leek

1 bay leaf

Bouquet garni

METHOD

1. Clean the vegetables and cut them into mirepoix (large cubes).
2. Cut the bones into pieces, split open the heads and clean them with plenty of cold water.
3. Cook all the fish and vegetables in cold water. Boil for 20-30 minutes, skimming the stock at the beginning of cooking.
4. Strain and cool the stock quickly, if it won't be used straight away, and store it in the refrigerator or freezer, properly labelled.

SEAFOOD FUMET Time: 3 hrs

INGREDIENTS FOR 2 LITRES OF STOCK

4 litres water ▪ *500 g prawn heads*

1 kg fish bones, heads or fish for soup

1 carrot ▪ *1 stick celery*

1 onion

1 leek

1 bay leaf

Bouquet garni

Fresh tomato or tomato purée (optional)

METHOD

1 Preheat the oven to 180°C.

2 Add the prawn heads and roast for 40 minutes with a few drops of oil.

3 Cook the vegetables over a low heat until they are completely cooked.

4 Add the ingredients (water, prawn heads and cooked vegetables) in a pot and cook for 2 hours over a low heat.

5 Strain the fumet and cool it quickly, if it won't be used straight away.

SAUCES

COLD, HOT, LIQUID, SEMI-LIQUID, SWEET, BITTER, CONSISTENT, LIGHT — IT'S DIFFICULT TO FIND TWO SAUCES THE SAME, AND THEIR FLAVOURS CAN VARY EVEN WHEN USING THE SAME INGREDIENTS.

Sauces are defined as a mixture of several substances dissolved in a liquid, sometimes hot, sometimes cold, and of a more or less dense consistency. They are used to coat, dress, season, complement or even to cook other dishes. Some sauces are bases, since they serve as a starting point or base for other sauces and preparations. There are mayonnaise and vinaigrette within the group of cold sauces, and the Spanish sauce, tomato sauce, velouté and béchamel sauce, among the ones prepared with heat.

Today, there are also special products, such as texturisers, that provide new structures to sauces. Thanks to them, the already great diversity of sauces has multiplied exponentially, allowing the most varied presentations.

MAYONNAISE

It is one of the most popular and simple cold sauces, and the base for numerous variations. However, there are some tips to its preparation. If it is too thick, add some hot liquid (water or stock). If it is too stiff and you can't bind the sauce, add one more egg yolk with a little lemon, but without oil, and start whisking again.

It is a very delicate sauce, since it is prepared without cooking and with eggs, so you must be careful when handling the products to avoid contamination risks. The eggs must be very fresh. It should be consumed the same day – it is not suitable for storing. There are some safe alternatives, such as using pasteurised egg products, commercial mayonnaise or a lactonnaise product (prepared with milk instead of eggs).

MAYONNAISE

Time: 10 mins

INGREDIENTS

200 ml sunflower or refined olive oil (non-acidic)

1 egg yolk - *Lemon juice (a few drops)* - *Salt*

METHOD

1 Emulsify the egg yolk with a few drops of lemon juice and salt.

2 Whisk the egg yolk and slowly add the oil while continuing to whisk with an electric whisk at moderate speed.

MAIN VARIATIONS

- **Tartar sauce.** Mayonnaise with capers, pickles and hard-boiled egg. You can add chives or parsley.
- **Chantilly.** Mayonnaise with lemon juice and cream. You can also add cayenne pepper.
- **Marie rose sauce or cocktail sauce.** It is a mayonnaise to which you add tomato ketchup, lemon juice, brandy, Worcestershire sauce, Tabasco sauce, salt and pepper.
- **Truffle mayonnaise.** It is made with chopped truffle, truffle oil or truffle water.
- **Herby mayonnaise, anchovy mayonnaise, bergamot mayonnaise, etc.** Just add the desired products, chopped or as flavoured oils.

1

2

3

MUSHROOM MAYONNAISE

Time: 1 hr

1 egg yolk - 10 ml water - Salt

100 g mushrooms · 100 ml virgin olive oil

METHOD

1 Clean the mushrooms and place them in a small casserole covered with olive oil. Confit them very gently for 30 minutes. Cool and strain the oil.

2 Emulsify the egg yolk, water and salt, adding the oil and making a mayonnaise with a stick blender.

3 When the mixture is blended, add the mushrooms and blend again until a very smooth texture is obtained. Season with salt and reserve.

VINAIGRETTES

By definition, vinaigrettes consist of a mixture of oil, vinegar and salt. In reality, there are as many possible vinaigrettes as there are days in the year. By simply varying the type of oil, vinegar (or another acid component, such as white wine or lemon) or salt, you can introduce appreciable differences. And, of course, you can make them unique by adding other ingredients: garlic, anchovies, gherkins, shallots, aromatic herbs, mustard, hard-boiled egg, onion, capers, etc. It is usually a cold sauce, though sometimes it is served warm, and it is normally used to dress salads.

VINAIGRETTE INGREDIENTS

OIL	ACID	SUPPLEMENTS
Virgin olive	White wine	Dried fruit
Refined olive	Sherry	Toasted sesame seeds
Pure olive	Lemon juice	Spices
Sunflower	Cider vinegar	Mustard
Corn	Modena vinegar	Beetroot juice
Groundnut	Modena Cream	Diced fresh fruit

BÉCHAMEL SAUCE

This is a classic sauce, based on the traditional roux (French name for a mixture of flour and butter, usually in equal parts; *see p. 334*), which can be reformulated with different ingredients according to the preparations it will be complementing. Learning how to make a béchamel sauce can help you to harmonise a multitude of dishes. The flexibility that this simple sauce gives you will provide an opportunity to make numerous original presentations.

BÉCHAMEL SAUCE

Time: 15 mins

INGREDIENTS

1 litre milk (milk and cream can be combined)
70 g butter ▪ 70 g flour
White pepper ▪ Nutmeg ▪ Salt

METHOD

1 Boil the milk with salt, white pepper and a few gratings of nutmeg.

2 Prepare a roux in a saucepan by mixing the butter and flour with a whisk. Use a palette knife to prevent it sticking to the edges of the pan. Mix until the roux is completely homogenised and without lumps. It is not necessary for the heat to be high, since, in most cases, is does not need to colour. Only in special cases, in which you want a blond or brown roux, you will need a high heat.

3 Add the hot milk to the roux and cook until the desired texture is achieved. The flour will not start to react until it exceeds a temperature of about 80°C, so it is important to provide the necessary heat for the sauce to thicken.

4 If necessary, strain the sauce. If you won't be using it straight away, cool it quickly. If you wish to keep it warm, put it into a bain-marie. To prevent a crust or skin from forming on its surface, cover it with clingfilm or a light layer of milk or single cream.

MAIN TYPES

- **Soubise sauce.** With onion purée.
- **Mornay sauce.** With grated cheese (Parmesan and Gruyère), egg yolks and sometimes butter.
- **Florentine sauce.** With spinach.
- **Béchamel Aurora.** With tomato sauce.
- **Béchamel sauce with kuzu.** (*See p. 337.*)

HOLLANDAISE SAUCE

It is one of the queens of French cuisine, although it is not easy to prepare. It is a hot mayonnaise made with butter instead of oil. Temperature control is important: it should be between 60 and 70°C, which means that it should be prepared just before serving. A food processor-cooker can make the task easier, since it maintains a stable temperature without running the risk of the sauce being cut by excess heat.

Like mayonnaise, hollandaise sauce is delicate in terms of storage, so it is not wise to save it for other uses.

HOLLANDAISE SAUCE Time: 15 mins

INGREDIENTS

250 g butter ▪ 2–3 egg yolks

Lemon juice ▪ Salt and pepper

METHOD

1 Clarify the butter — that is, heat it gently to separate its watery part. Remove the scum that forms on the surface and decant the butter to remove the liquid from the base. Keep it close to 65°C.

2 Using a whisk, whisk the egg yolks with the lemon juice, salt and pepper.

3 Emulsify the egg yolks in a bain-marie with the clarified butter. Slowly stir in the butter until the sauce is smooth.

4 If the sauce is too thick, add stock or a few drops of hot water. Keep the emulsion warm enough to prevent it breaking and the butter hardening, but not too hot, so that the eggs do not curdle.

MAIN VARIATIONS

- **Béarnaise sauce.** With shallots and tarragon.
- **Maltese sauce.** With blood orange juice.
- **Foyot sauce.** With concentrated meat juice.

COMPLEMENTS

BINDERS, TEXTURISERS AND OTHER COMPLEMENTS, SUCH AS CROÛTONS, SOMETIMES PLAY AN ANECDOTAL ROLE, BUT OTHER TIMES THEY ARE ESSENTIAL TO GIVE SHAPE, STRUCTURE AND UNIQUENESS TO A DISH.

If harmony is a primordial concept in cooking, binders, such as flours, starches, butters or oils, are our allies. These are used to bind the ingredients of a sauce so that it appears to be an indissoluble component of the main preparation. Texturisers, which are more novel in culinary use, can transform or mould the texture of a food – generally a sauce or liquid or semi-liquid textures – and can provide another interesting factor: surprise.

Sofritos (Spanish mixture of sautéed onion and garlic, sometimes with tomatoes and other vegetables), picadas and majados (types of ground ingredients) are also complements, even if there are preparations that would not exist without them. Finally, there are an infinite number of other minor complements, such as breadcrumbs or croûtons, which, perhaps, could fall in a second category. Regardless, the kitchen is like a great orchestra in which all the ingredients intervene in a decisive way at some point in the performance.

BINDERS

Certain products make it possible to join, bind or connect one thing to another: for this reason, we call them binders. They are elements that provide density and a specific texture to many preparations.

Binders can be of vegetable and animal origin. Perhaps the most common are the starches, which are present in the majority of the common flours (rice, wheat, corn) and are frequently used to thicken and bind sauces. However, the current trend towards lighter cooking has led to a reduction in the amount of flour used and to making reduced sauces that often do not use any starch. Regardless, starches continue to be common in many sauces and preparations.

BINDERS OF VEGETABLE ORIGIN

- **Oil.** Olive oil, like butter, finishes dishes, giving them taste and shine. It is usually used to take advantage of and emulsify the juice left by sautéing in the pan.
- **Rice and rice flour.** Rice is added to the liquid to be thickened. At the end of the cooking process, the mixture is ground and strained to obtain a thick liquid. However, rice flour only needs to be poured into a boiling liquid to serve as a binder.
- **Wheat flour, semolina, breadcrumbs.** They are used in different ways: either dissolved in a liquid, as part of a sauce, or just to give texture, as happens with bread in an onion or garlic soup.
- **Corn flour, polenta.** They are used in the same way as wheat flours.
- **Potato.** Potato starch is used in some cases to thicken liquids to obtain creams and purées.

BINDERS OF ANIMAL ORIGIN

- **Butter.** It is used to bind at the last moment of cooking, giving texture and shine to sauces. It is incorporated in the form of knobs, off the heat, and emulsified quickly. The cooking should not boil, so that the butter does not break. Sometimes butters composed of other flavours are used to add taste as well as texture.
- **Cream.** It binds the sauces by reduction. You must be careful not to overcook it, to avoid the risk of breaking it and separating its fatty part.
- **Eggs.** Both egg whites and yolks can add density and texture to preparations.
- **Blood and livers.** Currently, these elements are in disuse in their binding function. But they can still be used in game dishes, where the sauce of the stew is finished by binding with the blood of the animal itself. This is the case of civets. Livers are often one of the cuts.
- **Seafood coral.** Sometimes the coral (roe) of lobsters or rock lobsters is used to enrich or bind a stew. It should be added at the end of cooking.

COMPOUND BINDERS

This is the mixing of two elements to act as a binder. Among the various compound binders, the following stand out: sabayon and roux.

A sabayon consists of a mixture of egg yolks and cream that adds taste and density to a preparation. It is added at the last moment of cooking, ensuring that the liquid you wish to bind is hot so that it can act, but not boiling, so the egg does not curdle. It is used to finish creams and veloutés (typical French sauces), enriching them with the taste, spreadability and creaminess of these two fatty elements, and it also thickens the preparation.

A roux is a binding agent based on a mixture of butter and flour, which is added to the liquid to be thickened. The white roux is the basic one, and is used for a béchamel sauce, but to obtain a stronger taste, the roux can be lightly browned (blond roux), and to make its flavour even more intense you can toast the flour beforehand in the oven (brown roux).

TYPES OF ROUX

- **Roux 30.** 30 g of butter, 30 g of flour and 1 litre of stock. Favours a velouté with a creamy texture.
- **Roux 70.** 70 g of butter, 70 g of flour and 1 litre of milk. Used for a béchamel sauce.
- **Roux 200.** 200 g of butter, 200 g of flour and 1 litre of milk, or a mixture of milk and stock. It is a suitable binding for croquette dough.

THE ROUX PROCESS

1 Add to a saucepan the amount of butter needed according to the quantity of sauce desired, and melt it over a low heat. Add flour.

2 Mix until a uniform texture is obtained.

TEXTURISERS

As the name suggests, these are additives that can modify the texture of a food. In general, colourless and tasteless, their function is to change the density of the sauce and liquid preparations, such as creams, stocks, soups and juices, but also ice cream, cakes or dairy products.

These products are traditionally used in the food industry, but in recent years they have been introduced to professional kitchens, opening up a new range of possibilities for the usual preparations. They have revolutionised the restaurant industry or, at least, have allowed it to evolve by incorporating new processes and techniques. Little by little, they are beginning to arrive at homes and will soon accompany the most common products in our cupboards.

EMULSIFIERS

Basically, they stabilise the binding of fatty and aqueous molecules. Although this definition sounds like alchemy, it is something you do in your kitchen on a regular basis; for example, when you emulsify the ingredients of a mayonnaise with the help of oil so that they do not separate. Emulsifiers are often used in complex preparations, such as base mixes for ice cream.

SPHERIFIERS

Spherification is a culinary technique that allows encapsulating, in the form of a small sphere, different liquid textures inside a gel that acts as a solid layer to contain the liquid. This is a technique used in haute cuisine to create surprising elements, since the spherifying gelatine encloses the natural flavour of the food – sometimes an almost secret or unexpected flavour. When introduced to the mouth, the gelatine capsule breaks, allowing the liquid to flow and ultimately causing a small explosion of a very intense flavour.

Spherification requires products such as sodium alginate, a gelling agent derived from brown algae, and calcium chloride, a chemical compound used in medicine and also in the food industry for curdling cheese. Combined, they are responsible for causing partial gelation of the liquid and forming the sphere.

1

AERATORS

A variant of emulsifiers, products with aerating properties allow incorporating air molecules into an emulsion in order to increase its volume and give it a more ethereal texture.

Traditionally, cream or egg whites have served the function of increasing the volume of a preparation, but at the same time they added fat and flavour. However, products such as soya lecithin (a by-product of soybean oil extraction) can aerate emulsions without adding taste or colour. It is one of the most widely used emulsifiers in professional kitchens, since it enables fluffy textures to be achieved. By whipping juices or sauces with lecithin, you can obtain airs and foams *(photo 1)*.

THICKENING AGENTS

Simple to use and easy to incorporate in our kitchens, they are a perfect alternative to flours and semolina to thicken and bind sauces and preparations, as well as suitable for people with coeliac disease. Some of the thickeners on the market include gum arabic, locust bean gum, and guar gum, but perhaps the one most widely used and recommended is xanthan gum, due to its ease of use. Xanthan gum provides density and viscosity, and can be worked both hot and cold. You can add it, for example, to stocks, to give them more body, or to bind sauces.

THE XANTAN GUM PROCESS

1 Weigh or measure the liquid to which you wish to give density and prepare the corresponding quantity of xanthan gum according to the instructions on the packet.

2 Emulsify the mixture with a blender or whisk.

3 Allow it to rest, heat or vacuum if you wish it to lose any air it may have picked up during whisking.

GELLING AGENTS

These are food additives that make it possible to obtain different types of gelatinous textures: soft, hard, rigid or flexible. There are many types, which are also adapted to the needs of the processing: whether it is cold or hot, it must withstand freezing or must act in acidic environments.

- **Animal gelatine.** It is the classic gelatine, derived from collagen from the tissues of some animals boiled in water, such as fish's tails, which is processed in powder or in thin dehydrated leaves.
- **Pectin.** It is a gelling substance derived from fruit, such as apples or lemons. It is thermo-reversible — that is, it endures temperature changes, which is very common in jams.
- **Agar agar.** Vegetable gelatine of marine origin that has the advantage of maintaining its gelatinous property up to about 80°C.
- **Kuzu.** It is obtained from the root of a climbing plant of the legume family, typical of Asia. It is also used as a thickener.

BÉCHAMEL SAUCE WITH KUZU

Time: 15 mins

INGREDIENTS

1 litre milk - *70 g butter* - *35 g kuzu* - *Salt* - *White pepper*
Nutmeg

METHOD

1 To determine the amount of kuzu for a preparation, first weigh or measure the liquid you wish to add density to, and determine the proportion of kuzu following the instructions on the packet. In this case, for 1 litre of milk, there are 35 grams of kuzu.

2 Boil the milk with the butter, nutmeg, salt and pepper. You can reserve a small amount of the milk to emulsify the kuzu in.

3 Mix the kuzu with the reserved cold milk — or a small amount of water — and emulsify with a whisk.

4 Add the emulsified kuzu to the saucepan with the hot milk, filtering it through a sieve.

5 Cook over a low heat until the desired density and texture is obtained.

LOW-TEMPERATURE VEGETABLE STOCK WITH AUTUMNAL AROMAS

Time: 4 hrs | Level: difficult

INGREDIENTS FOR 4 PEOPLE

500 ml vegetable stock • 75 ml sunflower oil
1.5 g xanthan gum • 20 g Comté cheese
20 g capers • 60 g pumpkin
20 ml pomegranate vinegar • 15 g sugar
1 small Figueres onion
1 artichoke • 2 oranges
Chervil and dill leaves

METHOD

1 Season the vegetable stock to taste with salt and whisk it with the xanthan gum. Strain it and, if you have a vacuum canister, vacuum a couple of times to de-aerate the stock. If not, allow the stock to rest for 6 hours so that it loses the air that will have been incorporated when whipping it with this thickener.

2 Cut the cheese into very small cubes.

3 Crush the capers with a little vegetable stock until a dense texture is obtained.

4 Steam the pumpkin (you can also boil it) until it is soft, then cool it. Dehydrate it by microwaving it for about 30 seconds at medium power. Then grind it with a stick blender to obtain a thick purée.

5 Squeeze the oranges and put their juice with the sugar into a small saucepan. Cook over a low heat until you obtain a reduction of 80 per cent, so that when it cools down, it remains dense. It is important to do the reduction over a very low heat.

6 Impregnate the onion, cut into julienne strips, with the pomegranate vinegar. To do this, add both the ingredients to a vacuum canister and vacuum a couple of times.

7 Peel the artichoke (*see p. 110*). Cut it into slices and straight away immerse it into sunflower oil in a saucepan to confit it over a low heat for 10 minutes.

8 Place the stock in a deep dish.

9 With the help of kitchen pipettes, add a few dots of caper purée, pumpkin purée and candied orange. You can also add the diced cheese, the artichoke confit slices and the infused onion, and finally garnish with some chervil and dill leaves.

To the virtues of a stock cooked under vacuum and at low temperature, you can add the autumnal aroma provided by the ingredients, as well as the special texture of the xanthan gum. This natural thickener gives density to the stock, allowing it to remain a few seconds longer in contact with your taste buds, thus adding persistence to the tastes and allowing you to savour them better.

GNOCCHI WITH SAFFRON MUSSELS

Time: 6 hrs (12 hrs for cooling) | Level: moderate

INGREDIENTS FOR 4 PEOPLE

For the chervil oil

60 ml olive oil • 5 g chervil • Salt

For the saffron water

100 ml water • 1 g saffron

For the mashed potatoes

500 g potatoes • 70 g butter

30 ml extra virgin olive oil • 6 g salt

For the gnocchi

200 g mashed potatoes • 60 ml saffron water (from the above preparation) • 15 g kuzu

For the mussel sauce

250 g mussels • 40 ml saffron water

10 g flour • 10 g butter • 80 ml cream

60 ml Chardonnay wine

To garnish

Saffron • Chervil oil

METHOD

1 To prepare the chervil oil, finely chop the herb and mix it with the oil and salt.

2 To prepare the saffron water, preheat the oven to 180°C, put the saffron into a small bowl and heat it for 20 seconds. Heat the water and add the saffron; remove from the heat and infuse for 15 minutes.

3 To make the mashed potatoes, wash the potatoes and bake them in the oven at 180°C for 45 minutes. Peel them, pass them through a potato ricer or sieve, and add the oil, diced butter and salt. Cool and reserve.

4 To prepare the gnocchi, add the kuzu to the cold saffron water — reserve about 40 ml of water for the sauce — and blend with the blender.

5 Mix with the mashed potatoes and cook in a frying pan until the dough comes off the base of the pan and is compact. Allow to cool for at least 12 hours.

5

6 Place the dough in a piping bag and make cylinders. Cut them in slices 1.5 centimetres wide.

7 Clean the mussels and put them into a casserole with the white wine. Cover and cook until they open. Strain and reserve 200 ml of the juice.

8 To prepare the mussel sauce, in a small saucepan, mix 200 ml of the juice with the reserved saffron water and bind with a roux (*see p. 334*). Cook for 5 minutes and add the cream. Cook for a further 2 minutes until you have a creamy and velvety sauce.

9 Gently heat the gnocchi and mussels in the microwave or steamer. Place them over the sauce and add saffron and chervil oil.

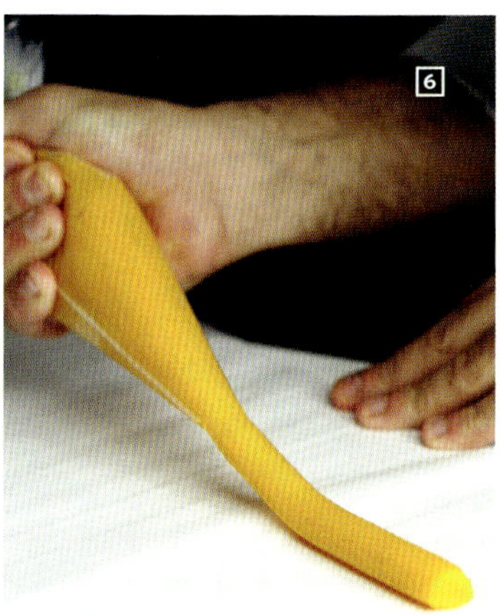

SCALLOPS WITH PUMPKIN AND MANDARIN TEXTURES

Time: 1 hr | Level: moderate

INGREDIENTS FOR 4 PEOPLE

300 g pumpkin
7 ml water
15 g sugar
4 large scallops
2 mandarins
Chervil leaves
Sunflower oil
Salt and pepper
For the pumpkin cubes
300 g pumpkin
Agar agar
For the caramelised seeds
30 g pumpkin seeds
7 g sugar

METHOD

1 To prepare the pumpkin purée, cut 300 grams of pumpkin into wedges and steam them. Blend them, season with salt and reserve the purée.

2 Squeeze the mandarins and cook their juice with the sugar over a low heat until reduced to obtain a concentrated mandarin juice.

3 Crush some chervil leaves with the sunflower oil and season with salt.

4 To prepare the pumpkin cubes, blend the remaining 300 grams of pumpkin to obtain 100 ml of pumpkin juice. Put the juice into a saucepan and add the agar agar.

5 Cook the juice until it boils, stirring constantly with a whisk so that the agar agar is completely dissolved.

6 Place the mixture in a flat pan and allow it to set. When it is ready, cut it into cubes and place them on a tray.

7 To caramelise the pumpkin seeds, place them in a saucepan with the water and sugar, and cook, stirring them often, until the sugar begins to turn white around the seeds.

8 Heat the pumpkin cubes in the oven.

9 Season the scallops with salt and pepper and grill them with a little oil.
10 Assemble the dish with a base of pumpkin purée. Add a scallop, pumpkin cubes, seeds and a few dots of mandarin reduction. Drizzle with chervil oil and garnish with its leaves.

In this preparation, the scallop combines with the softness and sweetness of the pumpkin presented in different textures: a soft purée, gelatinous cubes and crunchy seeds. Thanks to the agar agar, the liquefied pumpkin juice takes on body, giving the dish concentration and authenticity of flavours.

MINOR COMPLEMENTS

These all help to perfect recipes. They accompany, enrich, harmonise and distinguish. Most of them are incorporated towards the end of the preparation process, but there are also some, such as sofritos, which are the base of the dish.

COMPOUND AND FLAVOURED OILS

Finishing a dish with a good raw oil provides the taste and necessary unctuousness for the ingredients' textures to shine. However, not all oils are suitable for all types of preparations. A virgin olive oil, for example, is suitable for macerating black olives, but not for dressing a dish with flowers, which needs a neutral oil that is softer and more respectful of the fresh floral aromas.

Oils can be flavoured with an infinite number of compositions to better complement certain recipes. If you prepare or choose the aromatic oils that best combine with your dishes, they will gain a subtle added value.

These oils can be made cold or with a gentle application of heat. In the first case, the procedure is simple: it is sufficient that the combination between the oil and the aromatic element are properly matched. In the second case, using heat allows the volatile aromas from the product to be released more easily and aromatise the oil.

COLD FLAVOURED OILS

- **Spice oils.** Mix the spices with the chosen oil, or crush them together with the oil, strain the mixture and set aside.
- **Fresh herb oils.** You can use herbs such as basil, mint, tarragon or parsley, which add freshness and colour to the oil. They can be prepared in different ways: you can grind the herbs with the oil, or blanch the herbs, then cool them and blend the preparation. In both cases, after crushing the herbs, strain and reserve the oil.
- **Oils with complements.** You can add aromatic complements such as olives, truffles, piquillo peppers, etc. to the oils. The procedure is simple: blend the chosen product with the oil. In some cases, you need to strain the mixture, but you can also leave part or all of the crushed product. A special case is that of black olive oil, since you must first dehydrate the olives, then crush and mix them with the oil, and finally strain them (*see p. 313*).

HEAT-PROCESSED OILS

■ **Basics.** Heat the chosen product covered with oil at a low temperature (between 60 and 65°C). The cooking time will depend on the characteristics of each ingredient; for example, a flower oil will require much less time than a spice oil. With this process, you can aromatise oils with mushrooms, or with seafood and fish heads and bones. Sometimes, this process is also used to cook a raw product; in fact, this is how mushrooms are candied.

You can also use a food processor-cooker with temperature control, such as a Thermomix, to chop the herbs with the oil and heat the mixture to about 70°C. Afterwards, cool the preparation quickly, strain it and set aside.

■ **Bain-marie.** Vacuum pack the oil, or put it into bottles, with the food that will aromatise it. Then submerge it into a bain-marie and keep it for variable times, from 2-6 hours at 65°C. You can use this method to produce vanilla, truffle, cayenne, herb or spice oils. At the end of the cooking time, cool straight away and strain.

THE PRAWN OIL PROCESS

1 In a saucepan, lightly brown the prawn heads with a little sunflower oil.

2 Once browned, cover the prawn heads with more sunflower oil and allow them to confit at 65°C for 6 hours.

3 Cool and reserve. It is not necessary to strain the oil until the moment of use.

COMPOUND BUTTERS

The mixture of butter and other ingredients is widely used to make canapés. This is the case of Roquefort butter, sobrassada butter, tuna butter, anchovy butter, spinach butter, walnut butter, honey butter, hard-boiled egg butter, olive butter and pine nut butter. But compound butters can have many other applications. For garnishes, for example, we suggest making them of herbs and/or spices, of curry, of aniseed herbs, of romesco sauce, of lemon or peppers. There are also some classic formulas, such as the Maître d'Hôtel's preparation, a butter garnished with parsley and lemon juice.

To obtain a more ethereal and smooth texture, whip the butter with a food processor or electric whisk, as if it were cream, and to incorporate the product into the whipped butter. If you will be using it for glazing, add an egg yolk.

THE COMPOUND BUTTER PROCESS

1 Bring the butter to room temperature, but never with direct heat (do not put it in the microwave or on the hob, because if it melts it loses its buttery property). Rather, simply cut it into cubes and allow it to rest for 1 hour out of the refrigerator.

2 With the help of a spatula or whisk, whip it until you obtain an ointment-like texture.

3 Mix the butter with the chosen ingredient, which is usually blended to make the mixture more homogeneous.

4 Season with salt, pepper or spices.

5 Store in the refrigerator protected with clingfilm.

Citrus butter

200 g unsalted butter
10 g candied lemon
1 coriander seed
1 Sichuan peppercorn
10 g citrus peel
4 g salt

Dill butter

200 g unsalted butter
5 g fresh dill
5 g candied lemon peel
10 g mustard seeds
4 g salt

Curry butter

250 g unsalted butter
5 g curry powder
5 g coconut powder
5 g salt

Tomato and paprika butter

250 g unsalted butter
30 g tomato powder
5 g La Vera paprika
5 g salt

1

COMPOUND SALTS

To season or adjust the salt, in culinary terms, is the last detail before serving the dish. Even this simple gesture can be special if the salt is singled out with aromatic elements *(photo 1)*.

You can find a good assortment of flavoured salts in the shops: herbal salts, spice salts, lemon and pepper salts, sesame salts, etc. However, you can always customise your salts, since it is a very simple process that only requires mixing the aromatic elements with the salt and storing it in a cool place without humidity, or in airtight jars in the refrigerator. The type of salt recommended for this purpose is fleur de sel, as it offers the most neutral and natural flavour.

2

BOUQUET GARNI

This bouquet of aromatic herbs, simple and yet full of nuances, is a classic of French tradition, and one of our special guests in many preparations, such as stocks, stews and casseroles. It is composed of bay leaf, thyme, rosemary and parsley, and is introduced in these preparations tied and sometimes surrounded by vegetables to protect the herbs and prevent them from mixing with the preparation, or, more modernly, in special cooking bags that are porous, inert, flexible and heat-resistant, which allow the bouquet to release its aroma without its contents disappearing into the stock *(photo 2)*.

These bouquets can be updated with special flavours such as those offered by ginger root, spices and an infinity of aromatic ingredients from other cultures, which are increasingly present in our kitchens and can complement and singularise our recipes.

1

2

3

CRUNCHY COMPLEMENTS

Toasted bread croûtons are a classic, although nowadays there are finer and more sophisticated ones. Its objective remains the same: to introduce contrast, to complement, to differentiate. They never go unnoticed and contribute to the diner's attention to what they are eating.

TYPES OF CRUNCHY INGREDIENTS

- **Dried vegetables.** Vegetables dehydrated in a dehydrator machine, oven or microwave (*photo 1*).
- **Croûtons or toasts.** Bread diced or sliced, fried or toasted in the oven (*photo 2*).
- **Freeze-dried.** Industrial variant of dehydrated vegetables and fruits. By means of a complex system, the water is eliminated from the food, maintaining much of its flavour. The market offers very interesting and high quality products (*photo 3*).
- **Vegetable crisps.** Dehydrated fried vegetables for a crunchy texture. They can be served alone, as a starter or as a garnish.

SOFRITOS, PICADAS AND MAJADOS

In Spain, sofritos are first on the scene, and the picadas and majados are the last, but they all are important for the final preparation.

There are several types of sofritos (sautéed ingredients) depending on the ingredients added, but the basic sofrito of garlic, onion and tomato (*photos 1-9*) is popular. It is prepared slowly, confiting the onion – without frying it – (*photo 7*) so that its flavour permeates the preparation, and adding a small amount of tomato (*photo 8*), which prevents the onion burning and fixes the flavour. Food processor-cookers can reduce the long preparation time of sautéing by applying a gentle cooking temperature (*photos 4-6*).

It is worth making extra sofrito to save it for future preparations, since you can easily keep it in airtight jars or even freeze it in cubes.

The picadas (ground seasonings) and majados (types of paste) provide the final notes of flavour and texture to dishes. They often help to bind a sauce, but they can also be used as marinades to enrich food before cooking. There are as many types of these ground seasonings as there are geographical areas and local culinary cultures. Their preparation consists, simply, in grinding all the elements in a mortar or with a stick blender.

TYPES OF PICADAS AND MAJADOS

- Garlic, parsley and oil.
- Garlic, parsley and nuts (walnuts, hazelnuts, almonds or pine nuts).
- Garlic, parsley, nuts and crackers or fried bread.
- Parsley and saffron.
- Garlic, livers, nuts, oregano, and brandy or dry sherry.
- Garlic, parsley, crisps, saffron, fish liver and aniseed.
- Hard-boiled egg, parsley and lemon juice.

1

2

3

4

5

6

7

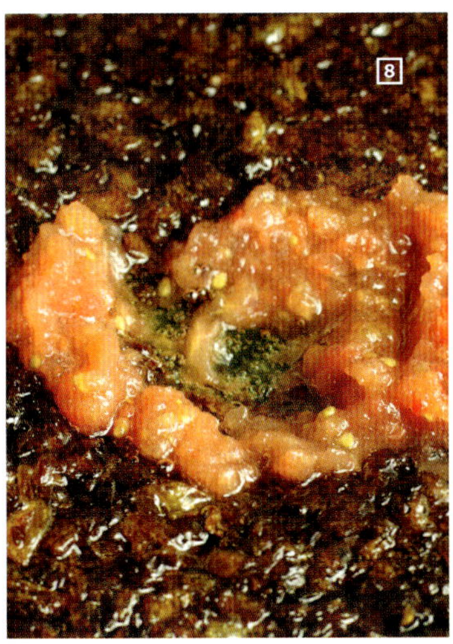
8

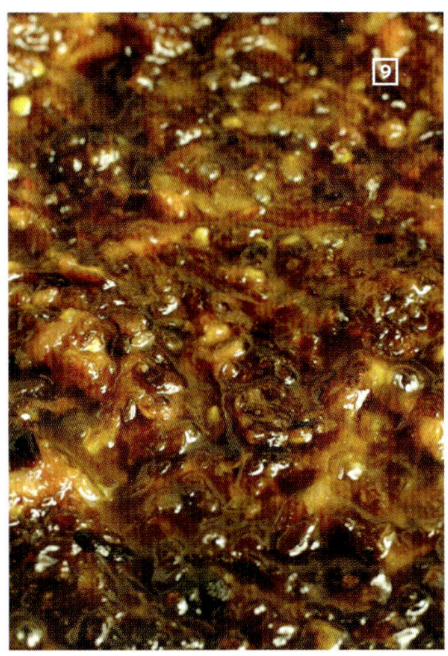
9

GLOSSARY

Acidity. Indication of the acid strength of a product. It is measured scientifically using a pH meter.

Agar agar. Food additive extracted from certain red algae. Fibre-like carbohydrate used as a gelling agent and, due to its properties, is a hydrocolloid. In cooking it is often used as a hot gelling agent.

Ageing. To give a meat (usually game) time to acquire a stronger flavour. It is also used as a synonym for resting or maturing.

Alginate. Organic salt derived from fibre-type carbohydrate used as a gelling, thickening and stabilising agent. It is extracted from brown algae.

Antifoam. Product that prevents or reduces the formation of foam in food.

Antioxidant. Product that prevents food oxidation. The most prominent antioxidant additives are the tocopherols, which include the two artificial products butylated hydroxyanisole (BHA E-320) and butylated hydroxytoluene (BHT E-321). Acidic products such as lemon or vinegar, as well as parsley, are also used as natural antioxidants.

Aroma. Perception received by the sense of smell, via the retronasal route, by capturing volatile substances that provide a certain odour that stimulates the sense of smell. It is related to the *flavour*.

Ascorbic (acid). Organic acid used as an antioxidant additive and vitamin supplement.

Assemble. Place the dish's components on a plate or tray for presentation.

Astringent. Taste nuance caused by products that contract the superficial layers of the tongue and cause a mixed sensation between bitterness and intense dryness.

Bain-marie. Also known as a water bath, a cooking method in which the preparation is placed in a container, which, in turn, is placed in another container holding hot water. This method is used to cook custards, terrines and creams. A bain-marie with cold water is also used to cool or set creams or jellies.

Bake blind. To bake a pastry in a tart tin without filling it.

Baste. To make a product moist or to glaze.

Batter. Coat a product with flour and egg.

Bead. Name given to the circle of dots that is drawn on a preparation to decorate a dish.

Bind. Add liquid gelatin to a preparation.

Bind. To hold or tie a product with kitchen string so that it retains its shape during cooking.

Bind. To thicken a liquid preparation.

Biodegradable. Product that decomposes over time due to the action of microorganisms. All food products are biodegradable, except salt, water and some additives.

Bitter. One of the fundamental flavours that we can detect. In the food industry, quinine is considered the standard for bitterness.

Blanching. Cook vegetables in plenty of boiling water, then cooling them to stop the cooking process.

Bouquet garni. Bouquet or bundle of aromatic herbs that is usually added to stocks and stews.

Braise. Cooking a food together with a wet base (such as vegetables, wine, broth, spices).

Braise. Cook in fat slowly.

Breading. Dredge a product in flour, egg and/or breadcrumbs and then fry it.

Brine. Solution of water and salt to which, sometimes, an aromatic element is added.

Bring to the boil. Heating a liquid to the boil point: at 90°C it boils and at 75°C it pasteurises.

Burnt. In cooked products, the term refers to when they are overcooked.

Caramelise. Process whereby food acquires a toasted and sweet colour with cooking.

Caramelise. Add sugar or liquid caramel to a mould to crystallise or brown it.

Carbohydrate. Biochemical compound that provides energy or fibre to an organism.

Carbonara. A creamy sauce that accompanies Italian pasta with main ingredients that include bacon, cream and egg yolk.

Citric acid (E-330). Organic acid present in many fruits, especially citrus fruit (lemon, orange), which is used as an additive to regulate acidity and also as a preservative.

Clarify. Operation with the objective of cleaning turbid substances so that they become limpid and clear. It is used in consommés, jellies and butters to make them practically transparent.

Cleaning. Remove inedible parts of vegetables.

Coagulate. Solidify a liquid by agglutination of the large clusters of molecules it contains. The liquid becomes a gelatinous solid, which can facilitate separation between the solid and the rest of the liquid.

Coat. To completely cover a product with a sauce.

Collagen. Protein with emulsifying, aerating and gelling properties.

Colloidal. Pertaining to colloids, which are the dispersion of particles in a continuous medium.

Colour. Cooking a preparation with a little fat to colour it.

Concassé. Type of more or less regular cut, referring mainly to tomatoes.

Concentrate. To reduce a liquid, juice or stock.

Cornet. Piece of paper in the form of a small cone used to decorate a dish.

Coulis. Concentrated sauce or jam used to enhance dishes or desserts.

Cover. To protect a product or dough with a cloth to prevent it drying out or to allow it to ferment, in the case of the dough.

Crystallise. To cover with syrup and keep it for a while so that when it is removed, it remains as a layer of sugar.

Deburring. Remove the egg remains in the form of fried and battered threads, or trim the barbels from fish and shellfish.

Decanting. To separate a liquid from its sediment, first allowing it to settle so that the impurities are deposited and then pouring it into another container.

Deglaze. Add wine to a roasting tin or frying pan to extract the fat or juice.

Done. Correct level of cooking.

Dust. To cover the surface of a product with icing sugar, cocoa powder or other powdered products.

Dusting. Sprinkle with icing sugar.

Duxelle. French term that designates a mixture of very finely chopped mushrooms, ham, truffles, and shallots. This is also the name given to the mixture of chopped vegetables used as stuffing.

Emulsifier. Product that enables the formation and maintenance of an emulsion or homogeneous mixture of two liquids that are not miscible with each other, such as oil and water. Lecithins and some fats act as emulsifiers.

Emulsify. Whisk in order to whip or bind.

Emulsion. Dispersion of a liquid in another liquid that is not miscible (homogeneous) with it. Like milk, composed of fat and water, or mayonnaise, composed of drops of oil dispersed in water.

Enrich. Adding a concentrate or essence to a product or process.

Enzyme. Protein that acts as a biological catalyst — i.e., it is able to break down or synthesise other substances without being affected.

Fat. Organic substance (lipid) formed by combining fatty acids with glycerine.

Fermentation. Chemical transformation carried out by microorganisms (bacteria, fungi) in combination, usually with carbohydrates. There are exceptions, such as the malolactic fermentation of wine.

Flambée. To burn a liquid with alcohol in a dish to give it a characteristic aroma and an intense taste.

Flavour. An Anglo-Saxon term that describes the set of organoleptic perceptions (olfactory, gustatory and tactile) of a food product.

Flavour. Taste and olfactory characteristic that is perceived in the mouth via the retronasal route and that allows food to be identified.

Food additive. A substance without nutritive properties that is intentionally added to a food product or food processing to ensure its preservation, facilitate or improve the processing, or modify its organoleptic characteristics.

Freeze. To coagulate a mixture until it solidifies using a low temperature, below 4°C.

Gamy. Game-like flavour that some game species take on as they age. Game bird.

Gelatine. Mixture of water-soluble proteins used as gelling agents. Its properties make it a hydrocolloid.

Gelling agent. Product that gives texture to an element by forming a gel. Due to its properties, it belongs to the hydrocolloid family.

Glaze. Coating meats with their own juices and putting them in the oven to finish them with a shine.

Glaze. To embellish a product by giving it shine through means of jellies, glazes, fats or syrup.

Glucose. Simple carbohydrate (monosaccharide). It is a type of sugar used as a sweetener. Known in gastronomy and in the food industry under the name of dextrose.

Homogenise. Procedure that standardises a mixture of substances that are in suspension.

Incision. Superficial cut in meats to facilitate cooking inside them.

Inverted syrup. Add lemon juice to a syrup to help it caramelise.

Julienne. Finely slice the vegetables into shreds.

Knead. To make a dough by amalgamating several ingredients, which can be worked by hand or by using a mixer.

Knock back. Knead or punch down the dough with your fists.

Lactose. Dairy carbohydrate.

Lecithin (E-322). Natural phospholipid additive used as an emulsifier and antioxidant.

Line. Cover the sides of a baking tin with a type of food: bacon, carrots, etc.

Liquid nitrogen. Element that when above -196°C is a gas, and that is carried at temperatures of between -196 and -210°C to keep it liquid.

Lyophilisation. Technique consisting of sublimation dehydration (direct transition from solid to gas) by heating under vacuum.

Maillard reaction. A very complex set of chemical reactions between amino acids and carbohydrates as a consequence of applying high temperature (grill, oven, barbecue, stew, etc.) to some foods, by means of which they adopt a golden colour and a characteristic taste.

Marinate. To introduce a product in a more or less liquid preparation — usually with oil — with the intention of preserving it, flavouring it and, in the case of meats, tenderising it.

Mirepoix. Cut vegetables into cubes.

Mise en place. Preparation of the necessary ingredients and utensils before following the steps to make a dish.

Moisten. To add the liquid necessary to a preparation for its cooking or to make the sauce or juice.

Moisturise. Increase water content.

Moulding. To put a product or preparation into a mould so that it acquires its shape.

Nozzle. Conical instrument, usually made of brass or plastic, which is adapted to the piping bag with the main purpose of decorating cakes or filling.

Nutrient. Any substance in food that is useful for organic metabolism. Nutrients can be divided into the groups generically called proteins, carbohydrates, lipids, minerals, vitamins and water, all of which are essential for the maintenance of good health.

Nutrition. Basic function of all living organisms to ensure their development and optimal growth through nutrition.

Odour. Sensation produced by volatile particles on contact with the organ of smell.

Offal. The viscera, heads, feet, legs, necks, combs and other edible parts of poultry and cattle, as distinguished from meat.

Organoleptic. The ability of a substance (a food) to be perceived by the senses (sight, smell, touch, taste and hearing).

Osmosis. The process by which water passes through a permeable membrane from a diluted solution to a more concentrated solution.

Oxidation (food). The process by which foodstuffs, in contact with air, age and lose their properties. This is due to a loss of electrons by one molecule or ion (electrically charged atom), which yields them to another and changes the characteristics of both.

Oxygen (E-948). Chemical element. Air component gas (21 per cent) and responsible for food oxidations. As an additive (E-948) is used to cause intentional and controlled oxidations.

Peel. Removing the peel from fruit or vegetables.

pH. A measure of the degree of acidity of a product in an aqueous solution.

Pickle. To put a product in a liquid to preserve it and to give it a characteristic flavour.

Piping. The process of working a dough, coagulated or semi-coagulated, with a piping bag. It is used to stuff pieces, to put them on a baking tray, to decorate a cake, to shape on a tray, etc.

Plate. Arrange a product on the plate or tray to offer service.

Poach. To cook a food in boiling water or other liquid.

Prep. Start the preparation of a dish.

Preserve. Procedure to extend the shelf life of a food or to ensure its durability in conditions suitable for consumption. It can be physical (sterilisation, freezing, etc.) or chemical (addition of preservatives).

Press. To subject a product to some kind of pressure to compress it for a specific purpose.

Protein. Biochemical compound with molecules that contain nitrogen and that contributes to the structure of an organism, as well as providing nutrients.

Prove. To subject a leavened dough to a suitable temperature to rise or ferment.

Quinine. A very bitter alkaloid extracted from the bark of cinchona-type plants (e.g., from the cinchona tree).

Rancid. Unpleasant organoleptic property caused by chemical alteration of fats.

Rancidity. Decomposition of fat molecules, usually due to enzymes; fatty acids oxidise and produce an unpleasant taste, which gives a rancid perception.

Reaction. Transformation of some chemical compounds into others by the action of reagents.

Rectify. Adjust seasoning or colour.

Reduce. To decrease the volume of a liquid preparation by evaporation.

Refresh. Place a product in cold running water to stop cooking.

Roux. Equal parts flour and butter. It can be white, blond or brown.

Saccharin (E-954). Artificial product derived from benzene (organic compound consisting of 6 carbons), used as a sweetener additive.

Salamander. Cooking appliance with a heating grill used in professional kitchens to glaze, gratinate or caramelise food. The oven grill, used with the door ajar, can perform the same function as the salamander.

Salt. A raw product used for seasoning.

Sauté. Cooking a food quickly with fat, with or without colouring.

Score. Refers to making incisions in fish or meat to improve its cooking.

Score. Make longitudinal cuts in the skin of fruit (especially citrus fruit) or vegetables (courgette, cucumber, etc.) for decoration.

Seasoning. To accentuate the flavour of a product by means of salt or other seasonings.

Shock. To interrupt the cooking of a soup or stew by adding water or cold stock.

Sieve. Separate, with the help of a sieve, the coarse part or the remains of products, such as flour.

Skewer. Rod for roasting small pieces of meat, fish or vegetables.

Skim. Remove impurities from the surface of the broth with the help of a skimmer.

Skinning. Remove an animal's skin.

Slice. A thin, broad piece of food, such as bread, meat, or cake, cut from a larger portion.

Soak. Moisten a sponge cake in perfumed syrup to give it flavour and consistency.

Soluble (product). A product that, due to its physical and/or chemical characteristics, can be dissolved in another product, which is called a solvent.

Spoilt. In the fresh raw products, it defines those that are close to the state of decomposition.

Starch. Complex and digestible carbohydrate that constitutes the main energy reserve of almost all vegetables. It belongs to the glycan group and, therefore, consists of only glucose chains. Its properties make it a hydrocolloid. In cooking, it is commonly used in preparing crème brûlée.

Starch. Starchy flour extracted from tubers (potatoes, tapioca, etc.).

Sterilisation. Conservation process by which microorganisms are destroyed.

Stew. Cook the food slowly, with little or no liquid, in a closed container.

Stir-fry. Cooking a food over high heat with little fat and making it 'jump' so that it does not stick.

Strengthen. Add some kind of concentrate to a sauce or soup to give it more flavour.

Stud. Insert cloves into lemons or onions to flavour marinades, stocks or stews.

Stuffing. Picadillo, or various ingredients mixed and bound together and used for stuffing.

Sucrose. Chemical name of sugar. It is a carbohydrate formed by the union of glucose (dextrose) and fructose. The latter is the one that provides most of the sweet taste.

Sweating. To cover a food (especially vegetables, such as courgette or aubergine) in salt and allow it to sit to lose its strength and eliminate its acidity. It is also said of cooking a product with fat and its own steam without colouring it.

Sweetener. Any chemical compound that produces a sweet taste. They can be divided into sugars and sweetening additives. Usually, the name sweetener is reserved only for additives.

Temper. To give the right consistency to creams, jellies and creams, with the help of ice.

Tenderise. The action of beating a meat to break its tendons, soften it and tenderise it.

Texture. Physical property (density, viscosity, surface tension, hardness, etc.) of a product that gives it characteristics perceptible by the senses, especially by touch.

Thicken. To bind broths or creams by means of the action of heat or coagulants.

Toast. Cooking foods with heat to give them a golden colour.

UHT (uperisation). Type of sterilisation applied to a product at a temperature of between 140 and 150°C for 2-4 seconds, in order to eliminate all microorganisms.

Umami. Basic taste according to the group of tastes established in Japan. It is associated with a metallic or mineral sensation in the mouth.

Volatile. Name given to molecules when, due to their evaporation, they are in suspension or in solution in the air.

Work. Stir or whisk the sauces.

Xanthan gum (E-415). Fibre-type carbohydrate used as a thickening and stabilising additive. Its properties make it a hydrocolloid.

Yeast. Name of a group of unicellular fungi very abundant in nature that are used to produce fermentations.

RECIPE INDEX

BASIC STOCKS

SAUCES AND COMPLEMENTS

GENERAL INDEX

ACKNOWLEDGEMENTS

Many people have collaborated on this book, and we are grateful to them. Without them, this book would not have been possible, and we would like to thank them sincerely for their help.

To Joan Pujol, for his extraordinary work, patience and involvement. There have been hours and hours of work, comments and discussions that have resulted in wonderful photography.

To all the people who have been involved in the process – which was not easy at all – of producing this book; in particular, to the duo Montse Armengol and Laura Hoet, and also to Àgata Olivella, who have been involved on the project for almost a year. Of course, to the people at Editorial Planeta, who have supported us at all times, Javi Moreno and David Figueras. To some friendly companies that have supported us: Lékué, Cata and the team at Suministros Girona, for their kindness and collaboration, and Quico de Sosa, for his very special products.

To the specialists who have helped us with the texts: Mireia Anglada, who has dealt so well with the topic of cooking and health, and Annette Abstoss, who has revealed to us the secrets of sprouts.

To the great team of people at El Celler, who have helped at all times in the preparation of the recipes and have provided a critical view. In particular, to Choi, queen of Asian cuisine and whimsical advice; to Ignacio, who has helped us and provided us with products, logistical support and happiness; to Dr Hernan, king of culinary irony; to Amanecer; to Mike; to Xavi; to Àlex, Gallego, and in short, to the entire wonderful team at El Celler de Can Roca.

And, of course, we would like to thank our family, with whom we share our kitchen and our life. Without them, our kitchen would be a kitchen without passion.

Joan Roca and Salvador Brugués